William Still and the Underground Railroad

Fugitive Slaves and Family Ties

LUREY KHAN

iUniverse, Inc.
New York Bloomington

Dedication.

For the late Evelyn Still Broy, and her sister, Grace Still Chatman, of Magnolia, New Jersey, descendants of Samuel Still, the first freeborn son of Levin and Charity Still.

Foreword.

William Still and the Underground Railroad Fugitive Slaves and Family Ties is the family history of a remarkable black family who lived, worked, and sometimes prospered before, during, and after the Civil War. When Sydney, the twice-escaped slave wife of Levin Steel, an emancipated Maryland slave, was reunited with her husband, they put down roots in the New Jersey Pine Barrens in Burlington County where they raised a family of freeborn children. Samuel Still, the first freeborn son of Levin and Charity Still, was born in Indian Mills, New Jersey, on 26 February 1807. Many other children followed in quick succession and they all began at an early age to carry their own weight.

The family under the new surname of Still, survived their hardscrabble circumstances from income, Samuel provided from the small plot he grew into a forty acre farm. Charity Still, however, never entirely escaped the threat of recapture by bounty hunters lurking in the Pines. She accepted the advice freely given her by Quaker abolitionists to use the loaded pistol or the dirk knife she carried on her person at all times should a slave catcher pounce upon her and return her to Maryland slavery.

William Still, the youngest of the eighteen children born to Levin and Charity Still grew up reading antislavery newspapers given him by antislavery Quakers whose abolition society had been established to protect innocent blacks from being recaptured and returned to the South. William Still left New Jersey in the spring of 1844 to make a new life in Philadelphia across the Delaware River. The position of groundskeeper rescued him from dejection which followed the many rejections William Still experienced in his hard pressed job search in the City of Brotherly Love. Mrs. Elwyn, his employer, opened her well stocked library to the country boy from the New Jersey backwoods when she noticed his interest in reading. In this situation, William made good use of his spare time to expand his mind and to stretch his poorly developed ideas. His wealthy, well traveled employer delighted in his intellectual growth and would have offered him more guidance in selecting appropriate books had she not abruptly moved leaving William Still jobless. He continued to teach Sunday School in the worst section of the black community and to practice assiduously his penmanship skills that he was soon to find use for when he found work at the Pennsylvania Antislavery Society's Philadelphia Vigilance Committee in the fall of 1847.

His superior, James McKim, the agent in charge of the Pennsylvania Antislavery Society, when he felt certain that his young underground railroad trainee was ready to assume more responsible duties, introduced young William Still to the intricacies of aiding and abetting fugitive slaves newly arriving into the city. The cliché of being in the right place in the right time applied to William Still. The Abolition Society was formed in Pensylvania in 1836. And the Fugitive Slave law of 1850 counteracted its provision for freedom of incoming former slaves. William Still's association with the Abolition Society began in the fall of 1847, only a few years before it increased its illegal, clandestine activity connected with the use of station 2, the Philadelphia underground railroad. The strategic location of Pennsylvania's southeastern border called the Mason and Dixon Line separated free states to the north from slave states to the south focused antislavery sentiments in New Jersey, and Delaware who funneled fugitives through their remote locations into Philadelphia, the hub of that section's busy underground railroad. The abolition movement here as in other areas of the country begun in the 1830s was driven by Evangelical

Christians who listed the emancipation of the slaves at the top of a long list of 19th century humanitarian reforms.[1]

William Still was born in 1821 in Indian M ills, New Jersey, that was later renamed Shamong. Although his parents had children in slavery, the majority of their children were born free in New Jersey.[2] Still's introduction to poverty in the squalid Lombard street section of the black community in Philadelphia made his rural poverty on his family's farm appear a Godsend in comparison. When he volunteered to teach at the Moral Reform Retreat he witnessed depravity in all its rawness that shaped the daily lives of fugitives and their children unable or unwilling to travel further north or into Canada.He developed his innate gift for social welfare programs that were manifested throughout his long career with the Pennsylvania Antislavery Society and on his own as a philanthropist designed to improve the lives of his unfortunate people.

Given the fact that William Still had always hoped to be reunited with his two brothers their mother had been forced to leave behind in Maryland when she made her second flight from Maryland slavery, he kept his eyes open whenever he met and interviewed incoming fugitive slaves. Although record keeping was prohibited, he chose to break this unshakeable rule by keeping secluded data he gleaned from runaway slaves. William Still never thought that these notes would ever be published because he kept the records to reunite future arrivals in search of their previous kinsmen.

William Still was amazed to meet one of his brothers their mother had left in Maryland when he was six. The chance encounter was facilitated when a black clergyman associated with the Philadelphia Vigilance Committee, Rev. Bias, delivered to his office a former slave, named Peter Freedman, a slave with free papers from Alabama who came to Philadelphia to find his mother and two sisters he last saw in Maryland more than forty years ago. William Still was certain that he was one of the two brothers their mother was forced to abandon. When Peter learned that William was his brother he had a hard time believing this to be true. A warm family reunion with his many freeborn siblings and his aged mother confirmed this to be true. [3]

William Still's contributions to the Philadelphia underground railroad were rewarded with a promotion to head station 2, and to become the Executive Secretary of the Vigilance Committee's Acting-sub-Committee in 1852. Because Philadelphia was the hub of the southeastern area of the American Antislavery Society's underground railroad operation.

When emancipation came after the Civil War, the war weary nation faced its difficult Reconstruction program. The transformation of millions of former slaves into American citizens gratified the abolitionists who joined ranks with the radicalized Republican Party that formed a Freedmen's Aid Bureau to help educate the slaves. William Still became a Freedmen's agent where he served in the Border States before he returned to Philadelphia to advocate education for the hordes of freed slaves newly arrived into the city. After the Civil War.

The Pennsylvania Antislavery Society at its last meeting in Philadelphia,1871, resolved that William Still publish his underground railroad records in a fugitive slave history book. He accomplished this monumental task in 1872 when he published a 780 page volume, *The Underground Rail Road.* Its Preface [4] ripples with horrific slave stories told him by neglected and abused runaway slaves from all over the South. Present day readers are advised to read some of the horrendous synopses contained in Still's 1872 preface. *Still's Underground Railroad Records* in 1878 also contains an interesting Preface [5] that urged the freedmen to assume the burdens and hard work expected of former slaves protected by the Constitution's Civil war Amendments that conferred upon them freedom, citizenship and voting rights. He used his family's transformation from slavery to freedom when slavery was expected to last forever as an example to follow in their own quest for better lives as freedmen.

William Still used his own funds derived from a lucrative coal distribution business to implement a series of social welfare programs he devised to ease the transition into the wider society of Philadelphia where they formed new lives in freedom. As the 19th century approached its turn into the 20th, many of the promised rights for the civil rights of slaves faded into oblivion with the 1896

Plessy v.Ferguson Supreme Court decision's separate but equal provisions for black people.

William Still and his wife Letitia, educated their four children who served as black leaders in Philadelphia when the mass of black people remained in a semi literate state. William's older daughter, Caroline Still Anderson, graduated the second of her race at the Women's medical College of Pennsylvania, where she earned an M.D. degree in 1878.William's brother, James. A successful herbalist in Burlington County, had the means to educate his son, James Thomas Still, at the Harvard Medical School where he earned an M.D. degree in 1871. William Still served as vice president and then president of the Pennsylvania Antislavery Society until he died in 1902, followed by his devoted wife, Letitia, in 1902. Their younger daughter, Frances Ellen Still, provided data about her father's long, busy life to Alberta S. Norwood, towards her MA degree at the University of Pennsylvania, entitled Negro Welfare Work in Philadelphia Especially as Illustrated by the career of William Still 1775-1902, which was accepted in partial fulfillment for her degree in 1931.[6]

The following is a partial list of achievements by William Still:

A trip to Canada in 1855 to investigate the veracity of the proslavery claims meant to denigrate the behavior of the fugitives living in Canada who, for the most part, had settled peaceably into their new home; an eight year campaign with the Managers of the Philadelphia City's Railway cars for the rights of black people to be seated where they chose on the city's street cars; the philanthropic contributions he made for the establishment of the Home for Aged and Infirm Colored People in Philadelphia; The tireless efforts at compiling information for the Social, Civil, and Statistical Society to determine ways and means for striking at the roots of prejudice in Philadelphia, which supplied the information needed to form a list of famous speakers to deliver talks on citizenship, race relations, human rights, etc., and its use towards the cause of universal suffrage; Still's service as the Post-Sutler, at Camp William Penn, a Civil War army camp for black soldiers during the Civil War.

The funding of worthwhile projects such as a donation of $500 towards the welfare of colored soldiers after the Civil War; $100 to the Executive Committee of the national testimonial to William Lloyd Garrison; his purchase of a share in the mercantile Library of Philadelphia, and his contribution of $1,000 worth of stock in the Nation; William Still's encouragement and support of talented black writers; one was William Wells Brown, author of *The Black Man;* another was Mrs. Frances Ellen Watkins Harper, author of *Sketches of Southern Life,* etc.; the financial contributions he gave towards the organization and funding of a permanent home for the Colored Soldiers and Sailors Home.

Still's active interest in the Home for destitute Colored Children, and the Shelter, both of which were located at the Cheyney Normal School where black Normal School students gained practice in teaching; the work William Still did as a trustee of Storer College at Harpers Ferry, West Virginia, in honor of the slain abolitionist, John Brown; William Still's literary labors included an extensive correspondence to the press on a variety of questions relating to the needs and problems of Negroes; he published the factual, fugitive slave history, *The Underground Rail Road,* which even now is considered an authority on the subject, and two pamphlets, A Brief narrative of the Struggle for the Rights of the Colored People of Philadelphia in the City Railway cars, and a Defense of William Still, and An Address on Voting and Laboring; they both contained ideas far in advance of his time, a fact that encourages opposition and censure from those not appreciative of his intellectual prowess.

The business acumen that William Still exhibited made possible the large and successful coal business at 1216, 1218, and 1220 Washington Avenue which according to Dr. Thomas Wister in 1895, "...supplied the Dispensary, myself, and father before me, honestly for thirty years"; Mr. Still's creditable representation of Negro achievements at the Philadelphia Centennial Exhibition when he feared that blacks would not have creditable displays to exhibit; the eye catching display of copies of *The Underground Rail Road* delighted the many visitors who viewed the varied-bindings artfully arranged in a specially made glass case for the Exhibition; the contribution to various ventures he believed would improve the facilities of the black community resulted in William Still's involvement on the purchase of a meeting hall in their community; his collaboration with other businessmen failed leaving Mr. Still to buy them out, fit up the meeting house with his own money, and to present Liberty Hall to the grateful community where a number of famous people came to speak.

He worked to organize and to implement the development of the Berean Presbyterian Church, with its Berean School, both located on College Avenue in northwestern Philadelphia; his help in establishing established a credit union for black workers to save to buy a house resulted in his election as its first president; the Berean Credit Union still stands today; William Still helped to found and to develop a plan for a black YMCA where black youth could meet to enjoy hobbies and sports; he worked tirelessly to offer political strategies for black males able to vote in the 1880 Mayoralty election in Philadelphia; and William Still's efforts to have hired on the police force in Philadelphia its first black police officers.

Above all, his fifty-four year inextricable association with the Pennsylvania Antislavery Society.

FootNotes.

1. The Concise Columbia Encyclopedia, Second Edition. (New York: Columbia University Press), 1989. p.2
2. Catalogue of the Children of Levin Still and his wife, Charity, Burlington, County, New Jersey. Peter Still Papers, Rutgers University, New Jersey. (Appendix 1.).
3. William Still, Philadelphia, to James O. Cousins, Cincinnati, Ohio, 7 August 1850. From Peter Still's younger, brother. Peter Still papers, Rutgers, New Jersey.(Appendix 2.)
4. William Still, *The Underground Rail Road,* (Philadelphia: Porter & Coates), 1872. Preface. (Appendix 3.)

5. William Still, *Still's Underground Rail Road Records,*(Philadelphia: Peoples' Publishing Company),)1878.Preface. (Appendix 4.).
6. Alberta S. Norwood, Negro Welfare Work in Philadelphia Especially as Illustrated in the career of William Still 1775-1902. In partial fulfillment for a MA thesis, University of Pennsylvania: 1931.pp. 105-108.

Lurey Khan,
Boston, Massachusetts.
2009.

Acknowledgements.

David McCord, my teacher in advanced writing at the Harvard Summer School, aided me in the publication of a book for young readers, *One Day Levin...He Be Free William Still and the Underground Railroad* (New York: E.P. Dutton), 1972.

I am also indebted to the support given me by a 1979 Mary Roberts Rinehart Foundation grant-in-aid for creative writers, and in 1985, a Mary Lizzie Saunders Clapp Scholarship on the History of Women in America at the Schlesinger Library, Radcliffe College, Cambridge, Massachusetts, now renamed The Radcliffe Institute for Advanced Study at Harvard University.

Much of the reference material used in this book was found in the stacks and card catalogues of these institutions:

The Schlesinger Library on the History of Women in America, Radcliffe College, provided me with a wonderful selection of papers on 19th century Women in Medicine, which furnished background data for the section on the medical education of Caroline Still Anderson, M.D. 1878 The Women's Medical College of Pennsylvania. Other material on 19th century women was found in the Blackwell Family Papers, the Alice Hamilton Papers on the History of Medicine 1868-1919, the Annual Report of the New England Hospital for Women and Children, 1862-1877, etc., and the Sophia Smith Collection on the History of Women, Smith College, Northampton, MA.

Material on African-American history was found at several first rate libraries: Suffolk University's Afro-American Reference Department, Harvard University's Widener Library, Cambridge, Massachusetts, Rare Books and Manuscripts Collection, at the Boston Public Library, the Philadelphia Library Company's Afro-American Collection 1553-190, The Van Pelt Library at the University of Pennsylvania, the Pennsylvania Historical Society, Harrisburg, Pennsylvania, the Ohio Historical Society, Columbus, Ohio, the Women's Medical College of Pennsylvania, Philadelphia, Oberlin College, Oberlin, Ohio, Howard University, Washington, D.C., and The Countway Library of Medicine, at the Harvard Medical School, Boston, Massachusetts, which provided data on James Thomas Still, M.D. (Harv.) 1871.

The General References and Bibliography Department of the Library of Congress, Washington, D.C., provided the following citations in African American Genealogy: The Dictionary Catalog of The Schomberg Collection, New York City Public Library, the Dictionary Catalogue of the Jesse E. Moorland Collection on Negro Life at Howard University, Washington, D.C., Robert W. Gleen Black Rhetoric: A Guide to African American Communication (The Skatecrow Press: Metuchen, New Jersey (1976).

Index to Periodical Articles by and About Negroes, (Boston, G.K. Hall), Race Relations and Information Centers Directory of Afro American Resources (New York: R.R. Bowker & Co., [1970] 485p.) ed. By Walter Shatz, and Black Genealogy in R.Q. for summer 1872 (v.11, p. 311-319), G.K. Hall & Co., Blacks in Selected Newspapers, Census, and Other Sources: An Index to Names and Subjects, compiled by James D.T. Abajian, Charles L Blockson, and Roy Black (Prentice Hall, New York: May 1977).

Contents

Chapter 1.
Slavery and Levin Steel.

Before the Civil War, the place of whites and blacks in America was determined logically and irrevocably by the laws that governed the institution of slavery. At the same time, the extrajudicial interpretation of the Constitution was sworn to by the members of the legislative and executive branches, who were duty bound to uphold the Constitution much the same as judges did in the course of their daily work.[1] However, it was the extension and slavery 'above all that lay behind the ever-increasing concern for states' rights; and it was slavery that brought the controversy surrounding slavery into the forefront of the nation's consciousness. The Wilmot Proviso, the Compromise of 1850, the Kansas and Nebraska Act, the Lincoln-Douglas debates, and bleeding Kansas enlarged the great debate over the issue of slavery before the Civil War in the minds and hearts of a concerned nation.[2]

Levin Steel, a slave in the potato and cornfields owned by his slave master, Saunders Griffin on Maryland's Eastern Shore apparently didn't know his place because he demanded his freedom when he was twenty one years of age. He refused to live under the yoke and was not shy about confiding his irate feelings on this subject in a face-to-face confrontation with his slave master in these words: "I'll die before I'll submit to the yoke!".[3]

An attempt to ascertain Levin's exact age when he chose freedom over slavery would make him about the same age of his slave master and the U.S. Constitution written in 1787 in Philadelphia[4].after it replaced the Articles of Confederation. No records known to the writer determined Levin's country of origin, nor the time he arrived in the new World from Africa if, indeed, he wasn't born in the U.S The facts reveal that he and his wife, Sydney had a baby named Ann in 1798 who either died or was sold away from them.

According to the concisely prepared Constitution's Preamble, its 7 Articles and 26 Amendments which, along with The Bill of Rights, became the document that stressed the right to own property to white citizens in the United States in its first nine Amendments added in 1791.

The clearly stated Constitutional Amendments, especially 1 through 8, prohibited certain federal actions analogous to those the colonists complained of in the Declaration of Independence. Amendment 9 gave these citizens rights not specified in the Constitution, while the 10th amendment (ratified in 1791) ensured the doctrine of States' Rights, which supported slavery, mandating that African slaves would remain held in perpetual bondage. The 14th amendment, after freedom came to the slaves, assured to all citizens rights that could not be abridged by the states, but were placed there to limit many state actions. Though unclear and briefly written, the language of the Constitution made itself adaptable to changing times, while leaving the mechanics of amendments difficult to actualize

Major American statesmen, even in those days, were concerned with the possibility of the extension of slavery westward. When the American Revolution ended, the signing of the Treaty of Paris in 1783 with England gave to the Americans the Ohio Country. This opening of the west, forced the Continental Congress to face up to the skirmishes that followed between them and the Native Americans who disputed their ownership of the territory. Many states, especially Connecticut and Virginia also had claims to it based on the permission of the King of England who had granted those colonies control of all land between their colonies on the East Coast and the Pacific Ocean. The Confederation Congress hoped to sell the land in the Ohio Country to raise funds in order to continue to function. The government also feared the appearance of large number of squatters who were daily arriving there.

Because they were so isolated from the rest of the country in the Appalachian Mountains, the Confederation Congress began to negotiate with the Indians and the states in order to claim the sole ownership of the land. Thomas Jefferson implemented the Ordinance of 1784 while these negotiations were going on which called for the land north of the Ohio River, west of the Appalachian Mountains, and east of the Mississippi River to be divided into ten separate states. The states would first be territories. They would remain territories until they had attained the population of the least populous state in America. When the territories became states, they would have the same rights as the original thirteen states. The Ordinance of 1784 also guaranteed self-government to the residents of the territories. The Land Ordinance of 1785 quickly replaced the Ordinance of 1784 and the Confederation Congress admitted no new states under the Ordinance.

The Northwest Ordinance, passed on 13 July 1787 by the Confederation Congress, created a governmental system for the Northwest Territory. It also stipulated the means by which the various parts of the Northwest Territory would become states. Earlier land ordinances such as the Ordinance of 1784 and 1785 only stipulated that the territory would someday become states and determined how the federal government would sell the land to private citizens. The Northwest Ordinance paved the way for Ohio to become the 17th state of the United States of America. It also, with minor modifications, established the process for admission to the United States for all states after 1787.[5]

These governmental generalities, though real, must have eluded the illiterate slave named Levin Steel. Levin did overwork to earn the undisclosed sum of money his slave master demanded for his freedom. When he was given his free papers, Saunders Griffin freed Levin while leaving behind him in Maryland his wife, and their four small children. Levin chose to immediately leave the South for fear of being recaptured. In addition, his conversation with Sydney will forever remain a secret. The family records document the pain his wife found too heavy a burden to bear when Levin went to a free state to settle down. She took Levin, eight, Peter, six, Mahalah, three or four, and Kitturah, or Kitty, with her on a flight she dared to take through the wilderness when she headed for New Jersey shortly after Levin had departed from the South Her difficult travel was recorded in the family documents in that pre-underground railroad time. The hardships they endured were legend, but did not deter the family from arriving in a place near Greenwich, New Jersey, where they were reunited with Levin. At Springtown, a black community this side of the Delaware River, across from Philadelphia.[6]

Levin who earned his keep chopping wood, secluded his family in a hired man's log house. The family reunion they joyously felt continued on for days. They hoped that it would last forever. But this was not to be because Levin returned to an empty, disheveled cabin. The reality of their abduction by slave catchers was inescapable in Levin's mind. Sydney, bereft of her children who were sent to live with their grandmother in the slave quarter, faced doom in her locked garret room where her master had her incarcerated to cure her of running off again. Memories of her father's brutal death at the hands of his drunken slave master surfaced in her mind. She tried to soothe her troubled her fears by singing some of the good old Methodist tunes she had learned at the slave church in her youth. Enduring her master's scrutiny, Sydney longed for another chance at freedom. Soon she had a chance to make a second bid for freedom when her hymns had convinced her irate slave master to leave her door unlocked.

When she arrived under cover of darkness at her mother's cabin, Sydney whispered to her a plan she had devised to run off with the little girls and to leave her sleeping sons behind. Her mother, Mary Washington's tears revealed the truth of her desperate daughter's need to lessen the number of children she felt capable of delivering to freedom on this more precarious flight. Sydney kissed Levin and Peter without awakening them from their deep sleep. Creeping out of the cabin, she joined her two sisters, Elsie and Nancy Washington, who had food and water enough for the early stages of the flight. Mahalah, three or so, and little Kitturah, or Kitty, a toddler, and taking them by the hand she prayed that the sleeping boys would one day devise and implement an escape plan of their own and find them near the Delaware River.[8] After Sydney had concluded this wrenching desertion of her two much loved sons, she joined her sisters, Elsie, and Nancy Washington at the edge of the fields with her two little girls in tow to begin the first leg of their perilous journey from slavery to freedom. [9]

Sydney piloted the party of escaping slaves through the route she had earlier taken with all of her four little children. Basing her journey on the experience she had gleaned previously, the stalwart woman followed her North Star through the wilderness which eventually took them to Springtown where an astonished Levin praised God for their recovery. Once he had fetched one of his daughters left in the care of a kind hearted family when she fell ill along the road, he hastily took his family on the advice of friendly Quakers to a more remote section of Burlington County located in the desolate Pine Barrens of New Jersey.[10]

Older sister, Elsie, and the younger Nancy soon found work in Burlington city. Levin chopped wood in the deserted Indian reservation to support his family he lodged in a log house owned by a black settler in the woods. The family survived their early years as settlers in Indian Mills with its sawmill and gristmill left behind when the Indians transferred to upstate, New York, where they joined their Oneida brethren. Levin's family found a measure of solace at the old Brotherton Reservation, a densely wooded area that attracted huntsmen from all over who came to shoot wild game and a variety of birds in that bucolic site of natural wonder. Other more ominous creatures were also attracted to the area in search of fugitive slaves such as the former Sydney Steel who now called herself Charity Still to protect her person from recognition as depicted on handbills carried by bounty hunters.[11]

Charity Still kept on her person at all times a loaded pistol and a dirk knife she had been trained to use when Levin was chopping wood. Living in Burlington County provided protection to the Still family in the Quaker abolitionists who had recently established an antislavery society there to protect the rights of black people who lived in New Jersey.The society fought for the rights of blacks accused of being fugitives when in many cases they were freemen. The Still family soon found solace and a measure of protection from the Quaker abolitionists whose headquarters was across the Delaware River in Philadelphia They had the great good fortune to have made the acquaintance of Benjamin Lundy, a noted journalist of antislavery newspapers and a devoted friend of the slave. He was a member of the Religious Society of Friends, also called a Quaker, who settled the present day states of Pennsylvania, New Jersey, and Delaware. In the 17th century under a charter given William Penn. the leader of the persecuted Quakers, by King Charles of England.

A large family was born to Levin and Charity Still beginning with Samuel, who arrived on 26 February, 1807. In the still family everybody carried his weight. From their youngest years, the boys Levin kept at home had chores until they were old and strong enough to work on the family farm Samuel had transformed from a small garden into a successful truck farm that sustained the family. Levin reluctantly hired out the girls to work in the kitchens of farmers because he could not early on support them. This fate was shared also by some of the boys who could not work the soil on the farm brother Samuel had expanded into a paying proposition After a stint at renting rooms for the family in black settlers' homes, Levin by dint of hard work and frugality, was able to buy a few wooded acres from the State government that encouraged settlers to farm the land left fallow by the former Indian community The log house his sons helped build sat on a clearing in the depths of the desolate New Jersey Pines The family lived through a series of name changes that transformed Indian Mills to Shamong before it was known as Washington Township in 1893, when Evesham Township, and in 1852 Little Egg Harbor Township, and Northampton Township (now known as Maple Shade Township) nestled in with the original Indian Mills In 1864.Washington Township also had included Bass River Township, and in 1866, Woodland Township; and in 1870, Randolph.

Philadelphia was home to America's premier antislavery society. Quaker abolitionists extended their antislavery agenda to oppose the recapture of former slaves by bounty hunters in neighboring New Jersey. In 1775, Pennsylvania Quakers founded their antislavery society and another one in New Jersey in 1794.Quakers on either side of the broad Delaware River that flowed down from its Catskill Mountain source in upstate New York splicing Pennsylvania and New Jersey along its route to Delaware Bay to empty into the Atlantic Ocean, wrote in their State Conventions the right to freedom of its black residents.

Levin Still's fugitive slave wife and two daughters were privy to slave catchers The family naturally accepted the protection of this Quaker abolitionists who frequented Burlington County on his way to Trenton to argue before the New Jersey Supreme Court for the release of blacks accused of being runaway slaves. The relationship between Mr. Lundy and William Still, who was born on 7 October 1821 in Shamong, New Jersey, was founded on this antislavery stand taken by a white man who clearly supported the freedom of his struggling black family.[12]

An important Quaker religious tenet was "Follow the Light!" This motivation drove the early Quaker settler in Pennsylvania to work relentlessly to end slavery which they found to be evil.[13] They formed the first organized abolition society in Philadelphia on 14 April 1775. The Religious Society of Friends petitioned the Legislature of the State of Pennsylvania in 1780 to incorporate the concept of "gradual" to further describe the abolitionist intention of their Society.[14] In this way, Quaker emancipators addressed the lingering reality of slavery within their ranks, while, at the same time, recognizing the temporary status of this reality.

Quaker slave owners were given adequate time to free their slaves. "The buying and selling slaves" was given a certain amount of time to end.[15] Those Quakers who continued to own slaves were told to free their slaves by 1781. If they failed to obey this dictate, those members would be forced to terminate their membership in the association until "the records show that the Friends had become entirely clear of the evil." [16] Benevolent Quakers formed an association at that time for the purpose of protecting freed slaves from agents sent into the State of Pennsylvania to recapture the slaves alleged to be the property of southern slave holders.[17]

Those Pennsylvania Quakers determined to act as protectors of runaway slaves living within their state, formed a regular society under the name of The Society for the Relief of Free Negroes Unlawfully Held in Bondage,[18] When the Revolutionary War began, members of this society were forced to suspend their operations until 10 February 1784 [19] when hostilities ceased. In order to accommodate individuals from other religious denominations who were showing an inclination to join, the Quakers revised their constitution in 1787 which permitted into their membership other denominations.[20] The Pennsylvania Legislature granted to the Society on 8 December 1789 an Act of Incorporation.[21] At that time, the Society, formed a Committee to investigate reports of illegal recaptures of alleged fugitive slaves in neighboring New Jersey. The subsequent study made concerning the incidents resulted in the decision made by the Society to offer protection to fugitive slaves liable to be summarily returned to slavery in the South. This Society defended in the Supreme Court in Trenton those Negroes about to be returned to slavery whether or not they were actually runaway slaves.[2]

The New Jersey Society for Promoting the Abolition of Slavery was formed when a Committee was formed in 1792 by the Quaker abolitionists in Philadelphia.[23] The Quakers left themselves open for federal prosecution when the United States Congress enacted the Fugitive Slave Law of 1793 with its provisions for the recapture of fugitives living in the North. Southern search agent were deputized to act in this manner under this federal law subsequent to the pattern set by the Northwest Ordinance, Article IV of the Constitution that required the return of runaway slaves which read as follows:

"No person held to service or labor in one State, under the laws thereof, escaping into another, shall, in consequence of any law or regulation therein, be discharged from such service or labor, but shall be delivered up on claim of the party to whom such service or labor be due." [24]

The law reasoned that "so long as slavery was permitted, one state could become liable for allowing itself to become a haven for undermining another state's laws." [25.] The Fugitive Slave Law of 1793, Article IV of the Constitution, for all its good intentions, did not specify exactly how slave agents were "to become deputized in order to deliver up" the fugitives in question. Instead, the law placed the responsibility on federal and state judges to enforce the owner's rights."

Chapter 2.
Life in the Pine Barrens.

One of Levin and Charity Still's younger sons, James, was born on 9 April 1812 in Indian Mills His self-published 1877 memoir, *Early Recollections and Life of Dr. James Still 1812-1885,* detailed the wrenching struggle for existence his parents endured upon their arrival in Indian Mills circa 1805. James wrote in graphic terms the hardships they and Samuel, himself, and the next few children shared in rented rooms in not one but two log houses his father rented for them until he had enough money saved to buy a few acres of farmland that sold in those days for a dollar or so an acre. Forced to hire out the children he couldn't feed, Levin relied on his Christian values and unshakeable frugality to weather the storm that seldom lifted until with the help of the older boys he was able to build a log house at the edge of a thickly wooded area in the Pines. Even then, he forced the boys to chop wood and do other chores to earn a few cents until they were old enough to work on the expanding family farm.

James obeyed his frequently overbearing father's stern rules and regulations to perform what was required of him when it came to chores. He recalled in minute detail the first years his family lived in their own house. The roughly-hewn homestead had an upstairs loft for the family to sleep in, while downstairs the two storey house with one door and one window in the room where his mother prepared the family meals on the pine-log burning hearth. James helped out on the farm. He enjoyed the excursions on the flatboat ferry with his father who sold the farm's produce at the Farmer's market in Philadelphia with the help of one of his brothers. Mahalah and Kitty had long since settled in Philadelphia where they began families, and Samuel, though married with a wife nearby, continued to work on the more than forty acre farm after he left home. James who grew up in rural poverty in agrarian New Jersey much the same as many other boys his age who lived on farms all over the North, regretted the fact that he could not be spared from chores unless the weather was too inclement for farm chores.[1,2]

James had much to say about a visit of a white physician, Dr. Fort, who drove up to the house in a fine horse and buggy to vaccinate the children against smallpox. He wrote extensively about the impression the medically trained doctor had on his future life plans to become a doctor when he was older. Although he emulated the inoculation procedure on his chums with spittle on the shard of a reed, he knew deep down that his race and poverty would preclude the realization of this plan. This frustration was born of his scanty schooling in the basics at the county school. However, the awakening of a desire to serve the sick and dying took root in his fertile, intelligent young mind despite the odds.[3]

A teen when his school texts consisted of *Comley's Spelling Book,* and the chapters and verses in The *New Testament,* James bristled under this desultory educational. He managed to overcome this deficiency in an unexpected way following a spat with his stern and authoritative father who caught him in his Sunday coat in the woods one day chopping wood. Before he knew it, James hurried over to Amos Wilkin's farm where he asked if the well known white farmer would take him on as a plow boy. To his surprise and gratification, the minor boy was told to ask his father's permission before he would be able to begin a three year indenture in his fields. When James told his father he was offered a three year term at the Wilkin's farm with a month of schooling at the end of each harvest time, his father agreed to let his son hire out if he was given a portion of his earnings. James was overjoyed because he desperately wanted to learn to do sums which he would be taught at the Brace-Roads School because he still held fast to the idea of one day practicing medicine and needed this basic skill.[4]

When James left home, his brother, William, resumed some of his chores on the farm and in the woods. He came of age after their father traded up the lumbering oxen for a horse that more rapidly transported cartloads of wood the boy chopped for sale at the Mount Holly sawmill. James welcomed this advanced method of hauling wood after impatiently waiting for the slow moving oxen to take the twisting country roads with any kind of speed. William, the youngest of eighteen children born to his parents in or out of slavery was given chores the same as his older brothers despite the fact that his father's truck farm had for some time proved economically fruitful. He gathered cedar logs from the nearby swamps, burned charcoal to make a few pennies, and chopped wood when not working on the farm. Much the same as James, William had to settle for a sporadic education at the poorly run county school. Inclined towards literature and not mathematics like James, William Still read every book he could get his hands on. He devoured chapters on history and geography in the *Young Man's Own Book,* he memorized while driving teams of logs to the saw mill. When the evening meal was over and the pine logs burning in the hearth provided enough light for reading, William Still pored over the *Colored American,* the antislavery newspaper he subscribed to and read with great interest. He was especially proud of Charles B. Ray, a secretary at the New York City Vigilance Committee, and his colleague, Philip Bell, also a black abolitionist in that city This widely circulated paper was filled with interesting information about the fugitive slaves who were fed and sheltered at that busy underground railroad depot. [5]

With most of his brothers living with their own family when William was growing up, he sometimes felt like an only child with a bit more security than the older boys enjoyed during the family's period of abject poverty. But his life was no bed of roses. James was enjoying the schooling his employer promised at the end of his first year on the farm. Instead of easing through the requirements of summing based on the need to carry tens, James simple failed to grasp the concept of carrying tens. James was taught to overcome this deficiency when his brother, Samuel, tutored him until he caught on. By the time James' term of service was over, he reluctantly left the farm in a new suit of clothes with ten dollars cash in his pocket. Sadly, he said goodbye to his mother at the homestead and started walking along the road to Philadelphia where he hoped to find employment to earn the money he needed to buy botany books from which he planned to learn the herbalist trade.

James, who had given the matter of a medical education much thought, decided wisely that he did not in any way meet the requirements to matriculate at a medical college. Because he believed in his innate ability to cure the sick, he decided to begin an African remedy business in Burlington County where he could use his concoctions to alleviate the pain and suffering of poor folks who lived in the backwoods of Burlington County. He was made welcome at his sister, Kitturah's home until he had work and could find a place to live. James looked for work to no avail. Eventually, he was hired to work in a glue factory where he became responsible for cleaning hugh caldrons where calves feet boiled at high temperatures. Because he had in mind the goal of buying books without which he had no way of improvising on the traditional formulas, James forced himself to endure the stench of glue making if he was to achieve his objectives.

James applied his father's lesson of frugality and hard work which helped him to remain employed and even promoted. He decided to leave his job when he had enough money to buy a few botany books he found at a book stall at the Philadelphia water front. Soon he was back in Medford, New Jersey, with a few dollars in his pocket and a slew of books with formulas he planned to study in a one room shack he built in the woods. James read medicine when he wasn't chopping wood with a new axe he bought to earn his keep. Farmers hired him to dig marl for fertilizer and to plow when spring came. James shoveled snow to clear the roads in the depth of the next winter when the weather was snowier than in a long time past. Though a young man not yet thirty, he worked to keep himself until he had established a home remedy trade he hoped would grow and prosper over time.

Once he met a fine, young colored girl named Angelina Willow, James decided that life without her as a wife was not an option. Laying aside his deep seated love of medicine, James renovated the simple wood house until the home they shared was as comfortable as he could afford. During the winter of 1837, her health began to decline. James read medicine to find the cause of the illness that was threatening her life After he had diagnosed her illness as tuberculosis, he paved the sides of the drafty log house to keep out the bitter cold winds generated that severe winter. They had a baby named Beulah to look after while the child's mother languished and soon died at peace with her soul. The many frustrations that had for long plagued James Still emerged from the depths of his soul to threaten his sanity. On the way back home from his mother's house after dropping off Beulah, James one day experienced a Road to Damascus conversion to the Christian faith his family practiced throughout his youth. Driven to open a Bible he kept on a shelf in his cabin, James opened it to Romans and read a verse that changed his life. The following verse gave him a new lease on life:"There is therefore now no condemnation to them which are now in Christ. Jesus, who walk not in the flesh but after the spirit."

He experienced a release from the negative thoughts that had for long enthralled his mind. Suddenly, he dismissed the weighty blame he had nurtured about his lowly status as a poor, black boy born to slaves. He stopped accusing the world for making him too uneducated and penniless to be able to afford a regular medical education. This transformation not only lifted his spirits but put James in a frame of mind to look for a good woman to tell his troubles to. When he met and married Henrietta Thomas, a wonderful woman who was working in the kitchen of a Vincent town farmer, James brought Beulah to the cabin where she looked after the motherless child Exactly a year after her mother died, in 1838, Beulah also died. She gave birth to a son, James Thomas, on 12 July 1840. In addition to her roles as wife and mother, Henrietta, worked side by side with her husband to collect botanical specimens growing wild along the Medford back roads. Henrietta fired the woodstove under the glass still James bought at a local hardware store which was needed to make essence of peppermint a Philadelphia druggist promised to see there.[6]

The quickly passing years found the Still family scattered in different directions. When they heard about their brother Joseph's death in 1841, they gathered together at the homestead to mourn his untimely loss. They were shocked to hear a year later that their father, Levin, was gravely ill. Again, Mahalah and Kitturah and their husbands, and Mary, a unmarried schoolteacher who also lived in Philadelphia, arrived on the next stage out. William, who worked for a farmer near the family farm, arrived on horseback which his supposedly ill father went out to help him with his horse. And Samuel, who with James had earlier been named as executor of their father's estate, appeared with the will prepared by a Notary.

The family members who lived in Philadelphia turned in early in order to get an early return to their home. They were satisfied that their father would recuperate in a short time. Charity was also pleased. However, nobody in the family anticipated a visit to Levin by the Angel of death by the time morning came. Words fail to adequately describe the mourning for his loss that preceded his burial behind the house he had built from the ground up with the help of his boys. According to Levin's Last Will and Testament, his wife, Charity, was given the house to live in for the rest of her days. A small inheritance to be accrued following the payment of his bills was to go to the unmarried children including Charles and Mary. When all of Levin's debts were paid, there remained no money left over. James bought his father's horse because he stood in need of a horse to draw his New jersey version of a Conestoga wagon painted grey and covered over its hoops with white muslin by his wife to shade him from the hot rays of the mid-day sun when he delivered his medicines to sick folk in the county. The home remedies James carried in a cigar box sat next to him on the seat next the driver. Jim Still felt confident that his African remedies would cure what ailed the farmers in the depths of the remote New Jersey Pines.[7]

The five dollars William had saved to tide him over in Philadelphia in the spring of 1844 didn't last long. The hopes he had that black men could find better opportunities there than in rural New Jersey were soon dashed when he experienced racial prejudice wherever he applied for a good job. His first winter in Philadelphia proved bleak, indeed. Subsisting on scanty wages earned at menial, low paying, and sometimes laborious work, William Still lived in rooms he rented in a rundown wood frame shanty on Lombard Street above Poplar while teaching Sunday School at the Moral Reform Retreat in the most squalid section of the black community. His lot improved when Mrs. Elwyn hired him to keep the grounds of her elegant West Penn estate at a decent salary. When his well traveled employer noticed an interest in her extensive library, she offered to let him select and read some of her books in his spare time. He as naturally pleased at the kindness Mrs. Elwyn showed him and took advantage of her help in selecting books she felt would expand his curious and intelligent young mind. Not only did he grow and develop as a person, but he also practiced the art of penmanship that later helped him in his secretarial duties that at the time had no apparent place in his life and future career. Although he soon found work of a similar nature, in Philadelphia, William Still kept his promise to Mrs. Elwyn that he would continue his work at the Sunday School established by the Philadelphia Vigilance Committee to improve the lot of the morally and spiritually deprived slave children of the city.[8]

A biographical sketch, later written years about the life and work of William Still credited Mrs. Elwyn for the contributions she made on behalf of her young employee which helped him to grow and develop new notions of men, public measures, and society in general, which he felt increased his sense of duty, order and economy, from a source so high in wealth and station that their studied existence there was a surprise to him.[9]

While employed by William Wurtz, on Walnut Street, William Still answered an ad he saw in the window of the Philadelphia branch of the Pennsylvania Antislavery Society in the fall of 1847 for a part time janitor and a mail room clerk. He was asked by the agent in charge of the office to write in a short letter the reasons he wanted to be hired to fill the opening.

This letter was received by the Executive Committee at the Pennsylvania Antislavery Society:

Philadelphia, September 21, 1847.

J.M. McKim, Esq.
Dear Sir;-

I have duly considered your proposal to me, and I have come to the conclusion of availing myself of the privilege, esteeming it no small honor, to be placed in a position where I shall be considered an intelligent being notwithstanding the salary shall be small.

Therefore, if you think it proper to condescend to confer the Favor upon me, I am at your service, Sir.

I have viewed the matter in various ways, but have only come to the one conclusion at last, and that is this: If I am not directly rewarded, perhaps it will be the means of more than rewarding me in some future day. I go for liberty and improvement.

Yours respectfully,
William Still.[10]

Chapter 3.
William Still in Philadelphia.

Whereas the national Body, or the American Antislavery Society was founded in Philadelphia in 1834, local branches were also founded in the middle and late 1830s all over the country. Executive Committees and Vigilance Committees within each branch were manned by carefully chosen individuals of demonstrated abilities useful to the undertaking of the local commitments to free the slaves. Generally speaking, the vigilance committees associated with the diverse branches were headed by blacks who worked closely with members of Executive Committees for their financial and other aid needed to supply the needs of the incoming fugitives passing through the cities and towns in the North. Many of the members of various vigilance committees were not only former slaves, but more often than not, Christian ministers trained at white seminaries in major northern cities. One of these was Rev. Charles B. Ray, [1] of Falmouth, Massachusetts who received his theological training first at the Wesleyan Academy at Wilbraham, Massachusetts, and later at the Wesleyan Academy at Middletown, Connecticut. In the 1840s, while serving as a Congregational minister, he co-edited *The Colored American,* an antislavery newspaper which for reasons best known to him, referred to the Negro or black man as colored. [2]

Rev. Ray, one of the few members of his race to attend the Convention of the American Antislavery Society in Philadelphia in 1833. A black abolitionist, Rev. Ray served as an underground railroad agent from 1839 to 1842 at the New York City Vigilance Committee where he helped shuttle fugitives from that city northward.[3]

Before the abolition movement had established itself in the national body whose aim was to free the slaves without any compensation given their former owners, Judge Samuel Sewall,(1652-1730), the English-born Massachusetts Bay Colony jurist known for the part he played in the Salem witch trials that sent 19 condemned women to their death, subsequently publicly repented his action, and became an antislavery advocate. The Quaker tailor-scrivener, John Woolman, placed Judge Sewall on a par with other pioneer abolitionists who lived and worked in that period of time.

The Quakers in Philadelphia met at the Sun tavern on 14 April 1775 to form a Society with a Preamble to its constitution based on its objective to end slavery in the United States.[4]

In 1787, its constitution was enlarged to allow for the inclusion in the Society of members outside of the Quaker faith And in 1789, the Society petitioned the Pennsylvania Legislature to recognize the changed name of this enlarged Society in an Act of Recognition as the Pennsylvania Society for Promoting the Abolition of Slavery, the Relief of Free Negroes Unlawfully Held in Bondage, and for Improving the Condition of the African Race.[5] Benjamin Franklin became its first president.

Antislavery societies throughout New England by1785 followed the lead set by the Pennsylvania Society in regard to the gradual form of antislavery first introduced by the Pennsylvania Quakers. The State Constitution of New York, and later New Jersey, Delaware, Maryland, Connecticut, Rhode Island, and Virginia all followed suit.[6]

When the need became clear that the diverse antislavery societies would gain strength in a single body, the New York Society proposed in 1793 a convergence of the various antislavery societies at a convention to be held at Philadelphia for the purpose of deliberating on the means of obtaining their common object, and of uniting an address to Congress upon that subject." [7]

The possibility of deliberating the means read as follows:

> Resolved, that the Society do agree to the proposition of the New York Society, and will appoint Delegates to the proposed convention, provided a majority of the Abolition Societies in the United States do agree to the measure.[8]

The Delegates appointed in December of 1793 [9] were given the authority on behalf of the Society to address the Congress on the subject of the slave trade, and on matters concerning slavery in the nation, and to work towards the common purpose of uniting in implementing any measures that served the common purpose of the various antislavery societies within its body. This convention of America's first American Antislavery Society at Philadelphia 1 January 1794 addressed the issue of slavery and those opposed to it, with a simple statement of the concerted aim of this body with respect to the subject of American slavery.[10]

Some of the events that followed the establishment of this Society led up to the transformation of the gradual form of antislavery work into a later, more militant form of abolitionism at a second national convention held at in 1833 at Philadelphia.

The importance of the first few steps away from this moderate or gradual form of emancipation of the slaves came from the evangelical Christians in the second Great Awakening in the 18th and early 19th centuries. John Woolman and his friend, Anthony Benezet joined with fellow members of the Religious Society of Friends in Maryland and Delaware in the 18th century, where they met to discuss the slow, or gradual form of abolition of the slaves. Members of other protestant denominations recognized the need to emancipate the slaves. Baptists abolitionists in Virginia as early as 1789, members of the Presbyterian General Assembly in 1795, Conferences of Methodists from 1780 to 1796, all became antislavery advocates, though with a Southern flavor.150 members of 4 antislavery societies in the North, and 130 members of societies in the South, brought to 6,066 members all told of individuals all told who focused on the gradual emancipation of the African slaves.[11] Some who were members of The American Colonization Society slowly purchased slaves from their masters mostly in the Border States, had in mind to send the trained slaves back to West Africa, specifically to the American Colony of Liberia, in West Africa, or even to the British Colony of Sierra Leone.[12]

A firebrand Boston based editor, William Lloyd Garrison, once aware of the scheme of the American Colonization Society to rid the nation of its African slave population, sailed to London to confer with British abolitionists then in the process of liberating their West Indian slaves. The pamphlet the Baptist antislavery advocate penned, *Thoughts on Colonization,* was applauded by the British abolitionists who were present when he read it to that assembly. The titular head of the abolition movement, William Lloyd Garrison returned to America as a disciple of the abolitionists he had met in England.st Indian slaves, the British abolitionists in 1830. The following year he published the first edition of the *Liberator,* which soon not only was widely read by northerners but especially by members of the black communities who subscribed to it in large numbers. The most telling improvement in Mr. Garrison's leadership capacities was his strident denunciation of a gradual form of abolition and the need to adapt a more militant and even immediate form of abolition of the American slaves with no remuneration to be made to their slave owners.[13]

The ramifications concerning the issue of the inclusion of slavery into the Louisiana Purchase Territories purchased in 1805 resonated throughout the 1830s in the North. Gradual abolitionists pondered the possibility of an alteration of the prohibition of slavery westward. Antislavery societies whose gradual form of abolition had been drafted into their constitutions, agreed with Mr. Garrison that the westward extension of slavery into the Louisiana lands was better suited to the reconciliation with actual justice of the law.

The Compromise of 1820-21 appeased the issue that confounded northern statesmen in the Congress. It prohibited the extension of slavery into the Louisiana Purchase lands north of 36° 30[1]. Missouri was admitted into the Union as a slave state and Maine was admitted as a free state as a counter balance to the slave to free- state issue. A concession by the antislavery movement to the

Congress was made by allowing Missouri into the Union as a slave state that bordered Illinois, Kentucky, and Nebraska to the west, and Iowa to the North.

Article 1V of the Constitution stated:

> No person held to service or labor in one state, under the laws thereof, escaping into another, shall, in consequence of any law or regulation therein be discharged from such service or labor, but shall be delivered up on claim of the party to whom such service or labor shall be due.[14]

The furor over slavery absorbed the attention of the members of the Pennsylvania Antislavery Society much the same as the members of each of the others. In fact, the Missouri Compromise failed to settle permanently the slave to free state issue once again being debated in the Congress. William Still found himself in the maelstrom as a trainee at the Philadelphia Vigilance Committee which, as station 2, The Promised Land to an increasing number of runaway slaves in search of freedom in the North. He kept the office tidy, and mailed out each Thursday copies of the *Pennsylvania Freeman* to the other antislavery societies scattered in northern cities and towns. During his first few years as an understudy as an underground railroad agent, his devotion to the duties assigned him as a reliable underground railroad agent impressed his superior, the overworked agent in charge, James McKim, who was responsible for the editorial content of the widely circulated antislavery *Freeman.* Members of the executive Committee fretted over political matters designed to support a new piece of legislation designed to enable Southern search agents to roam freely throughout the North to recapture alleged fugitive slaves. of slave holders, who, when they petitioned the Congress for the right to recapture their runaway slaves Petitions introduced to the Congress by antislavery Congressmen to ban slavery in the District of Columbia were tabled under the provisions of the "gag law", yet. John C. Calhoun, the noted South Carolina statesman, received for his efforts support for the right of slave holders to own and to recapture their slaves anywhere in the North. [15]

Militant abolitionists were ready to take up arms in their own defense. William Still's undercover operation flourished in open defiance of the imminent threat to the Pennsylvania State Constitution to the contrary. William Still's eyes focused on the needs of the incoming runaway slaves. His job was to meet and to listen to their reason for having fled slavery. Then he contacted reliable members of the Vigilance Committee who put the destitute former slave up in rooms in their homes until a train could be found to transport them to a more northern vigilance committee until they found a secure and stable location to stay permanently. Curiously, William Still reportedly confused the underground railroad and vigilance committees.. The differences though subtle were real. But this semantic did not interest William Still in the least.

The Congress sided with the proslavery advocates. John Quincy Adams, the representative to the Congress from Massachusetts fumed under this and other restrictions placed against the other antislavery members. In 1825, he wrote a letter to a member of the Quaker Abolition Society not to continue to place their trust in a peaceable solution to the issue of slavery because he felt certain that the inevitable solution would be war..[16]

Chapter 4.
Blacks and Abolitionism.

The Pennsylvania Legislature on 1 March 1780 in an Act of Incorporation granted to the Pennsylvania Antislavery Society the right to gradually liberate slaves who lived within the borders of their State.[1] Other northern states with similar Constitutions, also relied on the Acts of their state legislatures to protect their laws from being undermined by the laws of another state.[2]

The responsibility to enforce the rights of slave owners to claim a slave was placed under the jurisdiction of federal and state judges under the Fugitive Slave law of 1793. Article 1V of the US Constitution failed to require of the Congress the right to deter the implementation of the provisions determined in 1793.The passive voice in which Article 1V was written, left even more unclear the role of the persons who were to have the authority to "deliver up" the fugitives in question. In other words, when an alleged fugitive slave was brought before a magistrate, the only interest of the law was a demand that the paid agent confirm the status of the alleged fugitive to a magistrate, who could grant to the agent the right to return the fugitive back to his slave owner in the South.

The differences between the Fugitive Slave law of 1793, and the Omnibus Bill of 1850 with its infamous Fugitive Slave law rider, was that the specifications of the Fugitive Slave law of 1850 prevented state officials from enforcing the constitutional provisions of a particular state's statutes. Clarification was needed to determine the legally correct procedure for deciding whether or not the claimant was entitled to remove the illegal fugitive from the state or territory in which he or she was found.[3]

Members of the Executive Committee of the Pennsylvania Antislavery Society hastily assembled some of the best black talent available in the North to foil the attempts made by search agents sent into their State to recapture runaway slaves. When the infamous law was passed, the Pennsylvania Antislavery Society urged its Philadelphia Vigilance Committee to deputize reliable black individuals of known good character to defend their abolitionist agenda. Since Pennsylvania lay above the mason and Dixon Line, this strategic position placed its southeastern areas in jeopardy to slave catchers who readily crossed over from Maryland, a slave state, into the Commonwealth's lands.

William Still had been employed at the Philadelphia Vigilance Committee as an underground railroad agent four years previous to the passage of the Fugitive Slave law of 1850 with teeth in it. He had learned the ropes well enough when the Fugitive Slave law of 1850 rumbled over the landscape of Pennsylvania first, only to continue its destructive slave catching agenda into the rest of the North. Still's lack of fear of the ramifications if caught as ordained by the Fugitive Slave law of 1793, in force when he first signed on to the underground railroad, could now, if found and he was convicted for aiding and abetting fugitive slaves, land him in the penitentiary and cost him $1000 dollars in fines. In other words, this law was enacted to punish those who sheltered more than the earlier trickle that arrived at Philadelphia previously which amounted to a steady stream of runaway slaves into the North.

He was honing at the same time an innate capacity on his part to help the less fortunate members of his race in other ways besides running them off. His life when he first arrived in Philadelphia from the New Jersey Pines opened his eyes to the social and economic needs of the black occupants of the Lombard Street section of the black community. He empathized with those fugitives who intermingled with self emancipated Negroes who were uninitiated in the ways of ordinary citizens in Philadelphia. Recalling his inability to gain a good job because of his color, he was forced to survive by carting wood, selling new and used clothing, and even shucking oysters for their broth at a seafood stall at the river's edge.[4]

His experience at the Moral reform Retreat helped to develop his social activist skills.[5] Robert Purvis, the only black member of the General Vigilance Committee of the Pennsylvania Antislavery Society, founded the Philadelphia Moral Reform retreat in 1836. [6] William Whipper [7] from Columbia, Pennsylvania, was a black underground railroad conductor and one of the founders of the Philadelphia Moral Reform Retreat. David Ruggles,[8] was the Secretary of the New York City Vigilance Committee who also found time to become active in the Moral reform retreat in that busy underground railroad in the large black community there.

Whereas vigilance committee members focused on aiding and abetting the increasingly heavy influx of fugitive slaves in their communities, especially in Philadelphia, following the passage of the Fugitive Slave law of 1850, vigilance committees all over the North soon followed suit. [9] Executive Committee members of the Pennsylvania Antislavery Society debated on measures to be implemented over the lack of a jury trial provision in the infamous bill. Unprotected, accused fugitives risked being summarily snatched by Search agents paid by slave holders to recapture fugitives by the use of the presentation to the Court of a Repossession Certificate.[10]

Levi Coffin,[10] a well-known Quaker, whose Cincinnati station was a hub of active underground railroad operations, originally came from North Carolina. Referred to as the President of the Underground Road, by his devoted colleagues, Levi Coffin engineered the successful escape of scores of fugitives from Kentucky who fled slavery across the Ohio River before being shuttled to more northern locations and even into Canada. Thomas, [11] another well known underground railroad agent, ran station 1, at Wilmington, Delaware. Many if not most of the fugitives who came through his place of business originated in Maryland, Delaware, and Virginia, although parties of intrepid runaways sometimes began their flight to freedom from the Deep South Mr. Garret was caught at this illegal, clandestine work and fined heavily before spending a term in prison. Not to be dismayed, upon his return to his busy station, he continued to funnel new arrives through other depots with the end of their journey generally planned for station 2, in Philadelphia.

Kind hearted people all over the country fed and sheltered runaway slaves. They operated out of southern cities as well. Richmond, Nashville, Selma, Alabama, and New Orleans. The son of a slave holder in Alabama, James G. Birney, abandoned his father's cotton plantation to form an antislavery society in Kentucky before he relocated in Ohio. He found his forte in politics in upstate New York where he became involved in plans by the political wing of The American Antislavery Society to form The Liberty Party. The abolition movement attracted underground railroad agents who operated depots in Chicago, Missouri, St. Louis, Detroit, and elsewhere.

The intricacies of underground railroad work became a legend. Wilbur H. Siebert,[2] an authority on the underground railroad in America, long after emancipation came to the slaves in America, compiled data for his *Directory on the Underground Railroad, The Names of Underground Railroad Operators.* However, Benjamin Quarles, a respected black historian, corrected Professor Siebert for the lack of race of the lack of race in his listings in his the well known, black historian, Benjamin Quarles, found wanting in Professor Siebert's *Directory* the race of the individual operatives.

According to Mr. Quarles, the following agents should have been listed as negroes: J.G. Bias, Frederick Douglass, George T. Downing, Robert Morris, Robert Purvis, Charles B. Ray, Stephen Smith, and William Whipper. Also missing from Siebert's list was the race of these Vigilance Committee members: William C. Nell, and John T. Hilton, both of Massachusetts, Charles T. Bustill, C.L. Reason, William Still, Josiah C. Wears, and Jacob C. White, members of the Philadelphia Vigilance Committee.[13]

The Massachusetts branch of the American Antislavery Society was headed by William Lloyd Garrison [14] in Boston after he attended the Convention held at Philadelphia in 1833 at which time the American Antislavery Society formed its new, more militant form of abolition referred to as immediate with no compensation to be paid to former slave masters in the South.

Black people interested in helping incoming fugitives to find new homes in the North stepped up to the plate to join the vigilance committees connected with the various antislavery branches throughout the North following the passage of the Fugitive Slave law of 1850. Clergymen: such as Jahiel C. Berman, and his son, Amos G., served as the Pastor at the Temple Street African Church in New Haven, Christopher Rush, the Second Bishop of the Zion Methodists, and five Presbyterian clergymen: Samuel E. Cornish, Theodore S. Wright, Stephen H. Gloucester, a youthful Henry Highland Garnet, and Andrew H. Harris, an 1838 graduate of the University of Vermont, who had served as the Pastor of the St. Mary Church at Philadelphia, became vigilantes on the lookout for search agents sent North to recapture blacks they claimed to be runaway slaves.

Charles B. Ray left Massachusetts to serve on the New York Vigilance Committee. James W.C. Pennington, a fugitive slave, served at the Hartford, Connecticut Vigilance Committee with Samuel Ringgold Ward. Nathaniel Paul, a black Baptist, joined the Albany branch of the New York Antislavery Society's Vigilance Committee. New York Antislavery Society And another Negro, Negro, Alexander Crummell, also served as the Secretary of the Vigilance Committee at the New York State Antislavery Society, along with Daniel Payne, an Episcopal minister ordained in 1839. Curiously, while blacks felt excluded from white churches, were warmly accepted in the vigilance committees of the various branches of the Antislavery Society.

Sarah M. Douglass, the only black woman accepted as a member of the Religious Society of Friends in Philadelphia, admitted that she sometimes felt the sting of racism while at worship at Quaker meetings. She overlooked the social distance that existed between her and her white Quaker Friends out of respect for the many contributions 18th century Quakers had made on behalf of her less fortunate race.[15] Quakers, for the most part, kept to themselves. Even when they pondered a relationship with the Pennsylvania Antislavery Society at its foundation in 1836, some of the venerable

Friends had problems joining the militant, immediate Society because of their usual abhorrence of violent methods in lieu of more peaceable reforms. Many Quakers sheltered slaves in need of protection from bounty hunters in hot pursuit. They shuttled them to Philadelphia where the Philadelphia Vigilance Committee at the Pennsylvania Antislavery Society handled their transportation to more northern locations or even into Canada. Moreover, a number of influential Quakers once involved in running off slave, served on the Executive Committee of the newly formed Pennsylvania Antislavery Society.[16]

William Still, much the same as Sarah M. Douglass, praised the social reforms early Quakers had instituted in the black community. Whenever black folks could attend a funeral for a highly respected Quaker who had worked to elevate the lives of the destitute members of their race, they attended the service. out of respect for him. These deceased gentlemen included Elias Hicks, in New York City, and the Rev. Thomas Shipley, [17] in Philadelphia. Although Benjamin Lundy died in Ohio, black people in Philadelphia mourned his death in 1838.

Another well known Quaker, Isaac T. Hopper [18] was surrounded by faithful black residents of Boston with tears in their eyes when he was eulogized there, before being praised for his efforts to free the slaves by grateful black residents in Philadelphia.

Quaker pioneer abolitionists in Philadelphia were rightly praised for the following social reform agenda they initiated and implemented for black people in Philadelphia.

The Committee for the Improvement of the Free Negroes. Originally composed of twenty four members, who were to be sub divided as follows:

A Committee of Inspection, whose duty should be to superintend the general morals, general conduct, and ordinary situation of the free Negroes, to afford them advice and instruction, and protect them from wrongs.

2nd. A Committee of Guardians, for placing out children with suitable persons, that they may learn some trade, or other means of subsistence by regular but reasonable apprenticeship.

3rd. A Committee of Education, which was to superintend the school instruction of the children and youth of free blacks. This branch of the Committee was also charged to procure and preserve a regular record of the marriages, births, and manumissions of all free blacks. 4th. A Committee of Employ, which was to procure constant employment for those free Negroes who are able to work, the want of which would occasion poverty, idleness, and other depraved habits. This last Committee was disbanded after a time because some of its duties were discontinued.[19]

The talents of black innovators were encouraged by the abolitionists in Philadelphia. When they learned about the almanac compiled by a black man from Baltimore, Maryland, they used their considerable influence to find experts to analyze the almanac for the possibility of having it published. Once the integrity and honesty of the almanac were confirmed by experts in that field, it was published in 1792.[20] Two well respected Quakers knowledgeable in the area of almanacs, Dr. Rittenhouse, and William Waring, urged the Society to reprint the Banneker Almanac which they recognized as not more than meeting the standards for products of that nature.[21]

The education of black children in the public school system in Philadelphia induced the abolitionists to form A Committee for Improving the Condition of Free Blacks. In 1793 a plan was presented to the Pennsylvania Antislavery Society to first find a proper site for a school building, and after it was built, to place in it a black school mistress when that particular individual was found.[22]

Robert Purvis in Philadelphia helped to organize black members of various vigilance committees throughout the North as few before him. He held conventions with black vigilance committee members in the major cities who revealed their deeply felt need to improve the lives of the less fortunate members of their race in multiple ways. David Ruggles, the Secretary of the New York Committee on Vigilance, and Lewis Hayden, a member of the Massachusetts Antislavery Society's Vigilance Committee, met with Mr. Purvis in 1837 at the New York City headquarters of the American Antislavery Society to discuss with an assembly of other black vigilance committeemen to promote good mental, moral, and social health among the African slaves new to the civilization commonly accepted throughout the North.[23]

The newly formed American Antislavery Society was the brainchild of evangelical Christians. They proposed to demand the emancipation of African slaves from their slave masters free of charge. Theirs was an agreement with the four Gospels that emphasized salvation by faith in the atoning death of Jesus Christ through personal conversion, the authority of Scripture, and the importance of preaching contrasted with ritual. . The Protestant fundamentalism that marked these members produced in them a militant or crusading zeal to view slavery as an evil to be eradicated without delay.

Theodore Dwight Weld, 1803-95, the Connecticut born abolitionist leader who helped select the "Seventy", who were chosen to function as disciples or agents to head the various branches of the American Antislavery Society about to be formed. He was himself a disciple of the evangelical fundamentalists to assume leadership positions in various antislavery societies at the Lane Seminary to spread the Gospel to the new Society.

Lewis Tappan [24] elected to serve as the national Body's first president, was a Boston Calvanist, who settled in New York City with his brother, Arthur, a woolen cloth dealer. The antipathy they and their fellow abolitionists encountered erupted into acts of violence against their persons and their property. The militant form of abolitionism disturbed northern citizens now as never before.

Even the Congress refused to be swayed by this Gospel spread by the modern abolitionist. Their petition to end the slave trade in the District of Columbia was tabled under the provisions of the "gag rule'.

"gag rule".

The following remark made by John Quincy Adams is an example of the misuse of this procedure:

> A Right to petition the Constitution for a Redress of Grievances is secured by the people [by the first Amendment]. But, Sir, of what use is the right of petition, if their petitions are unheard, unread, and to sleep "the sleep of death," and their minds to be enlightened by no report, no facts, no arguments? [25]

Chapter 5.
The Fugitive Slave law of 1850 and Black Abolitionists.

The majority of black volunteers at vigilance committees along underground railroad routes were former fugitive slaves. Slaves who chose to run away from slavery were the most heroic of their enslaved race. They thirsted for freedom in the North. Those who remained in the North rather than to settle in Canada chose to help new arrivals from slavery under the tutelage of the mostly white members of Executive Committees at the various Antislavery Societies scattered throughout the land, who chose to donate funds to implement the activities of their Vigilance Committees. A good many of the fugitives in the North received theological training at some of the best known seminaries.

The New York State Antislavery Society posted on its border with Canada eight former slave vigilantes. J. Mitre, worked there with William Yates, both of whom published their autobiographies about their experiences as slaves in the South. Yates' *Slavery and the Colored People in Delaware* was well received. The Rev. Hiram Wilson's underground railroad depot at the end of New York State's border with Canada. Augustus Wattle proved ran the Ohio Vigilance Committee so efficiency that he was promoted to run a site in Indiana.[1]

Although large sums of money donated by prominent white abolitionists facilitated the day to day activities at vigilance committees everywhere, black abolitionists raised funds or received donations to pay for food and other necessities for runaway slaves at various from black friends in a position to contribute money towards this end. J.W.C. Pennington,a former slave, in the 1840s became the Secretary of the Hartford, Connecticut Vigilance Committee. [2]

Robert Purvis's role as the Secretary of the Philadelphia Vigilance Committee, relied on a fellow agent, Jacob C. White, to aid the fugitives streaming into the city. Other long forgotten black vigilance committee members at northern depots on the underground railroad included Stephen Myers, a conductor at Albany, New York. Jermaine Loguen at Syracuse, New York, sometimes known as The Canada of the North, because of its close proximity to the black settlements in Canada, Charles B. Ray, at New York City, and Henry Highland Garnet, who reportedly remarked when a young Presbyterian minister, "I never got a cent for my work. I gave them my last crust!" Before he turned to his literary work, William Wells Brown was an underground railroad conductor at the Albany, New York. George T. Downing, was a conductor at the Newport, Rhode Island Vigilance Committee, who in the 1840s, ran off an average of twenty-six slaves each week. By 1844, the poorly organized Philadelphia Vigilance Committee listed only these black clergymen who continued to serve: James G. Bias, Daniel Payne, and Stephen Gloucester.[3]

William Still differed from many of the above named, devoted friends of fugitive slaves in that he was born free. He and a small cadre of black men of prominence and means living in Philadelphia were also either born free or were self emancipated in the sense that they had free papers to prove this status to those who had a mind to want to know. This is not to infer that Mr. Still was in any way less involved with the problems connected with vigilance committee operations. In fact, he empathized with the social and economic problems he felt destroyed their upward mobility, and whenever he could, he lent a hand to improve their unenviable position. His superior, James McKim encouraged him to become involved in social issues which affected the rights of black people in Philadelphia. Therefore, when the Society became aware of the insertion of a clause into the Constitution of Pennsylvania in 1849 that denied suffrage to black males, they openly refuted this right to a suffrage for white males only clause that patently excluded black males from the right to vote. The Society felt that any astringement of that right to any portion of the inhabitants endangered to some extent, the liberties of the whole, and was injurious to all. [4]

The Memorial, or petition, they signed and sent to the Pennsylvania Legislature demanded that the rights of blacks earlier conceded in the Legislature's Act of Abolition in 1780 be returned. They presented a list of demands based on the wrongs they considered inflicted against Negroes by the revised Constitution. Moreover, they petitioned for the right of the disenfranchised to "receive that consideration which its importance demands and that measures be immediately taken to effect in a constitutional way an alteration in that instrument so as to erase the word 'white' in the article relating to the right of suffrage and thus to restore to them their ancient privilege and inalienable right to which they are justly entitled."[5]

The legislature refused to alter the changes requested to be included in the Pennsylvania Constitution.

The Society faced more pressing problems following the passage of the Fugitive Slave Law of 1850. Blacks living in Philadelphia themselves feared being recaptured by southern search agents whenever they claimed to have lost their free papers. Many blacks chose protect their freedom from bounty hunters in a violent manner. Violent emotions threatened the peace of the city. The hastily written pamphlet printed by Quakers contained in it advice for the mitigation of the very real problems faced by the black community.[6]

Fortunately, a majority of cool headed Negroes encouraged their overwrought people to control unbridled passions which had placed the community in more jeopardy than was necessary to come to a resolution of the problem.[7]

The petition to the senate and the House of Representatives presented to the General Assembly of the Commonwealth of Pennsylvania represented qualified and legal voters., who had signed the petition 'to provide to all persons arrested within this State, a jury trial, to prove they were, indeed, fugitives from justice.[8]

Concerned Negroes gathered together to unite in a common purpose to protect their liberty. The use of weapons to protect their freedom came up for discussion as a last resort. The Pennsylvania Antislavery Society's pamphlet, distributed in the black community entitled, "Address to the Colored People," cautioned the excited Negroes to listen to their more reasonable fellow blacks. Their ability to reason impressed many whites who previously thought black folk incapable of the use of reason with regard to the resolution of their difficulties.[9]

The Fugitive Slave Law proved especially lethal to black people in Philadelphia because of the strategic location of southeastern Pennsylvania. In addition, Pennsylvania was the first State in the nation to abolish slavery. Considering the large black community there, it was reasonable for the search agents to cross the Mason and Dixon Line that separated slave and free states. The Fugitive Slave Law of 1850 based it authority on Article 1V of the US Constitution which failed to provide clear and exact instructions concerning the person who was to "deliver up" fugitives. The responsibility given to state or federal judges in the previous Fugitive Slave law of 1793 was shifted upon federal and state judges, responsible for the enactment of laws against the kidnapping of free blacks on the pretense of claiming them as fugitive slaves.

The U.S. Supreme Court decision, Prigg v. Pennsylvania struck down the statutes forbidding state officers to participate in the enforcement of the constitutional provisions in any case. Southern statesmen argued in 1850 that the clause was a "dead letter," because not enough federal judges were available to enforce the law; therefore, "new legislation was needed to revive it.[10]

Vigilance committees were assembled to defy the provisions of the Fugitive Slave Law of 1850. The vigilantes who hid and fed escaped slaves obeyed the laws of northern states while disobeying the federal law contained in this infamous bill. The law mandated to return of any black person claimed by search agents sent to return these slaves to their rightful owners in the Sout The Rev. Samuel J. May, who ran an underground railroad station at Syracuse, New York, cursed the Omnibus Bill of 1850, the proper name for the bill that included in it the Fugitive Slave Law. But Henry Clay, a Virginia statesman in the House of Representatives. Known in the Congress as "The Great Compromiser," Clay conciliated Northern States to force them to accept the entire Omnibus Bill of 1850 that provided for the admission of California into the Union as a State with an antislavery constitution. In addition, two other territories would become States without the prohibition of slavery; the Southwest boundary of Texas would be extended to the Rio Grande; and slavery would be abolished in the District of Columbia, but not the interstate slave trade.[11]

Finally, slaveholders had a federal mandate in the bill to recoup their property anywhere in the North. This concession to the South, was signed into law on 12 September 1850, in the administration of President Millard Fillmore, who was helped by Senator Daniel Webster, a Massachusetts Whig. Webster leaned towards the slave holding South when he opposed the Missouri Compromise in 1819 when he was rewarded with the position of Secretary of State. Abolitionists hated him for his introduction of the Fugitive Slave law of 1850 because of its provision for "all good citizens" to be required to obey the law under pain of penalty, which denied to the fugitives in custody the right to a jury trial, and the right to testify in court.[12]

Commissioners and judges were easily bribed. The abolitionists feared that the $10 fee for handing over an accused suspect to bounty hunters might unduly influence the actions of those officials. The reduced fee of $5 went to the Judge or Commissioner if the proof adduced by the claimant did not satisfy him that the accused was, indeed, a fugitive from justice. Blacks could not speak up to defend themselves, or to swear that he had been emancipated by the will of a former owner, or by the purchase of his liberty.[13]

The use of underground railroads increased. William Still's home served as an underground railroad depot. His wife, Letitia, cooked and washed for the desperately used fugitives who poured into her home. She stayed up nights cleaning mud from the boots of fleeing men, and even small children, who chanced recapture for a chance to be free. Children slept with her small daughter, Caroline Virginia, who was born on 1 November 1848. Total strangers ate meals with the Stills at the family table. It made no sense to bemoan the Fugitive Slave law of 1850 that was known as "The Act Respecting Fugitives From Justice, and Persons Escaping from the service of Their masters." [14]

The true nature of the Omnibus Act of 1850 did not escape the members of the American Antislavery Society It was an argument over the extension of slavery into the territories. The really new thing about the slave retrieval hysteria in 1850 was the intertwined issues of slavery in the territories and the dispute over the border between New Mexico and Texas. These precedents were being set without recorded objection by Congress which had acquired the entire Southwest territory that extended from North Caroline westward. The annexation of Texas itself (by annexation, not treaty) had been defended based on the grounds that the acquisition of territory was incidental to its admission as a state under Article 1V.[15] Occasionally, forays erupted in the Congress over the right of the Congress to implement the constitutional provision to limit the state authority to reclaim slaves. Despite the constitutional arguments, the provisions to remove the alleged fugitive from the state or territory in which he or she was found, remained in force.[16]

Chapter 6.
The Kidnapped and the Ransomed.

William Still volunteered to help collect signatures for a giant petition in the black community to ascertain the needs of the most neglected residents in the community. The Philadelphia Vigilance Committee of the Pennsylvania Antislavery Society required this data for a plan they hoped to implement individuals in the black community most in need of social welfare programs to alleviate the gnawing poverty that plagued the lives of most of that community.[1] The mass of data accumulated by the petition was carefully scrutinized, and prepared for publication under the title of The Associations Among the Colored People of the City for Promoting Scientific and Moral Purpose.[2] Committees derived from the most pressing needs in the black community were subsequently formed to address these needs at various times and places in Philadelphia.

Rev. James Bias, a member of the Philadelphia Vigilance Committee delivered a middle aged gentleman who called himself Peter Freedman to William Still's office on early August afternoon in 1850 to see if William Still could help him find his family he last saw when he was six. The middle aged gentleman who said he had been separated from his master, Joseph Friedman, at Cincinnati after a steamboat ride from Alabama where he was a slave for more than forty years. A black man on the dock at Pittsburgh where Peter debarked advised him to take a stage to get a ride on a locomotive heading for Philadelphia where the majority of black folks lived. As was his custom when he met and interviewed fugitives, William Still made notes from the man's story which unfolded into a drama he had heard many times from his own mother's mouth. Peter described the loss of his mother and two little sisters, whose names he barely recalled, who left him and his brother, Levin, in Maryland never to see them again.

William contained himself while Peter droned on about their sale from owner to owner and their new, more difficult existence on a cotton plantation in Alabama where his brother, Levin, was whipped to death for visiting his wife without permission. He fought tears when he alluded to Levin's untimely death and his burial at the edge of the plantation in an unmarked grave. Peter's story about the death of his brother, Levin, due to serious floggings, and his burial at the edge of a cotton field in Alabama, in 1838, forced William Still to shout, "What would you say if I said I was your brother?" He touched upon his sale to Joseph Friedman, a Tuscumbia Alabama businessman who warned him not to debark before Pittsburgh, in the free state of Pennsylvania.

William was convinced at this point in Peter's story that he was sitting across the table with one of his two small brothers their mother had reluctantly left in Maryland more than forty years ago because she knew that if she took all four of her children, her chances of achieving her objective would have been diminished. When Peter confessed that it was his grandmother who had made him promise to free himself from slavery to find his mother at the Delaware River Peter barely remembered from his experience with the first escape of his family before they were recaptured and taken back to Maryland The life of slavery Peter related almost made his freeborn brother cry. Yet he controlled his feelings in order to hear Peter's life as a slave in Alabama. The fortuitous arrangement between Mr. Friedman and Peter, was the result of a plan the Tuscumbia businessman made with Peter's owner, who had been bequeathed the black slave when a man named Gist died and left him and the other slaves to Johnny Hogan. By dint of hard work and frugality as a hireling to people in nearby Tuscumbia who paid Peter small sums that added up to the $500 needed to buy himself, resulted in the former slave's arrival in Philadelphia and this meeting with a clerk at the Philadelphia Vigilance Committee. William, who could no longer contain himself, revealed to the trembling black man across from him, sent shivers of disbelief through the tired slave's mind and heart. Fearing at first his brother's confession that he was a brother with many freeborn siblings in Philadelphia and New Jersey, frightened Peter who had been trained by his slave masters never to trust another slave. Yet He believed William Still who offered to take him to meet his wife at their home across from the Antislavery Office until a meeting could be arranged with their mother, In New Jersey.[3]

Letitia made him comfortable while William posted the good news in a letter to his brother, James, in Medford, New Jersey. He described in glowing words the exhiliaration that welled up inside of him when he felt certain that the strange black man he met and interviewed was his own never before met bother. Perhaps William wanted the James O. Cousin, the underground railroad agent he addressed, to investigate the whereabouts of his brother's nominal master, Joseph Friedman, who was last known to be resettled in Cincinnati His letter was emotionally charged and his gratitude at his reunion with Peter, was an indescribable joy.[4]

The family reunion held at James' house where Peter and his mother met after a forty-two year separation, defies words. He answered her questions about the events that he had been forced to endure throughout his journey through the wilderness. Holding in his emotions, Peter reported to his mother Levin's last days on earth and his cruel death far from her side. "He is dead!" Charity Still then uttered the following words from Scripture, "Now letteth thy servant depart in peace, for mine eyes have seen Thy salvation, and in those latter days beheld the first fruits of my womb." [5]

William Still reported to James McKim the wrenching details of his brother's reunion with his family. Moreover, he confided in his superior Peter's plan to return to his family at his earliest convenience. Peter swore that he'd rather die than remain apart from his wife, Lavinia, his son, Peter, a teen, and his younger son, Levin. He also had a much loved daughter, Catherine about age twelve. James McKim, a man of discernment and common sense, chose not to advise the members of the Executive Committee of the Pennsylvania Antislavery Society about William's brother's predicament. Instead, he used his authority as editor of the *Pennsylvania Freeman* to inform its many readers about the details of the life of a slave who was separated from his family for more than forty years. *The Kidnapped and The Ransomed* was written to awaken an otherwise aloof population of northerners to the realities of the pain that followed the pain and suffering that followed in the wake of broken slave families. In other words, it was a propaganda piece for the uninvolved whites who continued to ignore the ramifications of slavery, especially now that the Fugitive Slave law of 1850 was now enforced.

Little did Mr. McKim anticipate the arrival in his office of Seth Concklin, a white man who offered to rescue Peter's family in Alabama. The idealistic brother of two members of the Executive Committee, Mr. Concklin read the article about the long years of slavery that had plagued Peter Still, and continued to separate him from a permanent reunion with his beloved family in freedom. James McKim in the presence of William still listened to a plan to be undertaken by Seth Concklin who had never been South to rescue Peter's family. When Peter heard about the attempt to run off his family by a white man, he applauded his generous offer while thinking it impossible to achieve. Peter was about to depart to Alabama after what he called an overly long absence from his close knit family. However, he realized that Mr. Concklin would not rescind his offer to run the family off, offered to return from his journey to the plantation with personal items from his wife which would force her to trust the white man who soon would arrive to take her and the children to Philadelphia and the other places where family members lived.

Peter's free papers protected him from recapture when he traveled through the South. He promised Seth Concklin when he refused to forget his offer to rescue Peter's family that he would be best served if he waited for his return from South Florence, Alabama with items his wife, Vina, would be sure to recognize when he handed them over to the Good Samaritan when he returned. [6]

Mr. Concklin accepted $1000 from the Philadelphia Vigilance Committee to help defray the cost of his travel and lodging expenses. He was told that when his money ran out, he had only to write the office from the location where he was staying at that time so that the abolitionists could replenish the funds. Choosing not to cause unnecessary concern to his sisters because of his dangerous journey to the Deep South, Seth Concklin departed Philadelphia with his carpet bag in his hand and faith in his heart that he would be able to rescue a slave family and return them to their rightful place beside their loving father and husband. He seemed not to regret the fact that he did not tell his sisters about his dangerous mission because they might implore him to think about the possible outcome of the trip. With $100 dollars in his carpet bag donated by the Philadelphia abolitionists to help defray his traveling expenses to Alabama, Mr. Concklin began an adventure into a region of the country where he had never before traveled.

William Still waited patiently for a letter from the man who had volunteered to free his brother's family. When one arrived at his home address, it was dated 3 February 1851. Post marked Eastport, Mississippi, it was filled with information Mr. Concklin gleaned from Levi Coffin in Cincinnati where the two abolitionists met and discussed various return routes of Peter's family when they were delivered to that station upon Mr. Concklin's return. William Still read with interest the mention of routes to be used when Mr. Concklin had the slaves in hand and was prepared to hand them over to underground railroad agents from their Ohio River arrival to agents willing to lead them through Ohio or Indiana and into Canada.[7]

Mr. Concklin's next letter was posted at Princeton, Gibson County, Indiana, dated 18 February 185. Apparently, Seth Concklin had run the slaves off from their South Florence, Alabama, plantation, and was no writing a harried letter from Indiana. He described the change of plans that a late arrival of the slaves at the Alabama dock had forced him to avoid detection by renting a skiff with Peter and Levin at the oars. This boat of slaves and their abolitionist leader were exposed to witnesses on the shores of the river that placed them in as much jeopardy rather than placing them in a similar danger on the steamboat in the exposing morning sun.

The blanketed women were seemingly concealed from intruders on the shore of the Tennessee River whereas the Ohio River up ahead was manned by underground railroad agents chosen to take the slaves through undisclosed locations through Ohio or Indiana where trusted underground railroad agents were privy to hidden sites designed to free the runaways to the next level of operatives in more northern places.

This letter had been handed over to an agent who had mailed it to William Still. He added to it details he felt would interest Mr. Still. The skiff was traveling northward to Indiana at the time to meet with agents who were prepared to meet them at the Wabash River opposite Detroit. The previous route through Illinois, or even through Cincinnati, Ohio, had been discarded because the route to Canada was too indirect. Mr. Concklin's route of choice once on land forty-four miles to New Harmony, Indiana, where, after a 13 mile trek east to the farmhouse of Charles Grier for a night's sleep, David Stormon, would relieve Mr. Concklin of his duties and hand the slaves over to an escort who promised to deliver them into Canada.

The next letter William Still received from Seth Concklin was dated 1 April 1851.It reported that Peter Still's family was on its way to Detroit. Bemoaning his fatigue, and lack of money, the writer gathered the energy to express the joy he felt at the completion of his mission. He asked for a replenishment of his depleted funds to be mailed to the address of the letter. He bemoaned the extreme physical hardship he had experienced on the long trip upriver, from Alabama to Gibson County, Indiana the underground railroad stop for the delivered slaves.[8]

The Philadelphia abolitionists cheered the successful delivery from slavery for Peter's enslaved family. Mr. Concklin who had earlier proposed to arrive at this destination in March,encountered unexpected difficulties when slave catchers vollied shots at the skill from the river bank. Forced him to pull over to the river bank, in response to a second more impetuous volley, which resulted in his capture with the escaped slaves by agents sent ahead by a telegraph by their slave owner, Mr. McKiernon Once the slaves were retrieved, the slave catchers wired South Florence where Mr. McKiernon waited for this news.[9]

The story of this slave recapture appears in an article written by Dr. Kenneth R. Johnson, A Slave Family's Struggle for Freedom. [10]

The Philadelphia *Ledger,s* article below described the disastrous result of Seth Concklin's failed attempt to free a party of slaves.

> RUNAWAY NEGROES CAUGHT…
>
> At Vincennes, Indiana, on Saturday last, a white man and four Negroes belonging to B. McKiernon of South Florence, Alabama, and the man who was running them off calls himself John H. Miller. The prisoners were taken charge of by the Marshall of Evansville….April 9th.

The tragic story of the aborted slave rescue reached agents at various underground railroad depots spread, they sent their condolences to the Philadelphia Vigilance Committee. One letter to William still was written by Rev. N.R. Johnston. a Presbyterian minister in the Covenanter sect He corroborated the event at Evansville, Indiana, in that 31 March 1851 letter about the unfortunate death of the martyr, Seth Concklin. He bemoaned the nearly successful escape of the slaves only a few hours earlier near Princeton. Rev. Johnston wrote, "they had been placed aboard a boat at 3p.m, while the writer got there at 6 p.m." The agent who opened the letter Mr. Concklin wrote and added the p.s. to it about a story a colored man on the wharf near the boat that he was planning to take to Paducah, Kentucky, out of St. Louis, and described the return to Alabama of the slaves accompanied by their owner, Mr. McKiernon, who took them with him to South Florence, Alabama. He remarked about this gentleman who boarded with the four youngsters and the woman slave, but not "the white man" named Mr.Concklin, whom he supposed had got away from them" about 12 miles up the river, at Smithfield, Kentucky, at the mouth of the Cumberland River.

Abolitionists at Philadelphia had already read in a newspaper the news about "the white man," arrested in connection with the capture of the slave family, who was found dead in irons on the river bank, his skull fractured. The certainty of the death of Seth Concklin made it necessary to prepare his two sisters at the Philadelphia Vigilance Committee office to receive the sad news. Mr. McKim and William Still knew that Mr. Concklin had refused to worry his sisters about his choice to make the dangerous journey into the South. Mr. McKim gently described to the grieving sisters the secret mission their brother chose to undertake; and they stressed the courage it took for him to even consider such a dangerous plan. Although their eyes revealed the pain inside them, neither sister shed a tear.[11]

Levin Coffin's 10 April 1851 letter to William Still contained a eulogy to Seth Coffin. He referred to an article that appeared in the *Times* that praised the underground railroad work being done at his Cincinnati station. The abolitionists at that station employed the services of one of their best trained underground railroad agents, Attorney L. B. Thornton, who agreed to contacted Mr. McKiernon, in South Florence, Alabama, with a request for a more reasonable price for Peter Still's family in South Florence, Alabama. [12] A 6 August 1851 letter from Mr. McKiernon to William Still stated in no uncertain terms that he would not take a cent less than $5000 for the sale of Peter's family. He further stated that he found Vina and her three children to be "likely looking" slaves who could fetch an even higher price at a auction .Mr. McKiernon alluded to a letter from a Mr. Thornton dated 6 June 1851 that requested a reduced price for the freedom of Peter's family which he refused.[13]

William still began his reply letter to Mr. McKiernon by describing the modest condition of Peter's brothers in Philadelphia. He appealed to the avaricious slave master's understanding about the pain Peter was experiencing every day more excruciatingly due to this painful separation. William still ended the letter with a request for the sale of Peter's wife and daughter, Catherine at a price the family could afford to pay. In the meantime, all Peter's family could do was to await another letter from Mr. McKiernon.

The Kidnapped and the Ransomed awakened the interest of readers all over the North. Kate Emily Reynolds, who married a man Named Pickard and settled in Camillus, New York, following her graduation from the school some years ago, contacted Rev. Samuel May at his Syracuse underground railroad station to report her previous knowledge about Peter Still, who was formerly known as Peter Gist. When they met, Mrs. Pickard described a kindly slave who was the subject of the article she had chanced upon in the *Freeman.* As a consequence, she expressed a desire to write a book about his years as a slave and his more recent dilemma over the loss of his wife and children to slavery in Alabama.

She confided in the curious underground railroad station-master at Syracuse near her Camillus, New York home that she had no idea then that the handyman at the school and at other places in Tuscumbia was saving his hard earned pennies to buy his freedom. Her recollections were based on his good character and work ethic that completely concealed his suffering as a slave. He blacked the boots of guests at the hotel, cleaned rooms and waited table for the guests at the Tuscumbia Hotel entirely unaware at that time that his brother, William Still was the clerk at the Philadelphia Vigilance Committee a world away from him.

When James McKim learned about the proposal for a book about William Still's brother, Peter, he shared this knowledge with his Unitarian colleague from the Boston area, Rev. D.H. Furness, who had no other real function at the Pennsylvania Antislavery Society than the moral support he lent to its membership. Now he found his forte with an offer to write the Introduction to the proposed book on the life of Peter Still that despite the tragic martyrdom of the Good Samaritan, Seth Concklin, who died trying to rescue from slavery Peter's wife and children. Plans were now laid for a volume on the subject of one man's long time life as a slave and the repercussions of slavery's effect on the break-up of black families. Mrs. Pickard made it plain to her confidants that she would be overly cautious about revealing anything about the fugitive slave status of Peter's mother, Charity Still, who could even in 1850 be pounced upon and taken back to Maryland slavery by slave catchers roaming about the New Jersey backwoods.[14]

All concerned welcomed the input of Rev. Furness whose praise of the courage of Seth Concklin's daring attempt to liberate a slave family in the depths of the South, became an accepted Preface to the wrenching experiences of a slave family was to be shared with masses of readers throughout the North who had previously buried their heads in the sand over the issue of slavery on black people in the South. [15]

Chapter 7.
From Pacification to Agitation and the Fugitive Slave law of 1850.

Northerners caught on to the newly granted rights given to search agents who invaded their region. As it became clear to these citizens that the Fugitive Slave Law of 1850. disregarded the basic human rights idealized in the 1789 U.S. Constitution's guarantee of liberty, property, and security rights to citizens in the new World, they vowed to take up arms against the invading enemy. More to the point, virtually every black resident in the North knew terror, whether fugitive of self emancipated. Many prepared to fight for their freedom they had come to enjoy by dint of hard work and sustained efforts to develop their native skills, intelligence, and considerable organizational capacities, etc.[1]

Even more imminently dangerous to the future safety of black residents in the North, in William Still's view, was the effect that the Fugitive Slave law of 1850 was "[The] breakdown of a man's sense of his own worth, [which] murders his aspirations and chokes the God in him."[2] Still's fear of the recapture of members of his family plagued him day and night.[3]

While abolitionists in the North trembled over the Draconian provisions in the Fugitive Slave law of 1850 which denied the sovereignty of their region, Southern Congressmen felt empowered by the law because of its connection between the annexation of Texas, and the acquisition of the Southwestern territories acquired from the War with Mexico. Abolitionists all over the North were empowered by its role as the precursor to the clash of the powers of darkness and the powers of light.[4]

Abolitionists prepared for battle. Otherwise uninterested citizens in the free states prepared to go to war to preserve their social and humanitarian values.[5] No sensible black person failed to understand his assigned role in the imminent conflict between the dominance of slave or free in the common territory of an expanding nation.[6] Astute abolitionists faced the reality that seemingly eluded southern slave holders,--the reality that the United states of that day had two frontiers to be defended-- a Southwestern as well as a Northeastern frontier.[7]

Slaveholders tried to compensate for the loss of labor that followed in the wake of the increasing number of slaves who fled the cotton fields of the South for their freedom in the North. Although slaveholders may have exaggerated the actual number, they chose to recapture as many black slaves in the North as time and money allowed. In this they were right because of the fact that the foreign slave trade had since its passage in 1808 denied to slaveholders the further importation into the new World of African slaves. Given their depleted southeastern soil, planters interested in the extension of the institution of slavery into the virgin soil in the southwestern lands gained after the Mexican war, were hard pressed to recapture as many allegedly runaway slaves to work in the cotton fields of the South.[8] Congress rang with debates by Southern Congressmen in its 1837 session over the annexation of the State of Texas into the Union. The eminent South Carolina statesman, John C. Calhoun opined thusly: "There is but one question that can dissolve the Union, and that is involved with slavery"[9] William Lloyd Garrison, and his gifted orator colleague, Wendell Phillips, preferred to live in a dissolved Union rather than to allow the domination of slavery in the land.[10] John Quincy Adams, the Congressman from Massachusetts, agreed wholeheartedly.[11]

Formerly reticent Bostonians reacted passionately to the intrusion of the slaveholding South into their region. Public statements flew from the lips of a formerly slumbering group of discreet bankers, businessmen, politicians, academics, and their fringe element cohorts alike, as they vowed to personally enforce the integrity of their state laws when they were defied by search agents seen roaming about in the Boston area who preyed on black people whatever their legal status. Dr. William Ellery Channing, an esteemed Harvard Medical School professor, praised the brave, black people he considered to be "among the mildest, gentlest of men, affectionate, easily touched, open to religion more so than white men, meek, and long suffering...patient [able to] endure scorn, etc.,"[12]

William Lloyd Garrison entrusted to his trusted black abolitionist cadre to assemble protest meetings at the African meeting House on Beacon Hill where many blacks resided on its North Slope.

About this time, a schism erupted between Frederick Douglass, a freed slave who had been associated with the Massachusetts Antislavery Society with Mr. Garrison. One of the reasons the black abolitionist removed to Rochester, New York where he established an underground railroad depot was his inability to convince William Lloyd Garrison that Boston needed another antislavery newspaper besides the *Liberator.* Some good came from this split between two devoted abolitionists with the publication in Rochester of Douglass' antislavery paper, the *North Star.*[13]

Vigilance committee members prepared to do battle with slave catchers in the North who tried to retake their black brethren. Martin R. Delany, a former slave, swore to risk his life to protect those former slaves who hoped one day to function as independent black folks despite his gratitude for the social and economic skills they had been taught by kind hearted whites in the North. Henry Highland Garnet, a Presbyterian minister, agreed with the independent stance taken by Mr. Delany who believed that the time had come for black people to implement a plan for economic stability on their own, although he suggested that an economic base for black people could be found in Africa, if not attained in this country.[14]

Abolitionists always worked to improve the lot of the African race in the North. They had for some time past implemented plans for black schools in Philadelphia and Boston to educate as many black children as they possibly could .in public school systems prepared for their needs. When the Fugitive Slave law was passed in 1850, these innovative social programs were put on hold in order to buy time for the real threat to the nation over the imminent problems concerned with the quest of the extension of slavery westward certain to result in a national conflict. In order for James McKim to focus on his correspondence with British abolitionists who had in 1833 freed their West Indian slaves, he offloaded some of his responsibilities as Corresponding Secretary at the Philadelphia branch of the Pennsylvania Antislavery Society in this country onto William Still's shoulders.

Wendell Phillips, when he served as the president of the New England Antislavery Society, opined, "Up to 1840, the antislavery movement had preserved a unity among its many-sided supporters..." Another notable, the former Dean of the Harvard Divinity School, Ralph Waldo Emerson, referred to Southern planters as "a barbarous people in the process of improvement, not accountable like those whose eyes have been opened to the best of Christianity. Enervated by their climate, demoralized by their habits, still they are as innocent in their slaveholding as we are in our Northern vices."[15]

Social activists in Boston had the luxury of more slowly dismantling the plan to desegregate the seating of black riders on their street cars because of their greater distance from the hordes of incoming search agents pouring into the North in hot pursuit of escaped slaves.[16, 17]

Overall, however, abolitionists moved from pacification to agitation as a reaction to the passage of the Fugitive Slave law of 1850 because they rightly saw it as a disregard for the autonomy of their region which empowered the slave holding South as never before.[18] The Compromise made by Daniel Webster, a Northerner, gave to the Southerner, John C. Calhoun, on 18 September 1850 the Omnibus Bill of 1850 to serve as a compromise that represented their resolve to restore equilibrium explicit in the dilemma of "How can the Union be Preserved?" The response of Northerners was the passage within their state constitutions of personal liberty laws to protect the rights of black people living within their borders.[19]

These laws provided legal protection in the form of jury trials to those abducted black people in need of an opportunity to prove their innocence. The provision to oblige all good citizens to participate in the recapture of alleged runaway slaves under the provisions of the Fugitive Slave law was counteracted by these personal liberty laws that provided for jury trials in northern states for the accused black person before being transported summarily back to the South. Accordingly, slave masters were forced to hire agents and to give them the right to represent "the claimant of any person who had escaped, or should escape from slavery, in any State of Territory, might apply in any court, or record, or judge thereof, describe the fugitive, and make satisfactory proof that he or she owed service or labor to said claimant, etc.,"[20]

Philadelphia, the site of the Convocation of the Continental Congress, was at that time the second largest English speaking city in the world, next to London. It served as the nation's Capitol for most of the period of 1777-80, and was the city where the Declaration of Independence was signed in Independence Hall. Yet it was the scene of several blatant slave catching episodes that stunned the sensibilities of its residents. Southeastern Pennsylvania, adjacent to the States of Maryland, Virginia, and Delaware, became known for its defiance of the Fugitive Slave Law. Rural farmers, tradesmen, merchants, and others, sheltered fugitives, and even gave them "passes" that served as letters of introduction to the next line of conductors ahead who ran similar underground railroad depots. [21]

An explosion of slave recaptures erupted in northern cities. A fugitive slave living and working in the Boston area, named Shadrach, was taken by a Commissioner, who was about to lodge him in a jail cell. A mob of determined abolitionists stormed the jail and snatched from it the bewildered black man who was quickly hustled through New York State underground railroad depots and to freedom in Canada. James Hamlet, a fugitive who also lived in New York, became the first victim of the Fugitive Slave law to be summarily arrested and quickly spirited away to the South. The escape from Georgia on the trains all the way to Philadelphia from Georgia became in antislavery annals one of the most daringly innovative escapes ever implemented by slaves in underground railroad records. William, who posed as his white looking wife's slave, protected his owner from using her inflamed jaw hidden under a muffler whenever search agents queried him when riding on the trains. A few interested members of the Philadelphia Vigilance Committee arrived in William Still's office to witness the removal of Ellen's muffler and the embrace she gave to her darker husband to celebrate their safe arrival in Philadelphia. Philadelphia abolitionists advised the happy couple to accept the offer of Boston abolitionists to move to that more distant location to foil slave catchers on the way to take them South. Their short stay in Boston where Theodore parker, a Unitarian minister married them legally, ended only steps away from the slave catchers who chased them to the wharf where they sailed aboard the next vessel going to London Another hapless slave, Adam Gibson, a free colored man, was snatched from his Philadelphia home by slave catchers who turned him over to the jurisdiction of Edward D. Ingraham, a Commissioner in Philadelphia, who ordered him returned to his alleged owner in the South.

The case of Euphemia Williams, the mother of six, had for long resided in Philadelphia. Her abduction by bounty hunters landed her in jail where she was represented at a court trial in Philadelphia by a team of talented abolitionist lawyers. She was eventually freed much the same as another fugitive, Adam Gibson. Hannah Dellum, also a long time resident of Philadelphia was snatched with her child and returned to slavery in the South. Thomas Hall and his wife, long time residents of Chester County near Philadelphia, were beaten up and dragged back to the South and slavery.[22]

These slave recaptures in the Philadelphia are astounded James McKim who lamented the invasion of the South into Pennsylvania. He wrote letters to members of antislavery societies in the British Isles about the gall of the South's incursions into the North since the passage of the infamous 1850 law. Mr. McKim seized the opportunity to gloat over the inability of proslavery lawyers at her trial to find as proof that Euphemia had a visible birthmark that had apparently faded on her body over time.[23]

The Executive Committee of the Pennsylvania Antislavery Society at a meeting on 2 December 1852, elected a new Vigilance Committee. The results of this meeting appeared in the Pennsylvania *Freeman* on 9 December of that year.

"We are pleased to see that we have at last, what has for some time been felt to be a desideratum in Philadelphia, a responsible and duly authorized Vigilance Committee. The duties of this department of Anti-slavery labor, have, for want of such an organization, been performed in a very loose and unsystematic manner. The names of the persons constituting the Acting Committee, are a guarantee that this will not be the case hereafter. They are:

William Still [23] (Chairman), 31 North Fifth Street,
Nathaniel W. Depee, 334 South Street,
Jacob C. White, 100 Old York Road, and
Passmore Williamson, southwest cor. Seventh and Arch Streets.

Robert Purvis was understood to remain as the Chairman of the General Vigilance Committee because he was nominated at the head of the list. Charles Wise was elected as the Treasurer of the General Vigilance Committee. William Still was elected as its Secretary, and Samuel Nickless, the Chairman of the Acting Committee whose members appeared above.

The full manhood of blacks was nowhere more evident than now when they worked together as a team to rescue their black brethren from slave catchers in hot pursuit. William Still, the station-master at Philadelphia underground railroad, was chosen to head the hub of the American Antislavery Society's southeastern underground railroad. He could hardly wait to assume the responsibility of sheltering the growing stream of runaway slaves searching for freedom. He was also responsible for keeping records of all financial transactions involved in the illegal, clandestine operation he had assumed. Moreover, he was asked to correspond to vigilance committee members throughout the North and other interested parties to these transactions on Executive Committees Up and down, left and right, William Still stood at the center of the nation's heart of freedom.

Temporary homes were found for fugitives interested in long and short term stays in Philadelphia until transportation could be prepared for the next step of the way.

The majority of the arrivals from the Upper South went through Thomas Garrett's place in Wilmington, Delaware.[24] Clergymen connected with the black churches in Philadelphia, Richard Allen, at the A.M.E. Bethel Church, and the Rev. John Gloucester, at the African Presbyterian Church, worked closely with William Still.[25]

The Rev. J.W.C. Pennington at Hartford, David Ruggles at New York City, and William Whipper, at Columbia, Pennsylvania, ran underground railroad stations and regularly dispatched "parcels" to Philadelphia where they basked in the warmth of freedom for a season or a reason. William Still was the responsible for the care and feeding of the wretched, runaways, until his correspondence with agents informed him about the feasibility of delivering more fugitives to their depots. Frederick Douglass, at Rochester, Robert Purvis, who continued to supervise the Philadelphia Vigilance Committee, Hiram Wilson, at Toronto, Stephen Myers at Albany, J.W. Loguen, and Samuel Ringold Ward, at Syracuse heroically displayed a high order of service on behalf of their fellow fugitives.[25]

Rev. Henry Highland Garnet, a Presbyterian like William Still, contributed to the work of sheltering runaway slaves in Philadelphia, but longed for more independence from whites at the Pennsylvania Antislavery Society than he felt blacks were receiving. In many ways, however, William Still felt closer ties to some of the born free blacks in the city who had, much the same as in his case, chafed less strenuously at the bonds of the white leaders than some of the runaways who had been lately accepted into the vigilance committee operations. Therefore, William Still found a more common cause in his acquaintance with Negroes such as Absolom Jones, Richard Allen, and James Forten, a wealthy sail maker in the city.[26]

Chapter 8.
Slave Hunting at Christiana.

The Fugitive Slave Law of 1850 evoked "the deepest feelings of loathing, contempt, and opposition within the abolitionist community". Publishers of antislavery papers, abolitionist lecturers and preachers, voiced their outrage openly. More and more slave catchers arrived on Pennsylvania soil in hot pursuit of fleeing slaves. The entry of a slave hunting party into this rural section of the State ended in defeat for the South.[1] A slave hunting party arrived at Lancaster, Pennsylvania, a few miles west of Christiana, where a bloody scene erupted between the slave catchers and their alleged runaway slaves. The details of the 1851 gun battle that ensued were written up in the pages of the Pennsylvania *Freeman*, were written by the new editor, Mr. C. M. Burleigh, when James McKim left.

A party of slave-catchers, who appeared in a Philadelphia Courthouse, sought the services of a deputy to accompany them to Christiana where the suspected slave, William Parker, resided. His slave owner, Edward Gorsuch, was accompanied by his son, Dickerson, and his nephew, Dr. Pearce, along with a group of sympathizers that included Nicholas Hutchins, all from Baltimore County, Maryland. The Commissioner Edward Ingraham deputized the notorious Philadelphia slave-hunting constable, a Mr. Kline, for this business.

William Parker knew that he would soon be hunted by the slave-hunting party. Employed as a field hand in the cornfields next the house where he resided, Mr. Parker lacked to time to run into the fields. He used the time at hand to stand before his open bedroom window on the second floor of the house where he lodged to blow a horn to warn his fellow fugitives in the corn fields of the presence of slave catchers. Fellow blacks returned to do battle with the southerners which left bullets caught in the clothing and boots of the blacks, who defended themselves with guns, corn-cutters, clubs, and axe.

The hour and a half battle peppered with diatribes of racial slurs and curses aimed at each other, was interrupted by the arrival on horseback of two white men, Castner Hanaway, and a Quaker, Elijah Lewis, a Cooperville merchant. Deputy Kline, then in the process of forming a posse comitatus, ordered them to serve as his deputies. Elijah Lewis refused because of his beliefs as an abolitionist, and a member of the Religious Society of Friends, which forced him to avoid the enslavement of human beings. Instead, both white abolitionists struggled to prevent the further escalation of violence between the warring faction despite the urging of Deputy Kline, remained at the edge of the corn field. Unfortunately, Edward Gorsuch was mortally wounded in the heat of battle. William Parker was spirited by a party of underground railroad agents along their selected routes all the way to safety in Canada.

After Edward Gorsuch's body was removed for burial, his son was taken to the home of a kindhearted neighbor who volunteered to care for his wounds. The authorities threw into the local jail every black man they could find on charges of resisting arrest by deputies chosen for this task. On Friday, 10 September 1851, a day after the slave-hunting tragedy at Christiana, William Still arrived at the battle ground accompanied by a group of abolitionists who was sent there to assess the exact loss of life and limb that followed in the bloody gunfight. Police roped off the scene to keep away curious onlookers while the black community was patrolled by the police who scoured it for Negroes involved in the deadly slave hunting foray. Those apprehended were arrested with or without warrants, and forced to remain in the few remaining jail cells until more could be found.[2]

Mr. Hanaway and Mr Lewis returned to visit the incarcerated bystanders at Lancaster Jail. William Still and other antislavery members got a deposition from the wounded slave holder's son, to the affect that no white people other than his father's slave catching party were involved in the bloody shoot out. The abolitionists counteracted Deputy Kline's sworn testimony, because they had proof that he was hiding in the woods far from the murder scene near the house, which Dickenson Gorsuch swore really happened. While at Christiana, William Still met with Mr. Jones, the U.S. Marshal from Philadelphia, who was accompanied by Comissioner Ingraham. Mr. Jones, a special Commissioner of the United States from Washington, D.C., and the U.S. District Attorney, Ashmead, arrived with forty-five U.S. Marines from the Philadelphia Navy Yard, and a posse of about forty of the City Marshal's Police. They were accompanied by a large body of special constables, all of whom were trained and ready to engage in the manhunt for fugitives not only in Christiana, but also in the areas of Columbia and Lancaster.

The large group of twenty-five broke up into smaller sections to diligently searched the area, including the private homes of every black resident. They took into custody every black male they found, several black women, and two white men. William Still lamented: "never did our hearts bleed with greater pity for the persecuted colored people, then when we saw this troop let loose upon them, and witnessed the terror and distress which its approach excited in families, wholly innocent of the charges laid against them."

The *Pennsylvania Press* carried the story of the Christiana slave-hunting tragedy to readers who were outraged by the whole incident while others were appalled by the ill treatment of black citizens. Cries of civil disobedience conflicted with the resurgence of the events that led up to the Revolutionary War.

The following report appeared in a conservative Philadelphia paper published by members of the Whig Party:

"There can be no difference of opinion concerning the shocking affair which occurred at Christiana, on Thursday, the resisting of a law of Congress by a band of armed Negroes, whereby the majesty of the Government was defiled and life taken in one and the same act. There is something more than a mere ordinary, something more than even a murderous riot, in all this. It is an act of insurrection, we might, considering the peculiar class and condition of the guilty parties, almost call it a servile insurrection- if not also one of treason. Fifty, eighty, or a hundred persons, whether white or black, who are deliberately in arms for the purpose of resisting the law, even the law of recovery of fugitive slaves, are in the attitude of levying war against the United States; and doubly becomes the crime of murder in such a case, and doubly serious the accountability of all who have any connection with the act as advisors, suggesters, countenancers, or accessories in any way whatsoever."

The following excerpt was published in a more Democratic Philadelphia newspaper:

We will not however, insult the reader by arguing that which has not been heretofore doubted, and which is not doubted now, by ten honest men in the State, and that is that the abolitionists are implicated in the Christiana murder. All the ascertained facts show that they were real, if not the chief instigators. White men are known to harbor fugitives, in the neighborhood of Christiana, and these white men are *known* to be the warm friends of William F. Johnston, (Governor of the State of Pennsylvania). And, as if to clinch the argument, no less than three white men are now in Lancaster Prison, and were arrested as accomplices of the dreadful affair on the morning of the 11th. And one of these white men was committed on a charge of high treason, on Sunday last, by the United States Commissioner Ingraham." Another daily newspaper of an opposite political persuasion wrote this article:

> "The unwarrantable outrage committed last week, at Christiana, Lancaster County, is a foul stain upon the fair name and fame of our State. We are pleased to see that the officers of the federal and State Governments are upon the tracks of those who were engaged in the riot, and that several arrests have been made.

> We do not wish to see the poor misled blacks who participated who participated in the affair, suffer to any extent, for they were but tools. The men who are really chargeable with treason against the United States Government, and with the death of Mr. Gorsuch, an estimable citizen of Maryland, are unquestionably *white,* with hearts black enough to incite them to the commission of any crime equal in atrocity to that committed in Lancaster County. Pennsylvania has now but one course to pursue, and that is to aid and warmly aid, the United States in bringing to condign punishment, every man engaged in the riot. She owes it to herself and to the Union. Let her in this resolve, be just and fearless."

A politically neutral newspaper provided this excerpt:

"One would suppose from the advice of forcible resistance, so familiarly given by the abolitionists, that they are quite unaware that there is any such crime or treason recognized by the Constitution, or punished by death by the laws of the United States. We would remind them, that only is there such a crime, but there is a solemn decision of the Supreme Court, that all are concerned in a conspiracy which ripens into a conspiracy which ripens into treason, whether present or absent from the scene of actual violence, are involved in the conspiracy and stimulate the treason, they may keep their bodies from the affray without saving their necks from the halter.

It would be very much to the advantage of society, if an example could be made of some of these persistent agitators, who excite the ignorant and reckless to treasonable violence, from which they, themselves, shrink, but who are, not only in morals, but in law, equally guilty and equally amenable to punishment with the victims of their inflammatory counsels."The Governor of Pennsylvania received a petition signed by a number of Philadelphia's most influential citizens stating that the Christiana affair was an insurrectionary movement. They demanded of him, as the chief executive magistrate of Pennsylvania to "take into consideration the necessity for the vindication of the outraged laws, and sustaining the dignity of the Commonwealth on this important and melancholy occasion. The authorities of the United States, Pennsylvania, and Maryland had the right to arrest as many suspects as they deemed necessary who were present at the Christiana melee. As a result, those held in custody included the following individuals: J. Castner Hanaway, Elijah Lewis, a number of colored and white bystanders along with colored women present at the bloody scene. The Lancaster hearing listed in its report those officials who represented the Commonwealth of Pennsylvania, and the defense of the incarcerated.

The report made the following day described the excitement at Christiana which resulted in the incarceration of several hundreds of individuals considered the perpetrators of this outrage.

The previous day's hearings and their outcome were published in the Philadelphia *Ledger*. It began with a description of officials chasing ordinary citizens all over Christiana whom they arrested summarily. It continued:"

> The Government hired its most able lawyers to defend the popular opinion of the public that William Parker and his loyal friends were responsible for the death of the slave holder. Thaddeus Stevens, the talented antislavery legal counsel defended the accused with the phrase which ought to apply to all citizens, not just white. Give me Liberty or Give me death.

The vast majority of the friends of freedom from the start of the court hearings that resulted from the incident believed that the killing of Gorsuch was not only wrong but unfortunate for the antislavery cause. But many changed their opinions after a few weeks time. The cry of the ordinary citizens who saw the breaking of the law as treason were counter balanced by the sympathy for the slave. The abolitionists snickered at the situation that landed three white men and twenty-seven colored men in jail while failing to capture the real fugitive slave, William Parker, who, by that time had passed through the Boston area, a free man on his way to Canada.

Judge Kane, and the Grand Jury, when he referred to the Fugitive Slave Law of 1793, and the other lesser known fugitive slave laws, before an indictment was handed down which found the accused chargeable of treason, stated that nothing remained so far as the men were concerned, but to bide their time as best they could in prison, wrote William Still, with respect to the settlement of the highly charged Christina incident.[3]

A copy of the Indictment which resulted in True Bills of Indictment against forty of the Christiana offenders charged with treason. A non resistant Quaker abolitionist, James Jackson, was one of the indicted.[4] The U.S. Attorney, John W. Ashmead, an Attorney for the Eastern District of Pennsylvania, was in charge of the Grand Jury.

Pennsylvanians recognized the significance of the Christiana affair as the most divisive issue till then presented to the nation over the future role of slavery in the American Union. Other Northern states including Massachusetts became involved in similar slave recaptures, albeit on smaller scales. Philadelphia, however, because of its strategic location co- terminus with slave holding states, continued to be the scene of dramatic slave scenes arrivals with slave catchers in hot pursuit.

This and other interesting cases found a home in the records kept by William Still based on Vigilance Committee. The Philadelphia Vigilance Committee, which were compiled in *The Underground Railroad* along with the story of William and Ellen craft.[5]

The 1 March 1850 edition of *The Liberator* carried in its pages the story of William and Ellen Craft, who were legally married by the noted Unitarian minister and abolitionist, Theodore Parker, who taught Ellen to be able to use the dirk knife he gave her at any time she needed it to defend her life. The Boston Vigilance Committee held a meeting at Fanueil Hall to call for the formation of a posse of "good men and true" to combat slave holders sent from Georgia to retake the Crafts. They soon realized given the incoming search agents into the city that the only freedom for the Crafts was in London via the next ship leaving Boston Harbor for England.[6]

Their arrival was duly noted in a letter dated 26 June 1851 addressed to William Lloyd Garrison in Boston from London abolitionistst.[7]

The Crafts were praised in abolitionist circles in London for their inventive escape from Georgia slavery. They were honored guests at the pavilion of the Great Exhibition. William Wells Brown [8] author of *The Black Men,* a well- received novel, was honored there. The multi-talented black man turned his considerable energies after the Civil War ended to the practice of medicine at Cambridgeport, Massachusetts.[9] William Still always supported in any way he could the production of art in the form of books or other productions. His efforts on behalf of Mr. Brown's early works were well known in the black community. The writer, Frances Ellen Watkins Harper, also a multi talented author became a protégé of William Still ever since her arrival at Philadelphia. Mr. and Mrs. Still named their younger daughter, Frances Ellen, for the renowned antislavery speaker, Frances Ellen Watkins Harper.[10]

Chapter 9. Peter Still and the Underground Railroad.

William Still kept in close touch with his brother, Peter, who cleaned stables in Burlington, New Jersey, to earn his keep. A letter from William written to Peter on 10 May 1852 at the Philadelphia Antislavery Society described a plan to persuade the slave holder of Peter's family to reduce the overpriced sum of $5000 for his family. William asked Peter to ask his employer for money towards the sale of his family.[1]

The failed attempt made by Mr. Thornton was written to another abolitionist, in a letter to Mr. Ely on 19 August 1852, a contact man in Alabama associated with the Philadelphia abolitionists.[2] William Still's letter of 12 October 1852 to Peter, stated that the Rev. Samuel J. May thought that the more realistic market value for the sale of Lavinia, Peter, Levin, and Catherine was closer to $2000 to $3000.[3]

Mrs. Pickard wrote a letter to William Still on 19 May 1852 [4] from Camillus, New York, in which she shared some of the memories she had of his brother, Peter, when she was a student in Alabama. For example, she wrote that Peter's slave master, Johnny Hogan, who had acquired him from his previous owner, a man named Gist, allowed Peter to hire out in Tuscumbia from Hogan's

South Florence, Alabama plantation. She found Peter punctual, a reliable worker, and a trusted employee until she last saw him when she graduated on 1 April 1850. She learned at that time that Joseph Friedman had arranged to buy Peter from Johnny Hogan to buy his freedom. This surprised and gratified her because she did not believe that one man had the right to own another as a chattel. She expressed her delight about his reunion with his mother and family in the North after more than forty years of separation from his loved ones.

Mrs. Pickard abhorred the custom that made it normal for slaves to sleep on rude pallets in their lowly cabins. She wondered how they felt when dawn came and called them down to their weary tasks. Did they pray for deliverance? She agreed heartily with Rev May that $5000 was much too much money to demand for the freedom of Peter's family. She also agreed with him that $3000 was much more reasonable, in her view. Mrs. Pickard added that she hoped to get a friend of hers in Tuscumbia to ask Mr. McKiernon to lower his asking fee for the family's freedom. She wanted to combine in her book as much as she could about Peter's long separation from his mother, his subsequent freedom from slavery, his reunion with his family in the North, and the problems he was facing at the present time over the separation from his own family. Mrs. Pickard promised to conceal the facts concerning his mother's fugitive slave status.[4]

The break-up of Peter Still's family first in Maryland, and later in Alabama struck a nerve in the minds and hearts of abolitionists when had heard his story. Black families in slavery had always been separated at the whim of their slave master, or at auction when slave families were parted for resale. The Democratic, industrial lifestyle taken for granted by white citizens in the North would be used as an antidote for their torpor and complacency. Therefore, abolitionists, aware of the need to bring before the uninitiated about slavery, would benefit by reading about the lives of black folk helplessly exposed to the Way of the South.

Plans were made to send Peter on an underground railroad tour of the North where he could meet with small groups along the way to tell his story about his life to interested people. Previous listeners would furnish a "pass" to Peter meant to introduce him to the next scheduled stop where he would repeat his heartfelt story of his life as a slave. Posing as a fugitive who arrived in Pennsylvania from Delaware who was conducted through Pennsylvania, New Jersey, New England, New York and finally into Canada, Peter Still would be recognized as a dependable fugitive when he received a "pass" accompanied by donations from the previous depot to begin fund raising anew at the next depot. Dr. Joseph Parrish, the brother of a member of the Pennsylvania's Executive Committee in Philadelphia kindly offered to keep a record of the funds donated towards the redemption of Peter's family.[5]

Peter Still's first donation at Burlington, New Jersey, the starting point of his underground railroad journey, was given on 6 November 1852, by E.E. Boudinet [6], who also gave him a letter of introduction for his next stop. It described Peter Still as a hard working employee, who was found to be honest, sober, industrious and capable as a house cleaner and a cleaner of his stable. One of Judge Boudinot's New Jersey friends, Mary A. Buckingham,[7] confirmed in her letter attesting to Peter's work experience, a reference similar to that given him by Judge Boudinot's letter. Courtlandt Van Rensselar [8] in a 6 November 1852 "pass" outlined Peter's integrity. Moving through depots in Rhode Island, Peter spoke to interested groups who provided him with donations and letters of introduction for his future stops in Massachusetts where Boston abolitionists gathered to listen to his life story as a slave. Harriet Beecher Stowe [9] then a famous writer, met with Peter Still when he spoke in Boston. Her 10 November 1852 letter of introduction attested to his honesty and true financial need, which she stated in her "pass" which she remarked: "...this unfortunate man, I am satisfied that his is a case that calls for compassion and aid." She added that the money his family's slave owner demanded was excessive. Yet she hoped that men who live free with their family ought to recall the Lord's words, "As ye would that men should do for you-do ye even so for them."

William Still, the station-master at station 2, Philadelphia, informed Mr. McKim that donations scarcely met the daily rations of the increased number of fugitives that the Fugitive Slave Law of

1850 had swelled beyond its former use. The inadequate funds at the Philadelphia underground railroad left nothing over to help his brother, Peter.[10] Quakers from the old Pennsylvania Antislavery Society volunteered their experience to the Pennsylvania Antislavery Society's Executive Committee whenever they could James Mott, a Quaker businessman in Philadelphia, served on the Board of the new Society, while his capable wife, Lucretia Mott led the Philadelphia Ladies' Antislavery Society.

Money, always scarce, was managed by the Secretary of the Philadelphia Vigilance Committee, Charles C. Wise.[11]

In spite of his many duties on the Underground Railroad, He and the other abolitionists at Philadelphia helped plan the itinerary best suited to his brother's accumulation of funds to redeem his family. William

His brother, William, wrote Peter on 18 December 1852 at an undisclosed address in which he urged his brother to consult with the Rev. Samuel J. May at Syracuse, New York, whenever he felt in need of spiritual guidance.[12]

Peter Still's tour of Boston impressed a number of prominent men of means, as well as their wives. One of these wives, Mrs. Bronson, was so moved by the story the former slave portrayed in all of its brutality that following his talk at Andover, Massachusetts, in December 1852, she not only gave Peter a "pass", but also reportedly said that Peter was a walking revelation of the barbarity of human slavery. John P. Robinson, who found that his reputation had even reached individuals professionally as far away as Boston. ssachusetts.[13]

James McKim, the Corresponding Secretary of the Pennsylvania Antislavery Society, found time in his busy schedule to contribute money to Peter Still while he was on tour. The Philadelphia Vigilance Committee was strapped for cash due to the overly large contingent of fugitives who were arriving there on a daily basis.

Chapter 10.
The Life of Peter Still.

Mrs. Pickard wrote Peter Still on 29 January 1853 [1] at the address he furnished to her. in the Boston area. Her letter was filled with facts taken from the manuscript she was writing on his more than forty years in slavery. She requested from Peter copies of letters of introduction given to him by people he met on his tour of the Underground Railroad in the North. Peter gave the "pass' a previous person furnished him which he was instructed to give to Stephen Fulton, at 30 Commercial Wharf, dated 31 January 1853.[2] It mentioned money donated to Peter's cause, and praise for the truthfulness of the former slave.

The ledger called The Receipt Book that contained monies donated and the names of the contributors in one section, was meticulously organized. It covered the expenses incurred in Peter's travel the distances covered, rail prices, and meetings arranged in the course of his ongoing tour.[3]

Mrs. Pickard included news about people in Tuscumbia they both knew. Some of the tidbits were sad, but most of the news was upbeat. Mrs. Pickard, herself a true Christian, urged Peter to keep his spirits up. And to keep his hand on the plough and never look back.[4]

Another inspirational letter to Peter Still came from Mr T.L.King, a Bostonian, whose letter, on 28 March 1853 reminded him, that as a Christian, he must persevere in his quest to raise the money needed to liberate his family.[5]

Ellis Gray Loring, a Boston Brahmin, received a letter from William Still in Philadelphia in his capacity of its station-master, which he wrote on 29 April 1853. Still's letter was written in a tone of deference. In fact, he said that he was writing to the esteemed Mr. Loring, on the advice of another prominent Bostonian, J. Bowditch, Esq. in which he asked for his opinion about the tour his brother, Peter Still, was taking through underground railroad depots in the North. William Still referred to the manuscript being written about Peter's long years as an Alabama slave. And he stressed the fact that the life of the slain abolitionist, Seth Concklin, had been selected to appear in the book's Introduction. He informed Mr. Loring that his superior at Philadelphia, James McKim, had taken the manuscript draft to England with him to be read by British abolitionists on his tour of Great Britain.

William Still learned that members of the Philadelphia Vigilance Committee were trying to interest a man in the South to purchase Peter's family at their ordinary market price. The former James G. Birney's son, formerly of Alabama, volunteered to get Mr. McKiernon to reduce the price he asked to free the slave family. The younger Mr. Birney, a Philadelphia attorney, was a partner at the Goodridge Law, Mercantile, and Collecting Agency. A letter from William Still to Mr. Loring in Boston indicated that this was a closely held secret from other agents including William Still promised not to share any information given him by Mr. Loring with anyone, not even the esteemed James McKim.[6]

William Lloyd Garrison, who was aware of the difficulties facing Peter Still, remarked, when he learned about the grossly unfair asking price the slave owner demanded for the freedom of Peter's family in the South, "How revolting!" In the capacity of President of the New England Antislavery Society, Mr. Garrison, who was appalled by the enormous costs involved in freeing the slaves, learned from Rev. May that his contribution of $200 brought to $1100 the total accumulated to date to free Peter's family. The issue of repudiating the proslavery Constitution of the United States troubled William Lloyd Garrison when the Rev. May last met with him at the last meeting of the New England Antislavery Society, forced him to table the matter until the next meeting of the Society on 30 September at the Syracuse Antislavery Society.[7]

Peter Still, at Syracuse, had with him a letter of introduction from Rev. May addressed to interested parties in which was noted a short summary of the hard pressed black man's tragic lifetime in slavery. Rev. May, made certain that his remarks about Peter Still's "excellent character" to convince others who were scheduled to meet with Peter Still that his words about the frustrated former slave were accurate. Rev. May outlined in the "pass" he wrote about Peter's kidnapping at age five or six to Maryland slavery from the free state of New Jersey where he had resided for a short time with his mother and sisters.

He described the boy's sale and resale on several occasions which ended in the cotton fields of Alabama far from his family in New Jersey. And the story of how the determined black man managed to save his money to buy himself, and about his trip to Philadelphia where he hoped to be reunited with his family. He found at Philadelphia a brother he never knew he had, and the story of his reunion with his mother and other siblings, but still found no peace because of his separation from his wife and 3 children held in bondage in Alabama.[8]

The efforts of compassionate individuals to have reduced the $5000 asking price for Peter's family came to naught. Their offer of $3500 was refused out of hand. Peter had collected a total of $1500 by the time he went to Syracuse which was increased by another $110 by 15 July 1853. William sent Peter a letter through the secret rerouting of his previous letters on November 1853 that contained the sad news that Mr. Birney, the secret agent to Tuscumbia, could not persuade Mr. McKiernon to lower his asking price for Peter's family. William Still wrote his brother for vital facts needed by the Philadelphia Vigilance Committee who were about to try another tactic to free his family.[9]

Peter Still's mail continued to be delivered to him at a secret address in Boston throughout his Massachusetts tour, and even throughout the New England states. One of the letters William Still sent to Peter on 19 September 1854 was a copy of a letter from Morris L. Hallowell[10] to Charles L. Gurley, at New London, Connecticut. William Still the chair of the Acting sub- committee of the Philadelphia Vigilance Committee was the recipient of letters sent him by agents in the South. Mr. Gurley's letter to William Still dealt with the problems involved in the inability of Mr. Birney to attain the goal he sought in Tuscumbia.

Another letter to Peter from Mrs. Pickard, dated 24 April 1854[11] cautioned the forlorn, former slave, not to lose hope, but to put his faith in the Lord that he would soon be reunited with his loved ones in the North. Negotiations continued between agents sent from Philadelphia to their allies at Tuscumbia still working on freeing Peter's family at a reasonable price. John Simpson[12] at Tuscumbia wrote to Morris L. Hallowell, on 27 March 1854, contained details from a conversation he had had with Bernard McKiernon, which failed to result in the lower and more reasonable price asked for the redemption of Peter's family. Bernard McKiernon charged an extra $1000 to his asking price of $5000 which the Fugitive Slave law of 1850 allowed to offset his expenses at retrieving the runaway slaves. He offered to send the family of four aboard the steamboat to Louisville where Peter Still's friends who were sent to dispatch them to Cincinnati could take the family to his destined location.

Mrs. Pickard's 22 January 1855[13] letter to Peter Still in Burlington, New Jersey celebrated the freedom of his family when the money for their redemption had been collected in full and paid. She wondered about the free status of his newly freed son, Peter, who was born on 11 March 1854 in Tuscumbia, Alabama. She asked Peter for the dates of birth of his children, Peter, Levin, and Catherine, because she wanted to place them in schools. She ended by writing, "Tell your children they ought to be the best children to their father that can be found in the whole country. I hope as their father has done that niggers are able to take care of themselves..."

Mrs. Pickard advised Peter to consider sharing the income from the book proposal she had discussed with the Rev. May with her, the writer. She asked for specific data about his life and that of his family which would enrich the text of the family history. These and other topics were discussed in the pages of her two following letters to Peter Still- one on 9 March 1855 [14], and the other on 18 April 1855.[15]

An undated letter written by Mrs. Pickard[16] in 1855 from her home in Camillus, New York, requested in it that Peter provide to her any information about the lives of his mother, Charity, his sisters, Mahalah and Kitturah, and even his aunts, Nancy Washington and her sister Elsie, all of whom ran off at the same time. She specifically asked for the facts concerning his father, Levin's life as a slave belonging to Saunders Griffin that, the family for reasons of their own chose to keep as a closely held secret. Further, she wanted to know the exact date he got is free papers, and whether or not the family had them still in their possession. How old was Levin when he bought himself? When did he marry Sydney? Did she have children at the time of her marriage? What kind of work did Levin do when a slave, and after he was freed? What was the season of the year when he left Maryland? Mrs. Pickard pondered about the length of time Levin remained in Maryland once he was freed. Further, she wanted to know when Sydney first ran off from Maryland slavery. Was it in the spring, summer, or fall?

The long list of queries contained questions about the chores assigned to Sydney when a slave in Maryland. How old was Mahalah when her mother took her to New Jersey the first time? How old was Nancy? How old was Sydney when she fled slavery the second time? Her age when recaptured the first time. What was she doing when the slave catchers snatched her and her four small children from Levin's cabin in his absence? These and other questions were asked by Mrs. Pickard who relied on facts for her narrative of the life of Peter Still. Readers wanted true stories about slavery and the effect it had on the development of the individuals it affected. Being an educated woman, Mrs. Pickard realized the importance of facts in her narrative of slave life.

She wanted for her audience every shred of evidence she felt necessary for the recounting of an honest recollection based on Peter's contributions on his family's suffering. Her research scoured every hidden corner of the family history. Therefore, she focused on the closely held family secrets concealed by the various family members until she had been told every fact the family wanted to share with the author of Peter's biography. She asked about the whereabouts of older sister, Elsie, and whether or not she had a family back in Maryland. Was Sydney faced with a more terrifying escape the second time? How did Levin find his way to the black community at Springtown, New Jersey? And she asked about the time it took for the escaped slaves on Sydney's second escape to reach Springtown?

Peter helped as much as he could without exposing the fugitives in his family to the imminent danger of recapture to the South. He continued his long friendship with William Handy [17] the friend he had in slavery who aided Seth Concklin when he tried to run them off. He asked another friend of Peter's, W.J. Baxter [18] who lived in Franklin County, Tuscumbia, Alabama, to write him in Burlington County, New Jersey, on 5 June 1855, a newsy letter about the events of interest to Peter concerning their old friends still living as slaves in the Deep South.

William Still, even when on a leave of absence from the Philadelphia Vigilance Committee, was not able to provide the author of her brother's biography when he was in Syracuse visiting the Rev. Samuel J, May with his brother, James, any more information for the book she was writing. Peter also heard from Mrs. Pickard in her 28 September 1855 letter which alerted him to a visit his brother, William, who had recently stayed at the May home.

William Still was assigned to decide for himself whether or not the reports about unruly black behavior in the settlements in Canada were true or connived by proslavery agents. Word had been spread in Philadelphia newspapers that the majority of fugitives from American slavery were ill equipped to live independent of their slave owners. Some readers of this negative press were beginning to wonder if expatriating runaway slaves was a good idea. William Still, armed with letters of introduction written by leading citizens of Philadelphia attesting to his responsibility and good character, eased his task of conferring with the white officials located in the area where a majority of former slaves had settled. [19] Some of the largest black settlements in South East Ontario were the following, Toronto, Saint Catharines, Hamilton, Kingston, Chatham, and Buxton.[20]

William Still prepared reports based on the interviews he had with resettled former slaves in Canada, all of which he found more truthful than the emotionally charged complaints of race conscious locals who feared their black neighbors. His data counteracted the tirades that appeared in the pages of the some of the proslavery newspapers in Philadelphia. Concisely put, Mr. Still presented his thoroughly documented report to the Executive Committee at the Philadelphia Vigilance Committee which was based on a positive attitude, in general, of the many incoming fugitive slaves.[21]

Chapter 11.
The Case of Jane Johnson and the Underground Railroad.

The Fugitive Slave law codicil carried with the Omnibus Bill of 1850 was included to deal with the question of the introduction of slavery into the newly acquired western territories acquired from the Mexican War. The Bill was passed in the Congress after the death in 1850 of President, Zachary Taylor. The enforcement of its least important feature, the Fugitive Slave law, became the most explosive law ever passed. *The Liberator* and the *Antislavery Standard* two of the most widely read antislavery society's newspapers published repeatedly the ramifications of this law to the recalcitrant Whigs and Democratic abolitionists alike the issues surrounding the settlement of the nation's struggle over slavery's extension westward.

Their bitter opposition to the Fugitive Slave Law rumbled throughout the North. . Abolitionists held heated meetings in Illinois, Connecticut, New York, Ohio, Indiana, Massachusetts, Michigan, Iowa, and Delaware. Never since the murder of the abolitionist/journalist, Owen Lovejoy in 1838, in Alton, Illinois, did abolitionists rally together their forces in the antislavery cause. Former dissenters within the abolitionist movement were unified despite their previous schisms and positions that clashed within their ranks. Northern States with the exception of Ohio, and Indiana, enacted Personal Liberty Laws. Eleven Northern States prohibited by law the use of public buildings for any purpose that might lead to a reunion of a fugitive with his or her master; and eight states used public funds for the defense of fugitive slaves residing within their borders. As a result, underground railroads newly funded and supported by prominent antislavery members flourished as never before. The sporadic use of vigilance committees ratcheted up to form a well-staffed and dedicated group of conductors ready to foil the slave catchers who increasingly rampaged into the North.

When the Congress passed the Kansas-Nebraska Act in 1854, minor and major issues complicated the organization of this territory. Southerners in the Congress were interested in a proposal through southwestern territories as a route for a proposed transcontinental railroad. Another was to oppose slavery and to organize it into a single territory much like the model used for the Missouri Compromise which barred slavery into new lands.

The doctrine under which slavery was permitted in territories was called by Stephen A. Douglass, the Illinois Senator who proposed popular sovereignty as a means of settling the disputes escalating between the North and the South. Abolitionists contemptuously called it squatter sovereignty because the final question of is legal status was to be left to territorial settlers when they applied for statehood. First proposed in 1847, it was incorporated into the Compromise of 1850, and the Kansas-Nebraska Act. Its chief exponent was Stephen A. Douglass from Illinois, who incorporated this concept into the Compromise of 1850 and the Kansas-Nebraska Act. Seeking Senate reelection in 1858, he engaged his opponent, Abraham Lincoln in the famous Lincoln-Douglass debates. At the Freeport, Illinois debate, Douglass asserted that territories could exclude slavery- a doctrine that made him anathema to the South. His bill conceded to the South when it created two territories, called Kansas and Nebraska, which repealed the antislavery clause in the Missouri Compromise and motivated antislavery settlement under the squatter sovereignty provision. Abraham Lincoln won when Stephen Douglass, nominated for the presidency, lost in the general election of 1860.

When the Kansas-Nebraska Act was passed in the Congress ,to establish the Kansas and Nebraska territories, controversy over slavery and the conflict over the route of the proposed transcontinental railroad had delayed territorial organization of the region, four attempts to organize a single territory had been defeated by Southern opposition to the Missouri Compromise, which would have barred slavery from the territory. An amendment repealed the antislavery clause in the Missouri Compromise. The Squatter sovereignty provision caused both proslavery and antislavery forces to try to swing the popular decision in Kansas in their favor. The bloody conflict between them called "Bleeding Kansas" resulted, and sectional division reached a point that precluded reconciliation and culminated in the Civil War.[1]

The Emigrant Aid Company in 1854 funded an organized antislavery immigration to Kansas from the Northeast. Antislavery settlers were financed to settle in Kansas in order to qualify the state as a free state when it met the provisions of statehood. The bloody clashes between pro and antislavery forces corroborated the belief held by William Lloyd Garrison that the slaves would never be emancipated by political means. He felt sure by this time that the nation would eventually break into two sections- one slave and one free.

Most Northern States including Pennsylvania, enacted Personal Liberty Laws in their legislatures to protect the freedom of blacks living within their borders. Members of the Philadelphia Vigilance Committee learned in 1855 that as southern slave holder, Col. John H. Wheeler, had with him on a boat docked at a Philadelphia wharf a woman and two boys, his slaves, who were traveling through the State on their way to New York. According to Pennsylvania law, underground railroad agents had the legal right to inform slaves brought by their slave masters into their state on boats or other conveyances that they had the right to choose to be free. Vigilance Committee members were within their legal rights when they told slaves they could choose freedom, which their lawyers could back up in the courts, if necessary. The case of Jane Johnson highlighted these aspects of the antislavery movement in America at this crucial crossroad of impending sectional strife soon to convolute the nation.

Whether or not Col. John Wheeler, the United states Minister to Nicaragua, knew about the law or not is moot. What is known of the case is the fact that he and his slaves were aboard a boat from Washington D.C. to New York that had stopped at Philadelphia in July 1855. William Still [2] who later wrote about the experience in the *New York Tribune* when he boarded the boat and informed Jane Johnson that she could choose freedom. His version of the melee that ensued when he led the slave woman and her boys from the care of the slave owner was heard in court when the case of Jane Johnson was considered an interesting and exciting case for the abolitionist movement. William Still included in his newspaper report a paragraph which the presiding Judge Kane thought requisite. It was the refusal of Passmore Williamson, a fellow underground railroad agent to respond to the Habeas Corpus issued by the court for his part in the melee.

The Case of Passmore Williamson[3]in the *Report of the Proceedings of the Writ of Habeas Corpus,* issued as the Opinion of Judge Kane, [4] is explained in the letter copied from *The New York Tribune.* Still's letter, dated 30 July 1855, from Philadelphia, formed the basis of the correspondence. In it, he explained the "facts and particulars respecting the agency of Mr Passmore Williamson and others, in relation to the slave case agitating the city, and especially as the poor slave mother, and her two sons have been so grossly misrepresented, I deem it my duty to lay the facts before you, for publication, otherwise as you think proper."

Still's narrative in *The Underground Railroad* [5] was nowhere in his previous work nearly as developed in style and content as in this lengthy and explanatory epistle concerning the Jane Johnson case. He introduced his view of the sometimes heart throbbing events that began with a letter delivered to him at the Antislavery Office by a colored youth employed at Bloodgood's Hotel, a hostelry near the dock where the ferry left for a Delaware River crossing to Camden on the New Jersey side of the river. Still stated that he hurried to his colleague, Passmore Williamson, whose office was at Seventh and Arch Street. The white Quaker Underground Railroad agent who read the short but passionate note written hastily by a slave woman afraid of leaving the state of Pennsylvania where she knew she would be free from Col. John H. Wheeler, her slave master who took her and two of her three sons with him on a trip on the boat to New York City, desperately desired members of the Vigilance Committee to rescue her from bondage.

Williamson waived the right to accompany William Still to the hotel to help rescue the woman and her sons because he said he had pressing business in Harrisburg. However, he advised William Still to get the woman's story and the name of her slave master to put in a telegraph to New York where agents could arrest the slave owner because Williamson hadn't time enough to get a Habeas Corpus in Philadelphia before he left town that evening. Once William Still learned that the party of slaves and their owner were aboard the boat, he went to the wharf where he unexpectedly ran into Passmore Williamson. The white man asked the passengers for a description of the slave woman, when William Still noticed the boy from Bloodgood's Hotel who informed him that the slaves were aboard the boat. Mr. Williamson shouted for someone to get their description, and a colored person appeared who described Jane Johnson as a tall dark woman with two little boys. When Mr. Still and Mr. Williamson failed to find the slaves, a passenger sent them to the upper deck where the dark skinned woman and her two young boys clung to her skirt. Not surprisingly, the slave owner, who had a cane-sword in one hand, refused to listen to Still's avowal that his slaves were in the State of Pennsylvania whose laws permitted them to choose immediate freedom from service to him.

Jane realized that she heard the last bell toll, indicating the imminent departure of the ferry, and that she had to act quickly. Visitors were told to debark. At that announcement, Jane Johnson declared her long held wish to be free! William Still helped the woman and her children off the boat and into a carriage at the wharf. Williamson, however, remained aboard to scuffle with the irate Minister to Nicaragua, who shouted expletives along with several sympathetic white passengers. While the carriage quickly turned down Delaware Avenue to Dock Street, and up Dock to

Front Street, leaving Passmore Williamson aboard ship restraining the angry slave master, Jane declared to William Still that she had seized an opportunity, while her master was elsewhere in the hotel to write the note and hand it to the colored boy to get help to free her and the boys.

Further, she added that Col. Wheeler left one son in Washington, D.C., where they lived as hostage in order to placate her with a promise to free her and the children upon her return to the South. She said she hoped to escape from New York, the end of her journey, but saw a chance to take advantage of the opportunity Mr. Still offered in Philadelphia. They stayed briefly in a Lombard Street safe house before retiring to the home of Mr. and Mrs. Still on Fifth Street.

The Pennsylvania Antislavery Society published *A Narrative of the Facts in the Case of Passmore Williamson.*[6]

William Still's p.s. at the end of his correspondence to the *Herald Tribune,* attempted to explain the mystery in the letter about the activities of Passmore Williamson, who tussled with the slave master while he was leaving the wharf in the carriage with the fleeing slaves. The undisclosed whereabouts of the slaves after they left Williamson on the boat which Williamson swore to in the Habeas Corpus which Mr. Williamson,s father gave to William Still in his son's absence, prevented him from receiving it in person, was elucidated in the court hearing that was followed by an order of Col. Wheeler who swore that his slaves were taken against their will on the wharf. Passmore's father, Thomas Williamson, gave the Writ to William Still, said he would be best able to take care of it in his son's absence.

Apparently, Passmore found the Writ on the following day when the city was in a state of agitation over the matter. He swore he had no knowledge of the whereabouts of the boys and their mother following their departure from the wharf. The skilled lawyers queried them to no avail. Mr. Williamson was subjected to the severest trial when Judge Kane was investigating the matter *"That the persons named in the Writ, nor either of them, are now, or was at the time of the issuing of the Writ, or the original Writ, or at any other time in the custody, power of possession, of the respondent, nor by him confined or restrained; wherefore he* cannot *have the bodies."*

Passmore Williamson endured the severest trial of his devotion to the cause of freedom when his "noble bearing, throughout [the hearing] won for him the admiration and sympathy of the friends of humanity and liberty throughout the entire land, and in proof of his fidelity, he most cheerfully submitted to imprisonment rather than desert his principles..." wrote William Still.

The purpose of this public trial over the Habeas Corpus was the aim of slave holders bent on teaching abolitionists and negroes, that they had no right to interfere with a chivalrous Southern gentleman, while passing through Philadelphia with his slaves. Now as in several antislavery cases after the passage of the Fugitive Slave Law, proslavery adherents tried to have their way when it came to slavery. Passmore Williamson went to prison on the flimsy pretext of contempt of court, and True Bills were found against him, and a half dozen colored men, charging them with 'riot' 'forcible abduction, and assault and battery,' and there were no lack of hard swearing on the part of Col. Wheeler, and his proslavery sympathizers in substantiation of these grave charges."[7]

William Still and five others were included in the colored men. They were brought into the court for trial. Still, who was called up first, but was duly defended by the Hon. Charles Gibbons, one of the most capable abolitionist minds. William S. Pierce, Esq., and William B. Birney, Esq., were chosen to defend the other defendants.[8] Lucretia Mott,[9] and a group of women from the Philadelphia Ladies' Antislavery Society, escorted Jane Johnson into the court house to give her story to the Judge.

The subjoined affidavit read as follows: State of New York, City and County of New York. Jane Johnson being sworn makes oath and says—

> "My name is Jane Johnson; I was the slave of Mr. Wheeler of Washington; he brought me and my two children about two years ago, of Mr. Cornelius Crew, of Richmond, Va.; my youngest child is between six and seven years old, the other, between ten and eleven; I have one other child only,

and he is in Richmond; I have not seen him for about two years; never expect to see him again; Mr. Wheeler brought me and my two children to Philadelphia, on the way to Nicaragua, to wait on his wife. I didn't want to go without my two children and he consented to take them; we came to Philadelphia by the cars;--"

She reported to the court that she had sent the note to the Antislavery Society to get help in her planned escape from her master, although her slave master had warned her not to contact a colored person in any way. She stated that she wanted to be free and that when she boarded the boat with her slave master, a colored man came aboard and nodded at her. A white gentleman told her owner that he wanted to inform his servant that she had the right to go free if she so chose. Her slave master replied that she knew her rights.

When Jane stated that she wanted to be free, those interested in her earnest words appeared to be in sympathy with her wishes. She made it clear to the court that her original plan was to go to New York before she came down to Pennsylvania where she could declare her right to go free. She stated that she didn't expect to be freed in Philadelphia. Her reason for disclosing these facts was to vindicate Mr. Williamson who did not force her to flee from Col. Wheeler's bondage. The case of William Still ended in his acquittal and at the conclusion of the trial all of the other colored men were also found not guilty of the first count "riot". Two men were found guilty of assault and battery on Col. Wheeler, and the others were found not guilty. The guilty were given a week in jail. Thus ended the Wheeler case.[10]

This extract was taken from the correspondence of *The New York Tribune.*[11] The fervor between the antislavery and the proslavery forces were nowhere as volcanic as in this court room trial. The U.S. Marshal was present with warrant and extra men to enforce it. The Officers of the Court and other State officials were present to protect the witnesses and the onlookers because of the expectation of a bloody battle at the door where Jane Johnson was escorted out by James McKim, the redoubtable Mrs. Lucretia Mott, and George Corson,[12] one of the Society's most manly and intrepid officers. Jane was hurried away in a carriage followed by another, filled with officers and guards to protect her in her new status as a free woman in Pennsylvania, Passmore Williamson, the white man who should have been protected by the provision of habeas corpus long before such protection was given to black people in the Fourteenth Amendment of the US constitution, was sent to prison by Judge Kane for Contempt of Court. His term began on 27 July 1855 until 3 November of that same year.[13]

William Still received from the Rev. N.R. Johnston a letter dated 1 September 1855 filled with sadness over the incarceration of Passmore Williamson in the Jane Johnson case. The Covenanter Presbyterian then mentioned a full scholarship at Geneva Hall's Ohio College now available for the education of one of Peter Still's sons. Rev. Johnson's church, founded in 1848, Ohio College began as Geneva College, or Geneva Hall, at New Richland, Ohio, near the church.[14]

Chapter 12.
Heavy Use of The "Road".

As the date for the publication of Peter Still's book approached, letters between Rev. Samuel J. May, and Mrs. Pickard, to Peter Still increased. Rev. May wrote Peter in Burlington, New Jersey on 9 March 1855 in which he applauded Mrs. Pickard's rendition written in a powerful style designed to attract more readers interested in reading about Peter's harrowing life. He inserted in the letter this clipping to appear in the book's Appendix the details on the life of Seth Concklin that read as follows:

> Memoirs of the Life of Peter Still, Forty-Two Years a Slave; of His remarkable Restoration to Liberty, and to His Aged Mother and Her Children; Together with the subsequent Liberation of His Family, by Mrs. Emily Pickard, to Which is Added a Sketch of the Life of Seth Concklin, Who Was sacrificed Himself in an Attempt to Deliver the Family of Mr. Still, by William H. Furness, D.D.[1]

Mrs. Pickard's 23 January 1856, letter to Peter Still [2] informed him that Hall & Co., the publisher, had been replaced by a Mr. Hamilton's firm, because Mr. Jewett, the former publisher's representative, lacked money enough for its publication. She added that another reason for Mr. Hamilton's refusal to publish the book was his fear that a legal ramification might in the future occur as a result of any mention of young Peter's son, who remained an Alabama slave.

Her 9 May 1856 [3] letter to Peter Still advised him of the 15 May publication date for his book. Mrs. Pickard wrote of his dislike of the images he had sent her of his mother and his wife, Vina, whose daguerreotype she found to be unflattering. She wrote that "she'd never seen a meaner set of darkies than he [the publisher who selected the daguerreotypes] made you all to be." [Further, she thought that] " Vina [looked] quite attractive in a turban, but [she] also had reservations about Charity's stern expression."

Mrs. Pickard offered her heartfelt condolences to Peter at his mother's death. She wrote, further, that his mother had suffered throughout her early life in slavery, and, throughout her years in New Jersey, especially through the early years in Indian Mills, New Jersey, a free state, when she helped her husband, Levin, eke out an existence for his new family. Peter never forgot the tender reunion he had with his mother upon his release from Alabama slavery after more than forty years. She wept when she learned that Levin, one of her two little boys left in slavery, would one day meet her in Heaven though his body was "moldering in the land of the slaves." [4] James had cared for his mother in his Medford home when she fell ill. She was surrounded by family members and dear friends when she died from a stroke early in 1857. Her body is buried next to her husband' Levin, near the homestead they loved in Shamong, New Jersey.[5]

After his mother's death, James returned to his busy herbal remedy trade in the outlying towns and villages of Burlington County. Called "The Black Doctor of the Pines" by his many patients. James Still worked six days a week to meet the demands of his poor but ailing patients in the backwoods. The long time overwork endured by Jim Still took its toll on his health. Therefore, when his brother, William, invited him to tour the Underground Railroad with him to visit the black settlements in Canada East, James was happy to accept the vacation from his busy practice. The 1855 trip through forests populated with species of trees James had never seen in New Jersey inspired his exhausted mind with their bucolic charm. He and his brother visited station-masters along the underground railroad route to Canada where they met with former slaves who, for the most part, traveled through Philadelphia before being transported to their new homes under the British Lion. William queried a group of trustworthy Negroes about their new lives in Canada. His investigation resulted in much new material that openly disputed the proslavery accusation in Philadelphia newspapers that disparaged the ability of black people's to adapt to a new way of life under the British Lion.[6]

James renovated his Medford house when he returned from Canada. He extended the rooms in back to provide a storage area for his medical supplies. He had chests built to accommodate supplies of pills, elixirs, potions, and liquid medicines he carefully labeled according to the contents of the cabinet drawers. Essentially, this was his drugstore; and the original back room where his wife, Henrietta, fired the woodstove to where plants were distilled into purified basic specimens according to James' formulae. He readily sold his African remedies to folks in the country townships who could not afford to pay for the questionable medicines given them by regularly trained physicians.[7]

Brother Samuel, the talented farmer continued to run the paying family farm with the help of his brothers who remained in Shamong. James was by now a successful purveyor of African remedies in Medford, New Jersey, and William Still ran one of the busiest underground railroad stations in the scattered network.

An increasing number of fugitive slaves from the South were arriving in Ohio. The two northern states carved from the Northwest Territory were Ohio and Indiana, the portal entry of these runaway slaves into the North. Escaped slaves headed westward into Indiana from Kentucky, a southern state to the east. Some crossed the Ohio River at the south into Illinois to the west, from which Case Western Reserve, the region in northeastern Ohio which included a part of Indiana, territory ceded by Connecticut upon its entrance into the Northwest Territory. in 1830., another busy portal for fugitives in search of freedom. This portal of entry for fugitives to the North compared with the underground railroad activity in Pennsylvania.

A major U.S. River, The Ohio, attracted fugitive slaves who followed its waters flowing 981 miles from the confluence of the Allegheny and Monongahela Rivers at Pittsburgh, Pennsylvania, and west to the Mississippi River at Cairo, Illinois. Until the Erie Canal opened, this was the main route to the West. The 650 mile long Tennessee River tributary leads to the Ohio River which it joins at Paducah, Tennessee to the North. The legislative seat of southwestern Ohio was Cincinnati near the Ohio River. Escaping slaves took this route from the Deep South into Ohio and then to other more northern routes into Canada West.

The issue of slavery into the territories exacerbated a series of political and legal events that emerged into the nation's psyche after the passage of the Kansas-Nebraska Act of 1854. The Dred Scott Case, argued before the Supreme Court in 1856-1857 involved the status of slavery in the federal territories. It was based on the majority vote that a Negro descended from slaves has no rights as an American citizen and therefore no standing in court. It further inflamed the sectional controversy leading to the Civil War. The caning of a Republican Senator from Massachusetts, Charles Sumner, by a kinsman of a South Caroline Senator, Preston Brooks, over Sumner's 19-20 May 1856 speech, "Crimes Against Kansas," infuriated the South who fought with the North in a near death struggle over the western extension of slavery. When Senator Sumner had recuperated from his attack, his Radical Republican colleagues planned to enact equal rights laws to blacks when the inevitable Civil war ended and emancipation came.

The Dred Scott decision further inflamed the sectional controversy leading to the Civil War.

The convoluted Dred Scott Case went to the Supreme Court for arguments beginning in 1856. Due to the complexities in the case, a second period of argumentation led to a deliberation in 15-18 February 1857 when the constitutionality of the Missouri Compromise came up for the discussion of its role in the case. As a result, the justices decided the case against Scott, a Negro, on the grounds that by the laws of Missouri, as now interpreted in the state Supreme Court, Scott remained a slave despite his previous residencies on free soil. The following two important questions were decided by the Court's majority: That the Negro whose ancestors were sold, cannot become a member of the political community created by the Constitution with an entitlement to the equal rights offered by federal citizenship, and that the Missouri Compromise which prohibited slavery in a part of the national territories was unconstitutional.

The Chief Justice, Judge Taney, declared that since Negroes were not citizens of the several states at the time of the adoption of the U.S. Constitution, they had no rights. Further, the Declaration of Independence used language failed to embrace black people as a part of the "People" of the United States.[8]

William Still paraphrased the Dred Scott as follows: "The black man has no rights the white man is bound to respect." [9]

The years between 1852 and 1857 found the Vigilance Committee busier than ever before in a similar time frame.[10] James McKim wrote a letter to the Massachusetts Vigilance Committee and to the New York City Vigilance Committee asking them to expect an increase in the number of "arrivals" on their way to their "depots" from the Philadelphia Underground Railroad. The 22 November 1852 letter McKim wrote to David Lee Child, a Boston abolitionist, stated that "20 able bodied refugees came through Philadelphia in a body from a Southern city on the Underground Railroad in a fortnight." The Journal of the Vigilance Committee at Philadelphia that William Still kept listed in its pages the arrival of 495 men, women, and children [who passed through the Philadelphia Station between December 1852 and February 1857".[11]

Thomas Garrett 's Station 1 at Wilmington, Delaware regularly funneled scores of Maryland, Delaware, and Virginia fugitives, to Philadelphia, where William Still expedited their future plans through Station 2.[12] Harriet Tubman, "Moses", as she was called, was a former slave. Harriet Tubman, a brave black conductor, regularly delivered parties of fugitives from various locations in the South to Thomas Garrett's Station, and from there through various stops along the route to Philadelphia. Station-masters revered the stalwart black woman who warned her "passengers" to "go through or die,' because she believed that "a live runaway could do great harm by going back, but a dead one could tell no secrets." Her record was never surpassed for bravery because she had safely delivered parties of slaves through dangerous southern territory into the North and "none had died on the Middle passage" nor had any become traitors to the cause. William Still had only words of praise for Harriet Tubman, a woman he held in high esteem. He thought her one of the bravest underground railroad agents he had ever met.

A letter from Thomas Garrett in Wilmington to William Still in Philadelphia dated 29 December 1854 [13] advised him to expect new "arrivals" led by Harriet Tubman from his station. William Still immediately looked for agents who had a place to shelter the incoming fugitives until trains could be made ready for the next stop. Finding shelter for the sick, exhausted fugitives came first, William Still then recorded in his Journal data derived from interviews he had with the runaways. Such facts as the means they used to leave slavery and to arrive at Philadelphia. The services provided for them by previous conductors. And any other facts he considered worthy of notation in their entry.

William Still had only a few months of formal schooling He mastered the art of penmanship on his own. When he was elected to serve as the Secretary of the Philadelphia Vigilance Committee, he found good use for his writing skill. Many of the interviews he had with incoming fugitives were compressed into pithy records with some of his humorous or sad remarks which gave them a personal touch. His secretarial duties were fulfilled by his voluminous note keeping and his financial records contained detailed information about any funds he received, along with the way he spent these monies for the food, clothing, and housing expenditures used on behalf of the most needy fugitives, in his view.[14] William Still's historical writings in the line of duty a as an elected official of the Pennsylvania Antislavery Society in Philadelphia revealed a man who was intently involved with the tellers of these heart wrenching stories some of which broke his heart.[15]

He wrote an article in 1857 that "in one month in Philadelphia his Underground Railroad dispatched to freedom in the North sixty fugitive slaves".[16]

Chapter 13.
The Convulsive 1830s.

According to the noted British historian, Arnold Toynbee, slavery in the United States failed mainly because of "the counter operation of the spirit of Christianity."[1] Moreover, he wrote that because this "redeeming spirit had been at work" it led to the emancipation of the slaves, but failed to negate "the tendency of the color bar to harden into a caste distinction." Although, even in the days of slavery, with no real hope of certainty, a good omen existed because "in the hearts of the dominant white majority, a Christian conscience that had insisted on abolishing Negro slavery had come to realize that a merely judicial emancipation was not enough, and on the other side a Coloured minority had shown signs of responding in the same spirit".[1]

Africans slaves, well trained in the cultivation of agricultural commodities in their homeland, transformed their skills at growing cotton in "Cotton Belt" states and thereby replaced the mixed farming labor previously done by white freemen. Slavery made possible the growth of a vast economic empire headed by wealthy white planters in the Deep South, and invited between the sections a trade war between the agrarian South and the Democratic capitalist system of the North.[2] Blacks resented with good reason their role in the Southern economy because the no pay system that cast them in the role of chattel property compared them to farm animals liable to be sold, traded, and bequeathed in their wills to family members.[3]

Black residents in Philadelphia were emancipated once within its borders. They had warm feelings towards the Quakers who had helped enact the law, but they lost this protection under the toothy Fugitive Slave law in 1850.Negroes joined the underground railroad in Philadelphia and other Northern states in the 1830s, 40s, and 50s no matter how stiff the penalties. They applauded the Personal Liberty laws passed in every Northern state except for Ohio, and Indiana.

Slavery was abolished in the British Empire in 1833. Militant English abolitionists outlawed the Foreign Slave Trade in 1807. Slave holders unable to buy more newly arriving slaves to cultivate their expanding cotton plantations resorted to recapturing their escaped property that ran into thousands living in the North. The 1837 Census records at Philadelphia listed only a few hundred Negroes who had free papers out of the 18,768 residents who could produce free papers.[4] Immigrants in the free state of Ohio had to subsist from low waged jobs. Many whites competed with others for the few jobs that paid a decent wage. Fugitive slaves were seen as more competition for the already scarce supply of job openings. Runaway slaves usually crossed the Ohio River to enter Ohio from Kentucky in the South, where the underground railroad helped them in the southwestern city of Cincinnati.[5]

Fugitives from Kentucky were dispatched through Cincinnati to Canada via a series of intricate underground railroad routes that converted the runaway slaves into underground railroad agents who returned through upstate New York to serve their people in this country. Henry Bibb, a runaway, returned to Syracuse from Canada to study theology, after which he served as an ordained minister at the Syracuse station. William Wells Brown [6] worked long and hard on the Syracuse underground railroad before taking up the pen, and eventually the practice of medicine.

Mr. Wells benefitted mightily from the advertisement of his works in local newspapers in the Philadelphia area. He arranged small reading groups of Quakers who had shown an interest in the literary output of the former slave. A poorly educated man, himself

William Still supported works of merit written by members of his race, especially those who had lived as slaves in the South. Moreover, he felt it his duty to dispel the racial prejudice aimed at members of the African race considered by some whites to be of an inferior intellectual nature.[7]

Many white philanthropists funded the books written by fugitive slaves about their experiences in the South. Black clergymen authors decried the unforgettable memories of slavery and the hunger for freedom that drove them from kith and kin from their plantations in the South. Henry Bibb's writings portrayed his former life as a slave in vivid words and his deeply felt hope for a better life in the North. Jermaine Wesley Loguen, another former slave, acquitted himself in the pulpit, and ran one of the busiest underground railroad depots in New York State.[8]

The spiritual advancement of the ordained ministers on the underground railroad impressed members of antislavery societies all over the North. William Still found fellowship with other Presbyterians ordained in this denomination. Samuel A. Cornish, Theodore S. White, Stephen H. Gloucester, and the Oneida New York Theology College graduate Henry Highland Garnet, were all Presbyterians.[9] Another notable clergyman, Andrew Harris, the Pastor of St. Mary's Church at Philadelphia, graduated in theology in 1836 at the University of Vermont. Other clergymen on the underground railroad included Charles Bennett Ray, the Congregationalist minister who edited the *Colored American.* Samuel Ringgold Ward was an underground railroad at Syracuse, and J.W.C. Pennington a fugitive slave from Maryland who served on the Hartford Connecticut Underground Railroad. In Boston, Nathaniel Paul, a Baptist agent, worked closely with William Lloyd Garrison, also a Baptist. The New York City underground railroad agents were blessed to have working there the Episcopals, Daniel A. Payne, and Alexander crummel.[10]

Black churches were often meeting halls for Vigilance Committee meetings. William Lloyd Garrison met with black underground railroad agents at the African meeting House on Beacon Hill. After the passage of the Fugitive Slave law of 1850, the city teemed with Southern search agents ready to pounce upon and return to the South any alleged slave they could find. A wall of the African meeting House carried a warning sign with these words: "Keep your third eye open!"[11]

When William Lloyd Garrison wanted to call a large meeting of black citizens, he left its organization to Charles Lenox Remond who He volunteered at the Salem Branch of the New England Antislavery Society's underground railroad. William C. Nell, and Lewis Hayden, were also devoted blacks who helped organize black assemblies at the Boston branch of the Massachusetts Antislavery Society. Abby Kelley, an Oberlin graduate, and feminist volunteered at the New England Antislavery Society's Lynn Massachusetts branch where she worked with her future husband, Stephen A. Foster, and another abolitionist, Parker Pilsbury.

Religion played a pivotal role in the abolitionist movement from the start. The growth of the antislavery movement was engineered by the melding of the evangelical Christians who combined their efforts to achieve a common objective-the cleansing of the American soul of the evil of slavery. Calvanists, Congregationalists, Unitarians, Presbyterians, Methodists, Baptists, and Episcopals in the North volunteered their services to the immediate form of emancipation for the African slaves. Although the Quakers, or members of the Religious Society of Friends, formed America's premier Antislavery Society in 1775 in Philadelphia, when the more militant, or modern American Antislavery Society was founded in 1834, it swelled with an assortment of protestant members many of whom were descendants of persecuted sects driven out of Europe by the Roman Catholic Church in the 17th century.

Of note at this juncture in the abolitionist movement is the mention of some of the persecuted protestant groups who settled in Pennsylvania because of religious persecution in Germany, Switzerland, Bohemia, and other locales in or around Central Germany. Because of their own religious persecution, they lent a hand in the abolition movement before the Civil War when they sheltered and fed desperately poor and hungry fugitive slaves. The Mennonites, a Protestant sect arising among Swiss Anabaptists, were for a time called Swiss Brethern. Their name is derived from a Dutch reformer, Menno Simons. Like the Quakers, Mennonites who believed in non resistance, refused to take oaths. The Bible was their sole rule of faith. In America Mennonites first settled (1683)) at Germantown, Pennsylvania. One of the most conservative denominations of the Mennonite Church is the Amish Church, which broke away from the main body in Europe in the late 17th century. The Brethern, or the Church of the brethren, is a German Baptist sect, organized in 1708 and fled religious persecution to make new lives in America. Bethlehem, Pennsylvania, was settled by members of the Moravian Church, from Moravia in Bohemia, now Czechoslovakia.

The Quakers or members of the Religious Society of Friends [12] provided for the long time benefit of the fugitive slaves a wide variety of social welfare programs carefully thought out to benefit the destitute black fugitives living within the borders of Pennsylvania where a sizeable contingent of Quakers put down roots.

William Still was associated with black churches in Philadelphia. He realized that when his people felt uncomfortable worshiping at the white churches, they formed their own black churches. As a result, black parishioners in Philadelphia New York City, Boston, Washington, D.C., and as far West as Ohio formed their own churches to avoid being forced to sit in the balconies or in the back pews of the white churches they visited.

Black Methodists in Philadelphia [13] attended the Zion Methodist Church [14] founded in 1816. The scene of the rebellion of blacks at a rally in 1816 against the American Colonization Society occurred at the African Methodist Episcopal Church when the congregation vociferously refused the offer made to them by members of the American Colonization Society to consider deportation to West Africa. Blacks anxious to establish their own church in Cincinnati accepted a donation of land in 1830 from the noted white abolitionist, John Rankin, who contributed mightily towards a church of their own. [15] In August 1794, black people in Philadelphia established the St. Thomas Episcopal Church. Similarly, in 1808, Negroes in New York City constructed the Abyssinian Baptist Church.

Abolitionists, black churches, and antislavery newspapers combined their forces towards the emancipation of the slaves. Black people Black contributed items that appeared in the pages of William Lloyd Garrison's antislavery paper, the *Liberator.* Not only did it sell well within the black community because it carried personal ads of interest to their community, black readers were able to keep abreast of the intimate activities important to their daily lives. Garrison had earlier contributed his editorial skills to the publication of two important antislavery newspapers, the *Emancipator* [16] and the *Genius of Universal Emancipation.*[17] African-Americans revealed their talents in many ways. Some were actively involved in work at local vigilance committees in various capacities. David Ruggles worked with Abraham D. Shadd, the editor of a black paper. Stephen Smith, a wealthy black conductor, and John B. Vashon [18] spent hours upon hours of their time along with as much money as they could afford to benefit of the Philadelphia Vigilance Committee.

The American Antislavery Society amalgamated a compendium of talent scattered throughout its marvelously organized Underground Railroad. Much of this concentrated effort was a function of the Society's response to the Fugitive Slave law of 1850. William Still at Philadelphia, Thomas Garret at Wilmington, Levi Coffin at Cincinnati, David Ruggles at New York City, William C. Nell and Lewis Hayden at Boston, Charles Lenox Remond at Salem, Massachusetts, Frederick Douglass and the Rev. Samuel J. May at Syracuse, Jermaine W. Loguen, Stephen Myers at Albany, and J.W.C. Pennington at Hartford.[19]

Lewis Tappan [20] and his brother, Arthur [21] were present in 1833 when the Convention of the American Antislavery Society was in Philadelphia. These and the other evangelical Christians reenacted the roles of "the seventy' in Scripture who became disciples acting as agents of the new national body who volunteered to lead the crusade against Southern slavery. Slavery headed a long list of sins in need of correction in the minds of the evangelical Christians who founded the 19th century humanitarian reforms. The Tappan brothers were pioneer abolitionists wealthy enough to fund several antislavery newspapers from their large financial reserves Money needed to publish *The Antislavery Record* and *The Emancipator* came from the coffers of Lewis Tappan, who was elected to serve as the first president of the American Antislavery Society at its

Brooklyn, New York headquarters. Unfortunately, in the early 1830s, proslavery opposition to the newly founded antislavery society aroused violent opposition in New York City, and even in Philadelphia where a meeting house was burned down when abolitionists met there..

Lewis Tappan, presided over annual meetings of the national body at the Society's New York base. Mr. Tappan wrote "Abolitionists, white and colored, both in slave and free states, entered into extensive correspondence, and set their sights at work to devise various expedients for the relief from bondage and transmission to the free states and to Canada [members of their race fresh up from slavery]...." He noted further that the Philadelphia Vigilance was capable of ingenious changes in plans for transporting fugitives along the accustomed routes in order to elude the slave agents sent to retake the slaves in hot pursuit. The incident he referred to concerned a party of fugitives who paid a trusted friend to take them to safety in Pennsylvania. They were fortunate that the underground railroad agents were able to confound the bounty hunters by changing the route previously planned to take them to Canada via Albany, New York, through New Jersey.[22]

William Still's position in Philadelphia, the hub of the Underground Railroad, responsibly acknowledged arrivals and dispatches of fugitives to agents at various vigilance committees from the South to the North. A Quaker, Elijah F. Pennypacker[23] served several terms at the Pennsylvania Legislature. He was a friend of the Governor of Pennsylvania, George Ritner and Thaddeus Stevens, the U.S. Representative to the Congress from Pennsylvania, who favored the social improvement of black people. Mr. Pennypacker's home near Phoenix, Chester County, Pennsylvania, functioned continuously as an underground railroad station for new arrival from southern districts of eastern Pennsylvania. Dr. Bartholemew Fussell [24] a Quaker medical doctor formerly associated with the old, Quaker Abolition Society, worked with the American Antislavery Society through William Still's station from his home at the southern section of Chester County.

William Wright [25] another Quaker from the old Pennsylvania Abolition Society, sheltered fugitives in his Adams County home near the foot of the Southern slope of the South Mountain, a spur of the Alleghenies that extended down to Chattanooga, Tennessee. He and his wife, Phoebe ran a busy underground railroad station along the route used by hundreds of slaves fleeing slavery through southeastern Pennsylvania. Their farmhouse served as an underground railroad station beginning in 1819 for fugitives from Baltimore County who were shuttled through York, Pennsylvania by agents who transported them to Philadelphia. J.W.C. Pennington [26] the fugitive slave who was sheltered at the Wright station, later out of gratitude added the initial "W" to the "C" in his name in honor of the man who transported him to Hartford, Connecticut where he eventually attended Yale University before he served on the Hartford Vigilance Committee.

The comings and goings of fugitives were duly noted in the meticulous records compiled in William Still's underground railroad work by William Still. He was especially grateful to Quaker ladies in New Jersey, some of whom were elderly but deeply committed to the emancipation of the slaves. A Quaker widow at Salem, New Jersey, Esther Moore [27] never failed to give to each fugitive she aided, a silver dollar to ease his entry into a new life in Canada. She never deserted her Quaker tenet, "Friends, Mind the light!" which she paraphrased as "Mind the slave!" Another Quaker woman, Abigail Goodwin [28] also from Salem, New Jersey, sheltered slaves in her home before mailing out the "parcels" to William Still at Philadelphia.

Daniel Gibbons [29] a Quaker gentleman lived in the area of Pennsylvania called Lancaster County. He worked with the early abolitionists at the original Quaker Abolitionist Society on its underground railroad. Daniel Gibbons remained true to the tenet of the Quaker faith, as espoused by George Fox, founder of the Religious Society of Friends in England in the 1600s. Daniel Gibbons Mill Creek home became a refuge for the poor and oppressed fugitives fleeing slavery. He described a desperately ill fugitive slave woman who knocked at the door of his farm house as "one of the poorest, most ignorant, and filthiest of mankind- a slave from the Great valley of Virginia who was footsore and weary, and could not tell how she came or who directed her there..." When she was felled with smallpox, he and his wife nursed her back to health within six weeks.

Another Quaker, John Hunn [30] known an "engineer on the "road", had a house "almost within the Lion's den" of slave holding Delaware. His "headquarters" was at Cantwell's Bridge, but, "as an engineer of the Underground Railroad his duties, like those of his fellow laborer Thomas Garrett at Wilmington, were not confined to that section, but embraced other places full of great peril, constant care, and expenses." For his and Garrett's role in aiding slaves to escape from their masters, they both suffered financial and other personal losses in 1848 as penalties for their illegal acts.

William Still regularly received fugitives from Samuel D. Burris [31] a black conductor from Delaware. Mr. Burris sent his "parcels" first to Hunn's place before the final lap to Philadelphia. Burris was apprehended by the authorities, incarcerated in a Dover jail, and eventually placed on the auction block where he was sold as a slave. He had the luck to be purchased by an abolitionist railroad agent who provided him with the money needed to remove himself with his family to the new State of California in 1852 to live out their lives in freedom. "A stockholder on the road," Samuel Rhoads [32] used his connections with the British abolitionists where he solicited funds needed in the American struggle for the emancipation of the slaves. Like other abolitionists who chose not to become involved directly with the underground railroad, Samuel Rhoads showed his sympathy with this branch of antislavery work by contributing money to antislavery newspapers, and to other social reforms designed to disavow the expanding hegemony of the Southern planters in the United South. A Pennsylvania Quaker, Rhoads funded the Pennsylvania Antislavery Society in Philadelphia. William Still benefited from the association of Mr. Rhoad's Friends who ran antislavery societies scattered throughout Great Britain. One of these important contacts in England was A. H. Richardson, whose wife, Anna D. Richardson [33] at Newcastle-on-Tyne, England, remained loyal to the Philadelphia Vigilance Committee in Philadelphia. Mrs. Richardson supported that station with inspirational pamphlets, letters from various antislavery societies in the American North who struggled with a lack of funds to service the influx of southern slaves daily flooding over the Mason and Dixon Line into the North before the Civil War. Her support to William Still through her correspondence helped to shore up his flagging spirits when his work was the heaviest and his funds sometimes wanting.

Professor Charles D. Cleveland [34] contributed to the antislavery movement in Pennsylvania in an ancillary manner. He had no real acquaintance with the cruelty of slavery until he went to Cincinnati in 1836 on a visit with Salmon P. Chase, the Governor of Ohio, who later became the 6th Chief Justice of the U.S. Supreme Court. Professor Cleveland realized that abolitionists who had failed to win the 1844 General election were stymied. On the other hand, he saw the power of the determined slave holders to retain slavery as a law of the land. He rightly feared the determination of the South to invade the North according to the provisions in the Fugitive Slave law of 1850 as a threat to the very basis of the political, social, and economic system of Northern culture, and the Judeo-Christian form of Western Civilization.

Chapter14.
John Brown's Raid at Harpers Ferry.

Three Quaker sisters, Grace Anna, Mariann, and Elizabeth R. Lewis[1] ran from their farmhouse in Kimberton, Chester County, Pennsylvania one of the busiest underground railroad depots in that part of the State. The Lewis sisters rerouted parties of single fugitives along convoluted routes beginning at Vicker's place in Adams County to Philadelphia with slave catchers after them in hot pursuit. Fugitives were secreted in the bottom of wagons under old blankets scattered with broken shards of clay pottery along seldom used back roads into Harrisburg in southeastern Pennsylvania along the Susquehanna River and then into Philadelphia.[2] Letter after letter arrived at Station 2 from Miss Grace Anna Lewis that informed William Still to expect whatever number of fugitives that Thomas Garrett at Wilmington had delivered to her farmhouse. She described the mental and physical traits of the dispatched slaves in her terse letters to Mr. Still for identification purposes to make certain that he met the correct slaves.[3]

Because these conductors held fast to Scriptures, they risked much to obey the Lord and to feed and clothe the hungry and naked. Evangelized Christian denominations clustered in the southeastern Pennsylvania farming communities lived and worked much the same as their persecuted Protestant brethren who evangelized the Indians and founded schools and colleges in the South for freed slaves according to the Great Awakening that flourished in the last decades of the 18th century.

Faced with the impotence of moral suasion intended to fire the movement towards its aim to free the slaves, a political wing or faction broke from the main body to implement a political solution. The first candidate in the general election of 1840 was James G. Birney, the candidate of the Liberty party in 1840 and 1844. Whereas William Lloyd Garrison disdained a political solution to the question of slavery, his colleagues led by Theodore D. Weld, in Ohio, and Lewis Tappan, the head of the National Body, were instrumental in the replacement of the Liberty party with the Free Soil party in the 1847 and 1848 elections.

The 1848 General election found the Democratic Party in New York State able to swing it to the Whigs who elected Zachary Taylor, president, leaving the more conservative faction of the defunct Liberty Party to morph into the Free Soil Party on President Taylor's death. When Millard Fillmore assumed the presidency, the Fugitive Slave law was in the process of being enacted in the Congress. Simultaneously, the death of President Zachary Taylor eclipsed his support of the Wilmot Proviso, a bill submitted to the Congress by the Pennsylvania representative, David Wilmot. The Wilmot Proviso pressed for the rapid admission into the Union of the Territories of New Mexico and Utah, and the admission of California as a Free State in the Union. It also dealt with the resolution of the boundary disputes between the State of Texas and Mexico.

This historical context inspired on a deep level the foolish resolution of John Brown, who led a bloody encounter between an antislavery mob against a proslavery group of settlers in Kansas under the provisions of the Kansa-Nebraska Ac. Having exhausted his resources, John Brown tried to solicit funds from the Emigrant Aid Company that was formed in 1854 to promote organized antislavery immigration to Kansas from the Northeast. The National Committee, formed in 1856 by various societies, became divided as to how to handle violence by proslavery forces. The movement virtually ended in 1857 and did little towards making

Kansas a free state, but it captured public attention and engendered much bitterness that contributed to the Civil War.[4]

John Brown decided to lead an army of blacks in the North and Canada into the South where they and their enslaved brethren could wage war against their slave holders. The lack of money needed to finance this plan forced him to consider other sources in the North.[5] Even his family thought him mad. They feared his obsession to free the slaves would end in a failed, massive slave insurrection.[6] Brown's Messianic fervor drove him to return to Philadelphia to resume a conference with a cadre of black abolitionists who had previously refused to aid his slave insurrection plot to raid the U.S. Arsenal at Harpers Ferry, Virginia, now West Virginia.[7] John Brown needed an army and sufficient weapons to arm slaves who were determined to gain their freedom from their slave holders. And Brown hoped to be "encouraged [in his plan], for he saw heads rising up in all directions to whom he thought he could with safety impart his plan".[8]

Brown met with a few black abolitionists at William Still's house in Philadelphia, according to a recollection by Frances Ellen Still, William's younger daughter. Brown then returned to Boston and next visited Brooklyn between February and March of 1859. On 15 March he tried a second time to enlist the support of William Still, Stephen Smith, Frederick Douglass, Henry Garnet, and others, but failed in this endeavor.[9] The meeting he called with Frederick Douglass at a stone quarry near Chambersburg, Pennsylvania also came to naught.[10] Brown's resolve was not shaken by Frederick Douglass' warning words because he had no fear of death. Yet John Brown insisted, "Come with me, Douglass, I will defend you with my life. I want you for a special purpose. When I strike, the bees will begin to swarm and I shall want you to help hive them."[11]

Oswald Garrison Villard, the journalist grandson of William Lloyd Garrison wrote in his book about John Brown in which he remarked: "To all these powers of an intense nature were added the driving force of a mighty and unselfish purpose, and the readiness to devote life itself to the welfare of others." He added, this "willingness to suffer for others," was the element that gave him the power "to draw men to him as if by a magnet," even if his actions put him in harm's way.[12] John Brown found a true friend in Shields Green, a South Carolina native Douglass once sheltered at his Rochester, New York underground railroad depot. Green said "I b'leve I'll go wid de old man".[13] That decision made in Philadelphia sent Shields Green with twenty-one followers of John Brown to the gallows following the raid aborted by Robert E. Lee on Harpers Ferry.

William H. Leeman[14] another zealous follower of John Brown, justified his decision as follows: "I have been engaged in a secret Association of as gallant fellows as ever pulled a trigger with the sole purpose of the extermination of slavery."[15] His piece in a letter published in the *Southern Slave State* explained his deeply felt abhorrence of slavery, whose raid, in his twisted mind, was "a just retribution for the South's retribution for their policy of violence in Kansas." [16] His loyal friends regarded Brown and his followers as "Martyrs in a Cause in its self noble." [17] Proslavery advocates described the raid as nothing "less than a wide sweeping rebellion to overthrow the existing government, and to construct another upon its ruins with Brown for its President and Commander-in-Chief, the proof of which was the provisional Constitution which was found in the old Man's carpet-bag." [18]

Antislavery officials feared the reprisals sure to follow when their association with a conspirator against the U.S. government was discovered.[19] White abolitionists on a high level in New England, New York City, and even Philadelphia fled to Canada or sailed for England.[19] William Still feared for his safety when he learned that a paper with his name on it, was found on the person of Captain John Henry Kagi, one of Brown's agents, which read: "wrote William Still Wednesday." [20] He hid his underground railroad records "in a loft in a building at the Lebanon Cemetery, then located at 19th Street and Passyunk Avenue." Had he not done this, the federal officers who searched his home and office for incriminating evidence would have used the evidence to send him to the penitentiary as an accessory to John Brown's treason against the United States.[21]

Two abolitionists, Lieutenant Francis G. Merriam, and Captain Osborne arrived at William Still's home under cover of darkness.

They came to report that two of Brown's confederates in Virginia had implicated him in the Harpers Ferry raid. The individuals were Mr. Redpath, and another individual whose name William Still failed to recall.[22.]

A biographical sketch of John Brown appeared in the Philadelphia *Ledger.* He was born in Torrence, Connecticut and raised in Ohio, and traveled to Kansas in 1855. His 1856 sack at Lawrence, Kansas, which ended with the slaughter of 5 proslavery settlers on the banks of the Pottawatami River, drove John Brown to declare himself "an instrument in the hands of God." His plan to use the arms he secured from the U.S. Arsenal, took him to the gallows following his 16 October 1859 raid. Brown didn't go alone. He and 21 followers, convicted of the Harpers Ferry, Virginia, raid intercepted the next morning by Robert E. Lee and his men were hanged on 2 December 1859. [23] William Still and his wife, Letitia, entertained Mrs. Brown and their daughter, Annie, in his home when James Mckim accompanied by a few abolitionists consoled the doomed man while he awaited execution.

William Still, a prominent abolitionist in Philadelphia at the time of John Brown's raid, ran one of the busiest stations in the Underground Railroad network, He and his wife, Letitia, used their home as a hotel where they fed, clothed, and sheltered 95% of all the fugitive slaves who arrived at Philadelphia until trains were found to transport them northward" [24] Philadelphia en masse turned out to pay homage to the slain martyr who body was carried aboard a train heading to Elba, New York, where he was to be buried. William and Letitia Still delivered to the train stop Mrs. Brown and Annie who boarded it with James McKim and the Honorable Hector Tyndale who remained with their friend, John Brown.

When the family had buried their dead, they wrote a letter of thanks to William Still for his hospitality while their loved one was awaiting execution. It was dated 20 December 1859 by Annie who included in it a lock of her father's hair.[25] Her p.s. asked William Still to deliver her family's regards to James McKim for his courtesies on behalf of her father before, during, and after his interment.[26]

Chapter 15. The Beginning of the Post-Slavery Period.

John Brown's dignity and sincerity he displayed during his widely reported trial led many people in the North to regard him as a martyr

Abraham Lincoln was elected by the State of Illinois as the 16th President of the United States in November 1860. The antislavery platform of the Republican Party brought terror to the hearts of slave holders in the South who feared the death of their way of life. South Carolina seceded from the Union on 20 December 1860. By 1 February 1861 six more states including Mississippi, Florida, Alabama, Georgia, Louisiana, and Texas seceded. Jefferson Davis of Mississippi, on the day he was elected to serve as the President of the Confederacy stated that he would never stand by and watch the end of slavery where it now existed, nor would he live to repeal the Fugitive Slave Law. On 12 April 1861, the fortification of in Charleston, South Carolina, Fort Sumter, became the scene of the first clash between the North and the South of the Civil War. The Confederates were victorious, but the fort was retaken by Union forces in 1865.The first skirmish between the Confederacy in the South and the arrival of troops from the North was at Fort Sumter, South Carolina, where the Civil War began.

The U.S. Congress passed the Confiscation Act of 1862. It gave the Confederacy sixty days to surrender. If this order was not obeyed, slave holders were punished for their refusal to surrender by the loss of their slaves to the North. The Civil War was the last resort to save the Union following many compromises designed to halt the escalating conflict between the sections based on an effort to deal with the westward extension of slavery. Once it was determined that only war would resolve these irreconcilable differences, President Lincoln knew that he could not win the war without the support of the War Democrats, and the loyal Border States (the slave states of Delaware, Kentucky, Maryland, Missouri); but he also knew he could not win the war by leaving slavery there as it stood. Federal Commanders when on the battle field were confused by the acceptance of the slaves there to join Union troops who claimed the Border States The Confiscation Act declared that all slaves who took refuge behind Union lines were captives of war liable to be set free. Thus was formed the basis for Lincoln's Emancipation proclamation on 1 January 1863 which included thousands of Southern slaves within the jurisdiction of the North.

The federal Government provided basic necessities to the destitute, homeless freedmen who also benefitted from the education provided them when teachers from New England arrived in 1862 to educate slaves in the Border States to read and write. In 1862 the New England Freedman's Aid Society sent agents down to South Carolina, Mississippi, and Georgia to open schools there for the freed slaves, to train slaves to help themselves open schools on their own. The North with its highly inventive skilled class of workers in the Connecticut Valley had earlier than 1860 manufactured advanced mechanical and technical items which gave them an advantage over the agrarian South. Dependent on slave labor to produce cotton, the South relied on the North for the cotton gin, the production of interchangeable parts for machinery, the steamboat, the screw propeller, the electric motor, the sewing machine, the method used for the vulcanization of rubber, and the manufacture of revolvers, the use of anesthesia, and other modern innovations.[1]

As the war took its toll on the Southern rebels, abolitionists turned the other cheek. "After these things the Lord appointed other seventy also, and sent them two by two before his face into every city and place, whither He, Himself would come, "adding- Go your ways: behold, I send you forth as lambs against wolves".[2]

Before William Still accepted a post with the Freedmen's Bureau in the area of education, he faced challenges that required his concerted effort to meet. After a black woman new to Philadelphia met with him about underground railroad problems, he wrote to a friend about a suspicion the woman he called in the letter a prostitute evoked in him. He believed that the female imposter wanted to present herself as a fugitive newly arrived in Philadelphia. But as it turned out, she was really a crook in search of monetary damages. Her lawsuit resulted in a True Bill which meant he had to pay the court $100 and he had to spend ten days behind bars for libel. Eventually, however, in response to a plea from Rev. May, William Lloyd Garrison paid William Still's fine from funds at the Massachusetts Antislavery Society's treasury, but William Still went to jail for slander.[4]

His many letters to Rev. May at Syracuse from his jail cell revealed the humiliation William Still suffered as a result of his trumped up charge.[5] Letters were also exchanged between William Still and Lewis Hayden in Boston in a vain attempt on William Still's part to vindicate himself of the charges aimed against him.[7] His pleas for understanding filled several letters to Rev. May .[8] And Still's 16 and 18 March 1860 letters to Rev. May, were written before and after he was jailed.[9]

Putting the unfortunate episode behind him, William Still wrote A Brief Narrative of the Struggle for the Rights of the Colored People of Philadelphia in the City Railway Cars, and a Defense of William Still.[10] In the pamphlet, he addressed the unfair seating of black riders on the city's street cars. Blacks were forced to ride on the outer platform next the driver because of their color. Reaction to his pamphlet was carried in part in an article that appeared as a Letter to the Editor entitled, Colored People and the Cars.[11]

William Still exposed the segregation of black people who paid the same fares as whites yet could not be seated next to whites on the City Railway Cars. He demanded a change in the policy that proscribed riders on the basis of their skin color. It troubled Mr. Still to see genteel colored people who paid taxes and owned nice homes treated as degraded individuals. He wondered why Philadelphia, a Northern city, proscribed the seating of riders based on their race, while New Orleans, a Southern city did not. Responses to his words appeared in a flurry of letters that were reprinted in the pages of *The Gazette.*[12]

In the 14 September 1859 edition of the *Gazette,* an article entitled, "Happy is the Man That Can help Himself," appeared in which the writer described himself as one belonging to the class which had the "right to use freely the passenger railway cars in our city." He wrote," If a similar intelligent and firm support of all their rights were characteristic of the colored race, it can hardly be doubted but that their condition in our community and in our country would be vastly improved."[13]

William Still's social reformist ideas were bringing to him responses from readers in their letters to the editor. The Social, Civil, and Statistical Association at the Pennsylvania Antislavery Society provided for him areas upon which to base future social welfare programs designed to improve the condition of his people. The petition's data laid the basis for a campaign to initiate a number of basic needs to help black people who had migrated into Philadelphia after the war. William Still was selected to serve as its Chairman with the aid of three of the black abolitionist assistants who had worked to circulate the giant petition that contained the signatures of nearly 360 leading white citizens. Stephen M. Smith, I.C. Wears, and the Rev. J.C. Gibbs assisted William Still over the many months it took to accomplish this objective.

The giant petition became the basis for uses other than the racially segregated seating of Negroes on the cars. When leading white people met to denounce the "proscription" of black riders on the cars, some of them were Union League members, interested in a civil rights agenda for the expected hordes of freedmen soon to swell the black community's streets of Philadelphia.[14] The value of the collected data provoked the Pennsylvania Historical Society to solicit this petition for their records because of its potential usefulness in "the struggle of a certain portion of the citizens for their rights.[15] The petition addressed to the Board of Presidents of the City Railways at their monthly meeting held at 25 Merchants' Exchange by William Still contained the arguments based on the data in the petition. Although Mr. Cambles of the Chestnut and Walnut Street Road, was impressed by the presentation, he lacked the power to make an immediate decision to remove the "proscription." [16]

The firing on Fort Sumter forced Philadelphia abolitionists to lay aside for the time being their proposed civil rights agenda being prepared for the hordes of future freedmen expected to arrive in Philadelphia. Black regiments paraded through the main streets in Philadelphia to demonstrate to the applauding public their loyalty. However, the fact of racial prejudice erupted when Gen. Louis Wagner, who organized the first black regiment, was prevented by the Mayor from parading the black soldiers down Chestnut Street. They were re-routed around Market Street onto a bridge to West Philadelphia, where black folks lived.[17]

This extensive troop movement of black soldiers ushered in an extensive recruitment of black troops. Mr. G.E. Stephens, Sergeant C. B. 54th regiment, Morris Island, South Carolina, wrote to William Still on 19 September 1863 about his plan for an extensive movement "for recruiting Negro troops." The long letter described a series of mishaps and difficulties in this regard in other Northern cities by superiors of black troops which could, by hard work, be overcome.[18]

Because of a lack of funds, and the reduced use of its services, the Pennsylvania Antislavery Society voted to end its work at Philadelphia. William Still, who had served as the Chairman of its Vigilance Committee for more than fourteen years, submitted his resignation dated 1 June 1861 to James McKim. The Executive Committee reported back to William Still in its letter of gratitude for his service to the Society that he would be missed. He wanted Mr. Still to " continue with them as coadjutors in the common cause"..."not bound together by any official tie."[19]

William Still received from Mr. George E. Baker at the State Department in Washington D.C. a letter dated 18 November 1862 in which he praised him for his work at the Pennsylvania Antislavery Society. This letter from the Freedman's Aid Society indicated that Still's name had been submitted to this relief society. An active recruitment of individuals with good reputations and extensive experience in helping blacks were chosen to provide assistance to the many former slaves in the process of being liberated.[20]

William Still, unemployed now, used some of his savings for a down payment on the building previously the home of the Vigilance Committee of the Pennsylvania Antislavery Society. A savvy businessman, William Still made a success of selling new and used stoves at a profit. He resold a lot he bought low to sell at a profit and used the money to buy the building. He used the lower level of the building to serve as a display room for his stove business. And he refurbished the upper level for the family's living quarters. He ran his business in such a way as to gain a profit from the stoves and room heaters which over a course of three years earned him enough to consult a business associate who advised him to lay up stock and merchandise to ward off an impending rumor that stoves would soon be in short supply because of the war.[21]

Spared an enlistment in the army to transact his business, William Still accepted the offer made him by E.M. Davis, Lucretia Mott's son-in-law, to serve as a Post-Sutler at Camp William Penn in Jenkintown, eight miles from Philadelphia. Although his business, now in its fourth year, was doing well and required his presence, he undertook the position left in a sorry state of widespread corruption that brought shame to the black army post. [22] The Commissary, rife with graft, resulting from the poor accountability of the last Post-Sutler, benefited mightily by Still's business practices. He investigated the mismanagement of the army store, and by dint of careful accounting, corrected the source of the bookkeeping errors used in the accumulated sales. The sale of liquor and luxury items such as jewelry, high volume sales, were researched until the mislabeled expenditures were found and reconciled in the accounting system. He reorganized the management of purchases and sales into a more efficient business model during his term at Camp William Penn until the Civil War ended.[23]

Still's 1863 letter in the *Philadelphia Press*, reopened William Still's long campaign with the Presidents of the City Railway cars. In it, he described his personal pain and inconvenience when he boarded a street car and was forced by the driver to stand on a platform with no protection from the inclement weather. He became so upset over this indignity that he decided to walk rather than ride on the car under those proscriptions. He reacted by stating that he was "feeling satisfied that nowhere in Christendom could be found a better illustration of Judge Taney's decision in the Dred Scott case 'that 'black men have no rights which white men are bound to respect,' than are demonstrated by the 'rules' of the passenger cars of the City of Brotherly Love "[24]

Still's powerful prose evoked a strong emotional response in the hearts and minds of readers as far away as London, England, who read his piece in the London *Times*. When William Still learned that his reprint was published in London, Mr. Davis directed him to the files at the Merchant's Exchange to find the paper which carried it. The Rev. Moncure D. Conway stated" It was one of only two American articles deemed worthy of publication in'The *Thunderer*" of that issue, and that "it had done the Union cause more harm than a defeat in Virginia."[25]

Readers of the Boston *Commonwealth*, similarly appalled, reacted to Still's description of the inhuman treatment he was subjected to on a Philadelphia street car. One reader man wrote that such rude treatment was out of order for any rider-white or black. Further, he blamed the incident on Still's color which he felt out of place at a time when America was engaged in a war over the rights of the slaves. He also wrote that "William Still (Colored) of Pennsylvania had published an article which appeared in *The Times* about his unfortunate ride on the outer platform of a street railway in Philadelphia, in the snow, because of his race. It was insane for the driver to make him pay a fare, given the fact that he got off the street car and walked most of the way on foot Further, the writer viewed the perturbing situation to which Still was exposed as an insult to his race at a time when the North and the South were dying to settle the issue of the rights of the black men in their land.[26]

Another English reader of Still's article published his comment entitled "English opinion on the American war." He made an allusion to the death of President Lincoln and the inauguration of President Andrew Johnson as a time of mourning when the sections ought to be "licking its wounds after the death struggle which resulted in the victory of the American Union." The writer compared the tragedy of the American situation to an Englishman's clinging to values such as being a" Liberal", or a "Conservative". A "protectionist" or, a "Free-Trader".[27] Moreover, the writer replied, "A slight majority of the whole British nation probably sided with the North, and that chiefly on antislavery grounds. A great majority of the more influential classes, certainly, sided with the South, and that chiefly on general grounds of antagonism to the United States."[28]

A committee formed from members of the old Pennsylvania Antislavery Society led by Alfred H. Love, proposed at its 28 September 1864 meeting that the candidates for the Legislature should be informed about the bill passed by the House of Representatives at the Pennsylvania Legislature which allowed colored people to sit where they chose on the city Railway cars. A committee appointed to learn about the views held by candidates running for the State legislature, the Mayor's office, and the District Attorney's position. This committee read their responses and reported that these responses made by "those candidates who replied promptly in favor of our cause were elected by an increased majority."[29]

Undaunted, the Car Committee continued its campaign by direct appeals, personal meetings and interviews with railway car officials. Information about the bravery of black troops fighting in the Civil War in the Union ranks was added to the issue of the Car Committee's crusade. A circular describing the progress being made in this struggle stated in part that "Since our petition was first presented, New York has removed every vestige of proscription from all the city passenger cars—although the rules of her roads, long before this final change, carried colored people generally without proscription,, except two roads...." It explained that in these exceptional cases, colored riders were permitted to ride in their cars designated by the words "Colored people are allowed." The report written and submitted by William Still, Stephen M. Smith, Isaiah C. Wears, and Rev. J.C. Gibbs, who comprised the Committee, concluded it by asking if "there was more less prejudice in Philadelphia than in New York?"[30]

Aided by James McKim, William Still arranged a meeting for Negroes at Concert Hall on 15 December with the signers of the petition for equality on the cars. The subject of the discussion before the Presidents of the City Railroads, that Friday evening was to form a committee to discuss "The Railway Rule." The committee asked for a resolution to be arrived at their next meeting.[31]

Chapter 16.
William Still-Social Reformer and Philanthropist.

The large audience that filled Concert Hall in Philadelphia on 15 December listened intently to the speech that William Still gave about his plan to continue his crusade against the "Railway Rule" which continued to proscribe the seating of black riders on the Philadelphia street cars.[1] Speaking for the other members of the Car Committee, William Still promised to eliminate this unfair practice in the City of brotherly Love.[2]

Senator N. Lowry from Erie County in the House of Representatives in the Pennsylvania Legislature wrote an article on the proscribed seating of black riders in the New York *Independent* on 30 March 1857 which ended with a caution to them to end this unfair practice.[2] He rebuked the Presidents of the Railway Cars for their unjust implementation of "Railway Rule" which he believed to be in need of change in order to "vindicate the rights of the Negroes of Pennsylvania by making it unlawful to exclude them from public conveyances." Having openly condemned the State Legislature for continuing to allow this proscription of black riders on the cars, Senator Lowry insisted on its revision of the use of this outmoded rule.[3]

The Car Committee consisted of the following members: William Still, Benjamin Coates, Joseph M. Truman Jr., and Alfred A

Love. They met on14 September 1864 to appropriate $16.50 towards a publication of a pamphlet composed to explain to the public the committee's views about the inability of black riders to choose their seating. At another meeting, the committee voted another $16.50 for its distribution of the expenses.[4.] On 18 March 1867, the Pennsylvania's House of representatives voted at a midnight session to prohibit the segregated seating rule on the city's street cars.[5]

The outcome of this longtime crusade to get for black riders the fairness in seating they deserved, instead of bringing praise to William Still, brought to him howls of execration from his own people. At a meeting he called to expel any false accusations aimed at his intentions, he openly accused of rejecting him after the many years of service he had given to them. He mentioned a rumor he heard about a segment of the black community who chose to "get their coal from copperheads" rather than to buy coal from Still's yards. William Still's obvious prominence in business circles in the city aroused envy in the hearts of some of the many unsuccessful black people in the community.[6]

Merrihew, a well known printing establishment in Philadelphia printed a pamphlet written by William Still entitled A Brief Narrative of the Struggle for the Rights of the Colored People of Philadelphia in the City Railway cars; and a Defense of William Still, Relating to His Agency Touching the Passage of the Late Bill. William Still appeared before a meeting held at Liberty Hall in the heart of the black community where he read from the platform from his 8 April 1867 pamphlet whose covers were printed with excerpts found below:

COAL UNDER COVER!

Wm. Still
Dealer in
Lehigh and Schuylkill Coal,
Nos. 1216, 1218, and 1220
Washington Avenue
Above 12th Street, South Side,
Philadelphia.
Orders received at 413 Lombard Street.

The opposite cover read as follows:

DESERVING OF COMPLIMENT- the *North American and United States Gazette,* 9 February 1867. This commendation of William still's work on social reforms to elevate his race and his excellent business skills as a purveyor of coal was well written by the one who showered him with heaps of great, but well deserved words of praise. [7]

A GOOD PLACE TO GET COAL The *Press,* 1 April 1867.

Abolitionist friends referenced William Still's business acumen which made him one of the most efficient coal dealers in Philadelphia. They applauded his social welfare reform programs on behalf of his people. They described his Washington Avenue coal-yard as one of the finest in use. It was fitted out by the proprietor all by himself, with a stable, car-track, and all the appurtenances and needs of a first class coal depot. It stated that his good quality coal that sold on liberal terms. The *Press,* 1 April 1867.[8]

Having dispensed with the proscription of black riders on the Philadelphia street cars, and the repercussions that followed in its wake, William Still focused on the right of suffrage applicable to black males based on the 15th Amendment to the U.S. Constitution. His association with members at the Pennsylvania Antislavery Society brought him into contact with individuals interested in helping and guiding the freedmen towards the best use of their newly endowed citizenship rights and privileges.

On 31 December 1866, $200 was appropriated by the former abolitionists to the Home for the Aged and Infirm Colored Persons. At that same meeting, another sum of $200 was voted to pay for information disseminated to black men concerning their right of suffrage then being ratified by the several states.[9] When the time came for the 15th Amendment to the U.S. Constitution to be incorporated into the Pennsylvania Constitution, William Still, who had earlier served on the committee to revise the Constitution, used his experience to good effect. Members of the 17 June 1872 meeting of the Political Action Committee offered to the Pennsylvania Constitution a list of proposed articles to be used in the revised document. It also was forced to consider changes based on the 13th Amendment to the U.S. Constitution which ended slavery in the American Union; and the 14th Amendment to the US Constitution in 1868 defined citizenship for the freedmen. It also provided habeas corpus, in Latin "you should have the body" which meant that a writ issued by a court commanding that a person held in custody be brought before a court so that it may be determine whether or not the detention is lawful. It ensures a person's right to due process of law. William Still, A.H. Love, and H.R. Warriner, submitted the following suggestions for revisions to the Pennsylvania's House of Representatives at their 11 November meeting:[10]

Art. 1, Sect.25, "Amend by inserting after the word " corporators' at the end of the first clause or period "and no corporation shall be established within this Commonwealth which shall make any discrimination in the exercise of its provisioner franchises against any citizen of the United States on account of color."

Add as a new section to Art. 2. Sect. 27. "No public hotel or tavern and no theatre or other place of public amusement, which by the laws of this Commonwealth is required to be licensed shall exclude or deter any person from the fullest privilege and enjoyment of its entertainment by reason of Race or Color."
Art. 3, Sect.1.Strike out the words "white freemen" in first line and insert "citizens."

Art. 7, Sect.1.The legislature shall as soon as conveniently may be provided by law for the establishment of schools throughout the State in such manner that the poor shall be taught gratis, but that no person shall be excluded from any benefit or advantage of such schools on account of color, nor shall any person by reason of race or color shall be debarred from attending any public school supplied by taxation and opened for the instruction of any portion of the inhabitants of this Commonwealth.[11]

The changes to the Pennsylvania Constitution made on 1 January 1874 remain in this format even now although some of the provisions were never fully implemented. This is not to say that these attempts to rectify the civil rights of black people were entirely ignored. An efficient public school system was begun wherein: "all the children of this Commonwealth above the age of six years may be educated."[12]

William Still was elected as the Corresponding secretary and the Chairman of Arrangements of The Social, Civil, and Statistical Association. Many constructive social welfare programs emerged from this Association formed to produce funds for its many broad areas of interest for black people. [13] As far back as In 1861, this committee voted to allow Still to draw up the giant petition from which he first crusaded for the rights of colored people on the cars.

A major contributor to the Association, William Still helped sponsor a program of speakers for a platform lecture series to a paying audience. The 1864 and 1865 lecture series was based on the following subjects: Citizenship, Race Relations, Human Rights, etc. Prominent speakers who proposed topics of interest to a general audience were assigned dates to appear at Philadelphia Lyceums. The program proceeded according to schedule in the early weeks but diminished due to weeks of inclement weather and illness. Some of the most popular speakers were unable to appear at Philadelphia during the cold spell that made it impossible for them to travel from afar: General Howard, Frederick Douglass, the Hon. Hugh I. Bond, Mrs. Frances E. Watkins Harper and others.[14]

William Still compensated for losses incurred by paying money from his own pocket. [15] He used these funds to prepare and distribute pamphlets prepared to explain to the freedmen the use of their newly acquired Constitutional rights.[16] $1,260 raised by blacks, was donated to Judge Kelley who offered to use the money for the purpose of printing documents based on the right of suffrage for freedmen.[17]

The Freedman's Aid Union and Commission enlisted the help of Bishop D.A. Payne, one of the most knowledgeable black clergymen in Philadelphia, to advise the freedmen on the best use of their rights. Other notables involved in the work of the Freedman's Bureau were William Lloyd Garrison, a founder of The American Antislavery Society, Chief Justice, Salmon Portland Chase, who became the 6th Chief Justice of the U.S. Supreme Court during the impeachment of President Johnson, James McKim, the former agent in charge of the Philadelphia branch of the Pennsylvania Antislavery Society, and William Still, the former Chairman of that body's Vigilance committee.[18]

A major use of his prosperity went to fund charities in the Philadelphia area William Still, a prosperous coal merchant, contributed money to The Home for Aged and Infirm Colored Persons founded on 28 September 1864 at 340 South Front Street. Still was elected to serve on the Board of Managers on 12 January 1865.[19] He also served as its President. Several years later, William Still contributed $100 to the Home and graciously accepted a life membership there.[20] Sundays found Mr. and Mrs. Still frequent visitors to the Home where they entertained the inmates who had no family to brighten up their spirits. William Still enjoyed reading to the old folks cheerful stories, or playing the piano tunes he had learned.[21] His contributions to the Home for Aged and Infirm Colored Persons were always substantial.[22] Some of his contributions were to be used specifically for entertainment programs for the residents.[23]

Committee members at the Home for Aged and Infirm Colored Persons agreed with William Still that their current building needed extensive repairs. In 1871 a lot was purchased for a new building mostly from donations by Stephen M. Smith, a wealthy black lumberyard owner in the city. He donated the lot and contributed $28,000 to finance the new building towards his $30,000 pledge. Considering the poverty of ordinary people in those times, this was a financial contribution from a black man considered nothing short of miraculous. [24]

Fund raisers kept their eyes on William Still, who became known for his generosity especially on behalf of the truly needy members of his race. He also contributed to white causes once he was known as a generous donor to good works. He purchased a stock certificate "which certified that on 10 May 1872 that he bought one share of stock in the Mercantile Library of Philadelphia."[25] His willing contributions to the Colored Soldiers' and Sailors' Orphans' Home resulted in his election as a Trustee.[26]

He gave freely of his time and money to the Home for Destitute Colored Children and the Shelter, charities devoted to the support and care of orphan boys and girls.[27] These homes were located at 53rd Street near Woodlyn Avenue until it was converted into the Cheyney Normal School, a teacher training institution for black teachers for the Philadelphia Public School system.[28] When Friends of John Brown founded Storer College at Harpers Ferry, West Virginia, Still contributed funds to commemorate John Brown's memory.[29]

William Still enlarged his mind and developed his writing style when he worked for Mrs. Elwyn at her West Penn estate. Scantily educated at the state-run school in the New Jersey Pines, he and his brothers were forced to make do with only the rudiments of reading, ciphering, and writing, as was the custom for farm boys in those times. Mrs. Elwyn when she noticed William's curiosity, allowed him to read books on subjects he had never before knew existed. Over time, he developed parts of his intellect which served him for the rest of his life in various capacities in his social reform activities in Philadelphia.

He saw these undeveloped mental skills in the underprivileged fugitives he met in the underground railroad duties assigned to him which awakened in him his own neglected abilities he was fortunate enough to develop to the maximum of his innate talents. Had they been exposed to the advantages, large and small, that he garnered from the people he admired and who respected his capabilities, they, too, could rise from the ashes of slavery into better lives for themselves and their families at some future time.[30]

William Still's record keeping skills were excellent. He more than fulfilled the requirements of his position as the Chairman of the Acting Sub-committee of the Philadelphia Vigilance Committee in Philadelphia's Station 2. His methodical cast of mind is made evident in the contents of a letter press or copy book beginning with his watch as the elected Chairman of the Vigilance Committee on 25 December 1852. He made notations on the envelopes of each letter he received from agents at various underground railroad branches. And he also made copies of each of the many letters he mailed out (about 900), which provided a cache of Underground

Railroad records that no other agent was able to furnish in their published recollections of underground railroad service.[31]

William Still, from the day he formed a personal and public association with his beloved Pennsylvania Antislavery Society, never relinquished this bond. Even after emancipation came, he continued his involvement with the needs of his less fortunate race.[32] William Still never failed to support black writers in any way he could. He recognized the problems facing talented black writers who struggled against the odds to produce works of merit. White readers generally refused to buy books by blacks because they believed African people unable to produce on a literary level books on a par with of whites. Mr. Still once bought 100 copies of a novel, *The Black Men,* by William Wells Brown, a freedom and temperance advocate, who spent his later life practicing medicine in Western Massachusetts.[33] He also supported Mrs. Frances Ellen Watkins who wrote prose and poetry before her marriage to Mr. Harper.

Miss Watkins early on revealed to wide audiences in the North a finely honed oratorical skill that praised the antislavery movement. When skeptical abolitionists listened to a maiden speech, at the Assembly Building in Philadelphia, they agreed that she was a gifted orator.[34]

William Still contributed $1000 towards the $100,000 sum needed to publish a monthly publication entitled *The Nation,* a periodical that focused on politics, science, art, and literature. William Still donated $1000 towards the publication costs of this independent, monthly publication.[35.] Edward Godkin, chosen to its first editor, produced the popular and widely circulated magazine after the Civil War that in the course of a few years set a new standard of free and intelligent criticism of public affairs.[36]

Chapter 17.
Still Family Progress and Reunions.

The fledgling herbal remedy business James still began with the sale of essence of peppermint to the Charles and William Ellis Drug Store in Philadelphia, erupted into a fullfledged African remedy business over time.[1]

Inspired to extend his home remedy business, he recognized a need to increase his knowledge of herbal remedies by reading text books with standard formulae from which he could innovate his own curatives. The Quaker bookstalls at Chestnut Street had on their book shelves standard botanical texts with the information James thought useful to his trade. Some of the books at the Thomas Cook Herb Store on Fourth Street that sold for a dollar each contained the exact material James needed to study before he had sufficient knowledge upon which to base his innovations.

After reading the books he bought in his Medford cabin, he returned to Philadelphia to buy another book that cost a dollar fifty when he had the money saved. After a period of careful study, James felt competent enough to incorporate the new material with his previous experience to concoct a new family of drugs and curatives he felt safe and efficacious enough to put up for sale. His diligent study resulted in the drug store of assorted pills, tinctures, salves, and liniments which filled the medicine chests in the renovated rooms he built in his house. Having mastered the medical research side of his business, James focused on addressing his deficient knowledge of physiology and anatomy which only medical text books could correct. He read up on subjects covered in medical school courses meant for doctors to gain a knowledge of the body before he felt competent to understand the etiology, or the cause of a disease or condition responsible for an ailment.[2]

Once James Still understood the reason for the illness that debilitated his clients, he developed home remedies he believed capable of relieving the pain or even swelling of a particular part of their body. He had good success in his treatment of scrofula, or swollen glands. He had similar success with the treatment or cure of other afflictions.. His grateful patients began to prefer his treatments over those of the regular medical practitioners in Burlington County. Money came in hand over fist. Soon he had the money to buy a new Rockaway wagon from a local merchant. Although he ran a good business, James lacked the income to raise his growing family in good style. He found at Dr. Cook's book store in Philadelphia a medical text that provided for him the more sophisticated material about the body he believed would be of value in his work.

James Still was accused of practicing medicine without a license by the regular physicians trained at the Medical College of the University of Pennsylvania. When he learned from a Justice he consulted that the practice of medicine without a license was a fineable offense, but that selling to his patients his African remedies was legal, he was told that selling to his clients medicines they wanted was legal. They also were forced to pay him for his time. Therefore, in order to assured that he was within the law when he sold his African remedies to his clients, James consulted John C. Ten Eyck, a Mount Holly lawyer, who had this advice to offer after hearing the details of James' problem:" You can sell medicine, and charge for delivering, and then you can collect it just the same as for anything else. There is a fine for giving prescriptions, but you don't give them: you sell medicine and there is nothing to stop you." Once James Still knew the definition of practicing medicine and purveying home remedies to his "patients," he focused on collecting the fees they owed him. These payments helped James reduce his debts. His only debt at that time was a payment of $160 he owed to Nathan Wilkins, Amos Wilkins' brother.[3]

The time had come for James to buy a plot of land on which to build a new and larger house for his family. Since he already had $200 and needed another $60 for the down payment, James found two businessmen who were willing to loan him the money. Once he endorsed the note and had the money in hand, he found a jobber who agreed to supply the materials needed by the contractor in order to assemble the new house. The refurbishing process took all summer and part of the fall of 1849. On 27 December of that year, James moved his family into their new home which was 30 feet wide in front and 18 feet deep in back where the old house was adjoined to the new one at the old kitchen.[4]

For the first time ever, a black man and his family lived at the Medford Crossroads.

James, who had adopted a sober minded approach to accounting, vowed to continue his thrift in the future. In order to remain solvent, he increased his patient load. Although he was inclined to dabble in real estate to increase his savings, he decided to expand his herbalist clientele even deeper into the Pine Barrens of Burlington County. He traveled to the remote sections of Burlington County such as Jackson Glass-Works, Waterford, Pumpbranch, and Tansborough. When he had extra money, James became involved in a public auction sale of a rundown tavern property with several adjoining buildings badly in need of repair. After he repaid the money to Amos Wilkins that he owed him, James borrowed another $1975 to make a low bid on the tavern property which he won on 24 April 1852.It was one thing to acquire the dilapidated buildings and quite another to pay for the renovations to the property necessary before he could rent it out. When Mr. Wilkins loaned James $500 for repairs to the buildings, James found a man who offered to pay him for rent $150 a year. James planned to repay the remaining $1475 loan against the property he anticipated would take another three years time. He next bought the Thomas Kline property near Medford in 1854 with $505 he borrowed from Amos Wilkins, because he wanted his family to live in the larger home he felt they deserved. Curiously, the deed was never registered at Mt. Holly, the

County seat.[5] After repaying the debt of $505 he owed to Amos Wilkins on 23 March 1861, James who used the rental income from the tavern property in 1860, was entirely free of debt.[6]

James always looked after ill members of his family. The failing health of his mother forced James to care for her in his home where he could watch her more carefully around the clock. However, she succumbed to a stroke despite his care, and she died on 23 April 1857.[7] Her sister, Nancy Washington, who worked in a home to earn her keep in Burlington, New Jersey, was also cared for gangrene of her feet and toes also died, a few years later, in 1865.[8] He also cared for his brother, Peter, who spent his last days with his beloved wife and children in Burlington, New Jersey, suffered but a short time from inflammation in his lungs, died on 10 January 1868.

Peter Still's decades of life as a slave took its toll on his mind, heart, and soul. However, he managed to buy his freedom, meet a brother in Philadelphia he didn't know he had, and tour the North to save the money needed to buy his family and to bring them North to live in relative comfort from the profits of his truck farm in New Jersey.[9]

A Slave Family's Struggle for Freedom by Mr. Kenneth R. Johnson, depicts the poignant life situation that transported young Levin and Peter steel from Maryland slavery to a Lexington, Kentucky brickyard owner who died in 1819 and left them to a kinsman named Levi Gist, a planter at Bainbridge, Alabama, near the Tennessee River. For the first time the little boys became accustomed to the brutality endured by cotton pickers on a daily basis in the Deep South. Peter's brother, Levin, was flogged to death by his slave owner when the young slave broke his rules and visited his wife in another plantation. After burying his brother, Peter vowed to one day return to the Delaware River where he hoped to be reunited with his mother, and two small sisters, he last saw at age six.

When his slave owner, Levi Gist, died, and his slaves were sold to Johnny Hogan, Mr. Gist's daughter inherited Peter with the other slaves. In 1840, when Johnny Hogan died, Peter was sold to Bernard McKiernon who had a plantation at South Florence, Alabama. Around 1842, Mr. McKiernon decided to hire Peter out to do odd jobs in nearby Tuscumbia. Generally, slaves who did odd jobs outside their plantation were obliged to turn their earnings over to their slave owner. However, Mr. McKiernon let Peter keep some of the money he earned cleaning hotel and dormitory rooms at the Tuscumbia Ladies' Seminary, where he made the acquaintance of Emily Reynolds later known as Mrs. E.R. Pickard, the author of his history. Always careful with his money, held onto his pennies until they added up to the $500 Peter needed to give to Joseph Friedman who bargained with Mr. McKiernon for his sale.

It took Peter until 1847 to save up the $300 needed to make up the sum of $500 Mr. Friedman needed to make up the balance of the price Mr. Friedman asked for his free papers. Alabama law dictated that a white man could own a slave from his previous master if he acted as a "surrogate' owner. Peter had saved the remainder of the asking price of $500 which made possible his self emancipation from Mr. McKiernon and his transference to his "nominal" master, Mr. Joseph Friedman. Peter faced a wrenching separation from his wife and children whom he promised to free when he had enough money. Then he took the steamboat with Mr. Friedman up the Tennessee River, and after his "nominal" master debarked at Cincinnati, Peter heeded his advice to remain aboard until Pittsburgh, where he debarked .His trip to the black churches in Philadelphia in 1850 resulted in the realization of a long dream that came true for the old slave name Peter friedman.[10]

Peter's meeting with his brother, William, at Philadelphia, was a miracle pure and simple. The heartfelt reunion with his mother at his brother, James' house, was even more miraculous. Peter's acquaintance with Mrs. Emily Reynolds Pickard and the subsequent publication of his life as a slave for more than forty years seemed more a dream than reality. More to the point, an even more preposterous gift from heaven occurred in early 1855 when Peter, his wife, Lavinia, Peter, Levin, and Catherine gathered at James' house to celebrate the redemption of a family member this side of Heaven.

The Kidnapped and the Ransomed opened the eyes of the uncommitted people in the North who before the passage of the Fugitive Slave law of 1850 had buried their heads in the sands over the issue of slavery. The 1856 memoir about the life of Peter Still sold briskly for several years. It was sometimes compared to the theme of Mrs. Stowe's *Uncle* Tom's *Cabin,* with its depiction of the abominations of horribly portrayed, eye- opening facts about American slavery. Though Peter's book remained in print until late 1860 when his message no longer was required to be read about, he received a letter from the Rev. Samuel J. May at Syracuse where Hamilton, the publisher was located, that diminished sales made it unprofitable to keep in print the book about Peter Still's life as a slave. He wondered if Peter wished to buy the plates to have the book reprinted.[11]

Though somewhat disappointed by the lack of royalties he received of late from the sale of the book, Peter relished his life he now shared with his family in the North. He exulted in the fact that his story helped to turn the tide of public thinking that was only fully changed by the shed blood of the Civil War.[12]

When the slaves were freed, Peter's book went out of print. The kind Dr. Parrish who had kept an account of the monies contributed towards the freedom of his family, offered to buy the rights to the copyright. Peter concurred, and his friends and family supported him in his last days spent at farming a plot where he ran a lucrative truck farm in Burlington, New Jersey. Rev. May, who had paid the tuition to the Onondega Girls' Academy while Catharine was a student there, wrote to her father that he regretted his daughter's inability to handle the advanced work expected of students her age. Catherine agreed to join her family on their farm in Burlington County, New Jersey.[13]

Chapter 18.
Still Family Activities After the Civil War.

New Jersey was first settled by the Dutch, but the Quakers and other members of Protestant denominations soon afterwards followed them. Quakers while sympathetic towards the plight of black families living in Burlington County New Jersey, also until 1847 held slaves there. Levin Steel first settled in Cumberland, Pennsylvania, "The Cradle of Emancipation," a rural and farming community of black settlers. He later moved his family to the Pine Barrens of Burlington County, New Jersey after leaving Maryland, across the Delaware River into Burlington County, New Jersey, where he and his wife began a family of freeborn black children. One of their older sons, James, began his medical practice in the following Burlington County Townships: Mount Holly, Medford, Evesham, Mount Laurel, Moorestown, Burlington City, and Bordentown.[1]

Although white settlers in Burlington County gave to black settlers the respect they deserved, their lives took different pathways. They worshipped in different churches. James Still worshipped in the Jacob's Chapel A.M.E. Church founded in 1813 near his home. It once was once the Colemantown Meeting House. Cyrus Bustill (1732-1804), when freed in New Jersey by his Quaker slave master, settled in Philadelphia, where he formed *The Free African Society.* The noted athlete and world class actor, Paul Robeson, a New Jersey native, was one of Bustill's great, great, grandsons.[2]

James Still had a natural gift for healing. He knew this ever since he was a child. When he came of age he learned the art of compounding African remedies he concocted to his own formulas. His experimentations with a variety of plants, roots, and herbs he collected from the sides of the Medford, New Jersey back roads provided for his medicine chest a veritable drug store filled with assorted palliatives, whose efficacy and resulting sales transformed the poor, black youth into a successful entrepreneur of home remedies. He rolled his wagon through the backwoods settlements in Red Lion, Smithville, Beaverville, Buddtown, Friendship, Chairville, Hampton Gate, Brandywine Run, and Retreat that dotted the farming landscape of rural Burlington County, New Jersey. Many of his patients lived in Eayrestown, Lumberton, and Vincentown. Old timers such as Doc. Ed Haines, walked with "Dr." Still along the densely wooded backwoods where he recalled watching the "Black Doctor of the Pines" put a fish inside the shoes of some of his patients to make certain that his cure would "take."[3]

In 1869, when James had made enough money from a series of real estate transactions, he made extensive renovations to his house at the Medford Crossroads. He had installed a new forty foot extension in the front of the house which allowed for a Mansard roof that was all the rage in the best homes in Medford. He was also able to afford an extension to accommodate a twenty-six foot wing in the back for a new kitchen and dining room. The modern water work system he installed compared with the latest indoor plumbing in the most modern homes in Medford Township. Remarkably, he had the wages to pay the workers every Saturday evening for the previous week's' work [4] James's real estate holdings increased in 1867 when he bought a cedar lot in the Bear Swamp for $300.[5] He also acquired that year, a nine and ten meadow and upland lot in Shamong Township from C.and B. Shreve; and a $2,200 lot from Joshua Stokes, for cash.[6]. James' purchase of the tavern property back in 1852[7] brought in rental income from the addition to the building next the tavern of a seven unit apartment.[8]

When his son, James matriculated at Boston's prestigious Harvard Medical School in 1868, his father paid for his tuition in gold pieces. His son graduated in with a Harvard M.D., in 1871, the second black man to achieve this singular honor.[9] Because James Still wanted for his other children a better education than he and his siblings had at the county school in the Pine Barrens. he paid a tutor to prepare his son, James, to meet the educational requirements for incoming students at Harvard University. And he wanted his other children to have the best teachers he could find to offset some of the prejudice against black people who were generally considered to be less intelligent than whites.[10]

James' oldest daughter, Angelina, and his youngest, Lucretia, both lived at home because they remained single. Emmaretta attended the Ashburnham, Massachusetts secondary school that boarded white and black youth from middle class homes.[11] Joseph and William, James Still's two sons who also became be purveyors of patent medicines, set up practices in Mount Holly, not far from their father's Medford, New Jersey home. Eliza Ann, one of James Still's older daughters, married and began a family when she married John Moses.[12]

In 1871, James held a family reunion in his home. Driven to meet with them at this juncture in their lives because of the quickly passing years, the residents of Philadelphia took a stage over the Delaware. River to get them to his Medford, New Jersey home. Mahalah Thompson and her husband, Gabriel, arrived with Kitturah Willmore, a widow. Mary, who taught in the black schools in Philadelphia, arrived with William and Letitia Still.

James and his wife, Henrietta, broke open a bottle of aged wine reserved for such a time as this, and, although they both were teetotalers, they toasted their loving parents, Levin and Charity Still, who had struggled against the odds to raise a God fearing family of freeborn black children in and out of slavery. They raised glasses to their future health and to the memory of the late president Abraham Lincoln, "The Great Emancipator." The afternoon found them reliving episodes in their youth in Shamong, New Jersey

Some fought tears when mention was made of the homestead and life on the family farm. As the afternoon wore on, smiles returned to their faces when each recalled times of humor that only a close knit family could appreciate about times long past. The humor that overtook their initial pain at the loss of so many of them faded, soon ended when the shadows of night forced the Philadelphia bound to hurry home.[13]

James returned to his many real estate transactions that required constant effort on his part to run. He was forced to spend $2,500 for the extensive repairs and renovations needed for the upkeep of the buildings and land in 1872. He soon became aware of the toll on his heath that his real estate dealings and his expansive African remedy business required. Unable to ignore his physical complaints, James agreed with his wife, Henrietta, that he needed to rest at a spa in Long Branch, New Jersey, known for its recuperative cures. James had this to say when he returned and made a notation in his diary, "My short respite was of no avail…I would gladly have relinquished my labor a longer time, but there seemed no way in which I could do it. I continued as best I could with my office work, suffering continually from great prostration."[14]

He continued to apply the knowledge he read in medical books that helped him to diagnose a problem before he even tried to treat the affliction. Regular physicians applied what they called "the nine day rule" before treating a fever with their medicines. During that time span, the patient either survived or died. James relied on sparing the heart and other organs from increased activity or depletion while the fever raged. He believed that, as the physician, he ought to aid nature while it was in the healing mode. Instead of simply waiting for the fever to subside, James Still treated the symptoms by relieving" the shivering, or rigors, followed by hot skin, a quick pulse, a feeling of languor and lassitude". These symptoms made the patient unable to eat, thirsty, restless, devoid of secretions, and a diminishment of every function as a result of the body's distress.[15]

Although not at all practicing medicine as a physician, James Still had to be familiar with the body in order to know which of his concoctions he compounded would be used to alleviate the patients' pains. The sudorifics he made from herbs, were diuretics administered to produce sweating, and perspiration on the skin. They also calmed the stomach muscles along with the entire digestive system. James' medical research taught him the secret of curing fevers was the restoration of secretions and excretions. When properly given, Still's sudorific drops restored to healthy functioning a fever-wracked body that returned to health after only a few days of convalescence.

James' emetics were given "to cleanse the stomach of any bilious, feculent, or irritating morbific matter." The cathartics he administered to his patients sometimes substituted for emetics because Dr. Still believed, that after the ingestion of "one single dose of a vegetable emetic will prove to be of more benefit than half a dozen purgatives" which "remove feculent matter contained in the bowels, stimulating the exhalant vessels of mucous membranes of the intestines, causing them to pour out copious effusions from the blood or circulating mass"

He had faith that the removal of the irritating cause, remained the single most important effort in his medical practice. Therefore, he expurgated the deleterious matter with his home remedies in order to help nature to prevent or deter the production of secretion of morbid matter.[16] if any of his patients came to him for cures for rheumatism. They wanted him to provide medicines to alleviate the pain due to the swelling of their sore, red joints. Debilitated patients found relief in the bathing of their feet in tepid water inundated with ashes before being put to sleep with a cup of catnip tea before wrapping them in warm blankets to warm their bodies during the night. James sometimes used liniment he concocted to rid their bones of the constant pain induced by swollen joints.[17]

Cancer perplexed James Still as no other affliction did. He recognized the virulence of the dread disease which sometimes spread rapidly throughout the body and "discharged a thin, acrimonious matter that excoriates the surrounding integuments, and emits a very foul smell." He tried but failed to cure patients afflicted with cancer of the female breast, the face, the uterus, the lower lip, the eye, and the tongue. Finally, he concluded that the only treatment that could alleviate cancer was the cutting away of the diseased part, in order to keep the constitution more or less affected; while questioning the propriety or prospect of such success because he found it cruel and unnatural to an extreme.[18]

Basically, his herbal trade was composed of vegetable concoctions which he used to treat the complaints of his patients. The harsh chemicals used by the regular doctors contained mercury or calomel, all the rage in medicine as it was practiced in those days. Went out of his way to concoct compounds he was certain were not only pure and safe for the patient, but also gentle and efficacious in their treatment. He made sure that his home remedies did not harm the surrounding organs such as the bones, muscles, constitution, and other parts of the body. He used apple-root as a purgative to cleanse impurities from the liver in lieu of calomel which eroded bones.[19]

William Still was contacted time and again by Philadelphia publishers who had also contacted other underground railroad agents with similar data. However, the Resolution made at the May 1871 meeting of the Pennsylvania Antislavery Society commissioned William Still to publish his fugitive slave records for posterity.

The following resolution appeared on the Society's Minutes:

Whereas, The position of William Still in the Vigilance Committee connected with the "Underground Railroad," as its corresponding secretary, and chairman of its active sun-committee, gave him peculiar facilities for collecting interesting facts pertaining to this branch of the anti-slavery service; therefore

"*Resolved,* that the Pennsylvania Antislavery Society request him to compile and publish his personal reminiscences and experiences relating to the "Underground Railroad."[20]

The Underground Railroad was published in 1872 by Porter & Coates, an antislavery publisher of note. William Still's Preface[21] (see also Appendix 3.) burst wide with living testimony from the quivering lips of fugitive slaves about the terror they knew as slaves in the South. William Still wrote simply for posterity the testimony of the fugitive slaves whose heroism astounded him throughout the most tragic period of American life up to that time.

Chapter 19.
William Still and *The Underground Railroad.*

William still used the hiatus the miners' strike that prevented the functioning of his coal business, to compile his underground railroad records into a history book.[1] His Title page encapsulated briefly his work as "A Record of Facts, Authentic Narratives, letters, etc., narrating the hardships, hair-Breadth Escapes, and death Struggles of the Slaves in Their Efforts for Freedom, as related by Themselves and Others, or Witnessed by the Author, together with sketches of some of the largest stockholders, and most liberal aiders and advisors of the road."[2] He signed his name, William still, adding, For many years connected with the Anti-Slavery Office in Philadelphia, and Chairman of the Acting Vigilant Committee of the Philadelphia Branch of the Underground Rail Road".[3]

The photograph of William Still in a tuxedo taken when he was about fifty, reveals in his penetrating glance the soul of a true hearted man as heroic and unafraid as the many fugitives who fought for their freedom against the odds against them.[4] He praised the slaves and their rescuers in the heartfelt Preface he wrote in vigorous prose with no embellishments. Moreover, he ended his homily by recognizing the emancipation of the slaves with the help of Almighty God.[5]

A list of photographs and illustrations, and engravings were methodically arranged in the next section of the introductory material.[6]

The author gave credit to the co-operation of the members of the Acting Committee, but chose for reasons best known to him, to place the photographs of white and black underground conductors towards the end of his book.[7] Also included at the end of the book were photographs and sketches of prominent station-masters, anti-slavery men, and some of the other supporters of the U.G.R.R.[8]

The arrangement of fugitive slave incidents was based on William Still's personal choice, and not for any other reason. The role played by the Good Samaritan, Seth Concklin, who lost his life trying to run off Peter Still's family, received first place in William Still's monumental fugitive slave history about the underground railroad.[9] He introduced the reader to pages of facts he had compiled over the course of his term as the Chairman of the Philadelphia Vigilance's Acting Sub-committee. He wrote: "Here are introduced a few of a very large number of interesting letters, designed for other parts of the book as occasion may require. All letters will be given precisely as they were written by their respective authors, so that there may be no apparent room for charging the writer with partial colorings in any instance, indeed. The original, however, ungrammatically written or erroneously spelt, in their native simplicity possess such beauty and force as corrections and additions could not possibly enhance."[10]

Thomas Garret's 3 March 1856 advised William Still to "...soon expect the arrival in Philadelphia a party of 11 fugitives from Norfolk, now sheltered in homes around his city."[11] Another underground railroad letter from Miss Grace Anna Lewis, at Kimberton, Chester County, Pennsylvania. She worried that if they took the direct route to Philadelphia the fugitives might surely be apprehended. She also feared they might fall prey to an ignorant colored man, Daniel Ross, whom she believed incapable of exercising the proper precaution, due to ignorance of the situation rather than for any maliciousness on his part. She queried William still about the addresses of Hiram Wilson and his fellow agent, Mr. Jones, at the Elmira, New York depot, both of whom, she believed, were to be trusted to dispatch fugitive slaves to Canada. Miss Lewis referred to reports that L. Peart sent three on to Norristown." She repeated her fear that some of the colored agents did "not understand the necessity of caution...."[12]

Grace Anna, Mariann, and Elizabeth R. Lewis the Quaker ladies whose Underground Railroad depot served as a hub of Underground Railroad activity between Thomas Garrett's depot at Wilmington, Delaware, frequently routed fugitives along safe, and individually selected side roads leading directly to Philadelphia, or via ancillary routes to Harrisburg, Elmira, New York, and finally into Canada.[13] William and Phoebe Wright, his wife, ran a busy depot at their Adams County farmhouse that sent fugitives through York, Columbia, and the Southern parts of Lancaster Counties as well as from the "several lines, from Adams County connected to Wilmington." Which converged upon the homes of John Vickers of Lionville, whose "Parcels" lay hidden under pottery in the backs of wagons heading for Philadelphia, or via the Harrisburg route by way of the Susquehanna Valley through the Southeastern districts of rural Pennsylvania.[14]

William Still's 24 November 1855 letter to E. F. Pennypacker, at Phoenixville, gave him the signal to deliver to Philadelphia two fugitive slave boys. They had to remain in the City until a "train" was made available to take them to Canada. He advised his Quaker Friend, "Any time when you may have anyone to forward if you drop me a line in advance, I will meet them or send someone else to, at the cars."[15]

Another letter Still sent to E.F. Pennypacker on 2 November 1857, referred to "those unprovided for. " Still thought it "safe to send them through to Philadelphia any time toward the latter part of the week " because he found the job situation in Philadelphia at that time unsafe. He mentioned, the usual amount of danger hanging over the heads of the fugitive. A plan was made to dispatch them in small parcels – that is, not over 4 or 5 in a company." He stressed the need for Mr. Pennypacker to keep an eye on the hour and train the arrivals will come.[16] William Still wrote in his 6 November 1858 letter to the Quaker abolitionist for funds to help Mr. William Wells Brown's literary meetings then begun at Berk's

County, Pennsylvania. He added that perhaps Mr.E.F. Pennypacker could arrange for a gathering of literary minded people near his Phoenixville, Pennsylvania home.[17] Mr. Still wrote him again on 20 November for a reply which failed to arrive.[18]

Letters to William Still at the Philadelphia Vigilance Committee office included one written to him left Washington, D.C., yesterday with a child of her relative. The writer referred to a woman with a sick child from Washington, D.C., who headed for Syracuse. He also asked for the whereabouts of "ten packages" he had sent to Still's address last evening, one of whom was a relative of Susan, who was routed to Syracuse via the Harrisburg route which meant that she would not get to Philadelphia till Monday or Tuesday. Still was asked to inform the writer about whether or not the "packages' had arrived safely at hand.[19]

S. H. Gay Esq., an Ex-Editor of the *Anti-Slavery Standard*, and the New York *Tribune*, wrote to William still on 17 August 1855 about two women who had arrived this morning with Syracuse for their destination. Adding that, he sent the two men who came yesterday to Gibb's place. Mr. Gay showed concern for sufficient spaces in local homes for the many fugitives he was sending, and queried Still about being able to accommodate them at his place or at Gibb's. The telegraph code he devised went like this: "One M. (or one F.) this morning W.S.," These men or women, as the case may be, have left Phila. By the 6 o'clock train—one or more, as the case may be.[20]

A former slave, John H. Hill, who had settled in Canada, wrote Still about his plan to marry a former slave woman from Petersburg, Virginia, named Miss Wever. Mr. Hall also enquired about an enslaved brethren in the South who was mentioned in a letter from him to Miss Wever, who wanted desperately to save poor Willie Johnson from the hands of his cruel master in the South.Mr. Hill stated, "It is not for me to tell you of his case, because Miss Wever has fully related the matter to you. The letter ended with a promise from John Hill to reimburse William still for the costs involved in contacting his relatives in Petersburg and Richmond.[21]

Letters to the Corresponding Secretary of the Philadelphia Vigilance Committee poured into William Still's office. Race, gender, class, and social or economic prominence mattered little on the Underground Railroad, or their interactions with each other or with their superiors. Still read a letter from an agent who was highly placed in life. J. Bigelow, Esq., wrote to Mr. Still 22 June 1854 from Washington, D.C. The writer asked about the over worked underground railroad operative, William Wright, at York, Sulphur Springs, Pennsylvania who had informed him about the transportation of some *property* from this neighborhood to your city or vicinity.[22]

Ham & Eggs, a slave and Underground Railroad agent, wrote a letter to William Still on 17 October 1860 from Petersburg, Virginia. His focus was on some "hams on hand that I would like very much for you to have." He asked William still to reply to his latter as soon as possible about the following subject,:"You write to me, Mr. Brown, and I will inform you how to direct a letter to me. No more at present until I hear from you; but I want you to be wide-a-wake."[23]

Elijah H. Pennypacker's letter from Schuylkill, Pennsylvania, written on 7 November 1857 was about "...three colored friends at my house now, who will reach the city by the Phil. & Reading train this evening. Please meet them." His p.s. noted that 43 passed through our hands, transported most of them to Norristown in our own conveyances within the past 2 mos.[24]

Joseph C.Bustill, a black Underground Railroad agent at Harrisburg was stationed at the Reading route when forwarding fugitives to Still at Philadelphia. His letter to William Still referred to "what signs or signals you make use of in your dispatches, and in any other information in relation to operations of the Underground Railroad." His use of the Reading Road had saved him and fellow agents five hours time by its use.[25] Relationships continued to be strong between slaves in the South and those who had successfully landed in Canada. An18 October 1860 letter from a Richmond slave relative of John C. Hill, then a resident of Hamilton, Ontario, enquired of William still about the whereabouts of a kinsman in Norfolk, Virginia, who arrived at his Philadelphia station.[26]

John Thompson wrote William Still from Syracuse, New York, about the "Jeny from Syracuse to thank him for delivering this letter to his mother in Verginia for me." Before he ended his letter by saying, "I am one of your Chattle," the illiterate writer stated, "beg her in my letter to Direct hers to you & you can send it to me iff it sutes your Convenience."[27]

"Wm. Penn" (Of the bar) in Washington, D.C., was a lawyer who wrote on 9 December 1856 to Still in response to Still's 6 December letter that his long delay to a response to it was due to the research involved in finding a correct answer to Still's query. As to his acquaintance with a number of people in Loudon County, Mr. Penn "confessed he had never practiced law in any of their courts." Further, he asked for "the *facts* in the case, (In that order) I can better judge of my ability to help you; but *I know not the man resident there, whom I would trust with an important suit.* As for the "packages" that left his vicinity four or five weeks ago, "fifteen to twenty in number [who] were directed to your office," left behind them a disturbing atmosphere to the neighborhood which was " at a time of uncommon vigilance."[28]

William Still published these and scores of other Underground Railroad pieces of correspondence in order to reveal to the reader the inner workings in the minds of the individuals with whom he was in touch during the heaviest period of the use of the "road". He also included in the pages of his book, high profile cases that exemplified various facets of antislavery operations at Philadelphia. Henry Box Brown, [29] gained notoriety because of his dangerous and innovative escape from Richmond, Virginia in a box supplied with a tube for breathing, and little else to sustain him all the way to Philadelphia where he arrived at the Vigilance Committee via Adam's Express. His wooden box was opened in the presence of James McKim, Mr. E,M. Davis, William still, and Professor C.D. Cleveland.[30]

A dying slave, Romulus Hall, alias George Weems[31] who had been flogged countless times when a slave owned by Henry Suthern, near Benedict, Charles County, Maryland. He stayed at "Still's Hotel" from the day he managed to get into the bed in March 1857 until, not long afterwards, he died a painful death. When William still, who tended him daily asked him at the end of his days, if he would again escape in his deplorable condition", the dying Hall tugged at Still's arm, and said in a firm voice, "I am glad I escaped slavery!" Plagued by his separation from his wife, a slave in the South, and his failure to get to his destination in Canada, the hapless fugitive with only a five cent piece to his name, died in peace for having arrived at Philadelphia.

Not a few brave conductors were commended by William Still. He called Harriet Tubman [32] "Moses of the colored people." Thomas Garrett's letter to William Still advised him to expect Harriet Tubman who left his station in Wilmington, Delaware, to arrive at Philadelphia with a large group of fugitives. William Still, who had received many arrivals from Harriet Tubman, wrote about her faithful service to the slaves, "She had faithfully gone down into Egypt, and had delivered these six bondsmen by her own heroism. Harriet Tubman was a woman of no pretensions, indeed, a more ordinary specimen of humanity could hardly be found among the most unfortunate-looking farm hands in the South, yet in point of courage, shrewdness, and disinterested exertions to rescue her fellow-men, by making personal visits to Maryland among the slaves, she was without her equal."

Marveling at her leadership capacities that began when she was in command of one or a party of runaways, she read them the riot act based on this tenet: "giving out and going back" which made them understand the need for the fugitives in her care "to go through or die." Moreover, she was heard to say to her charges, "A live runaway would do great harm by going back, but that a dead one could tell no secrets." William Still once wrote about Harriet Tubman, "...her like is probable was never known before or since."[32]

The many individual or groups of fugitives who arrived at Still's station in Philadelphia were dwarfed by the case of Jane Johnson, a slave brought into the state of Pennysylvania by her slave owner, Col, H. Wheeler, who exemplified the persecution of the State's personal Liberty laws Her case in the courts personified these laws in effect in most Northern states. Her plight, naturally, appeared in *The Underground Rail Road* under the caption: The Trial of the Emancipators of Col. J.H. Wheelers' Slaves, Jane Johnson and Her Two Little Boys.[33] Her widely publicized trial unfortunately resulted in a jail sentence for the Quaker Underground Railroad agent, Passmore Williamson, who was incarcerated on a technicality.

Another well publicized story was that of William and Ellen craft,[34] sub-titled Female Slave in Male Attire Fleeing as a Planter, With her Husband as a Body Servant, made a stir not only at Philadelphia where the slaves arrived after a long train ride from Georgia as husband and wife. Abolitionists as far North as in Boston, where the canny slaves found shelter, soon realized that slave catchers had been dispatched to the North to recapture the runaway slaves. In order to provide for the frightened pair the safety not available even in Boston, antislavery agents sent them to London on the next sailing vessel about to leave Boston harbor.

William Still queried a host of former antislavery society members hoping to get from them the permission to enclose their contributions in his book about the Pennsylvania Underground Railroad. He wrote to his revered superior at Philadelphia's Vigilance Committee, James McKim, on 10 November 1871, for a biographical sketch of his life and a publishable photograph for the book. A resident of New York City when he was asked for the data, James McKim[35] advised William Still in a letter that he would comply with his request when he came to Philadelphia in the near future. Dr. William H. Furness, who was widely known for his sympathy with the cause of the slave had helped proof read William Still's final draft of *The underground Railroad,* was called away on business suddenly, and was forced to ask his son, Horace C. Furness, a highly respected editor in his own right, to finish his father's editorial work on the book. His endorsement and voluntary aid thus by these highly esteemed friends, was appreciated by the author, William still, who felt indebted to them for their gracious contributions to his fugitive slave history book.[36]

Dr. Caroline Still Anderson, William Still's daughter, contributed to the grammatical and syntactical requirements of her father's compilation of his underground railroad records. Her Liberal Arts degree at Oberlin College proved beneficial to the neatly composed sections of her father's factual history of the fugitive slaves he met and helped escape from slavery. Boxes and boxes of notes were scoured for the material contained in William

Still's Underground Railroad records. Posterity owes a debt of gratitude for the tireless labor involved in the vigilance committee responsibilities shouldered by the agents at Philadelphia under the leadership of a self taught black man born free in the New Jersey Pine Barrens. Hard work and frugality taught to William Still as a boy growing up on his father's farm and his identification with fugitive slaves erupted into the public consciousness of black and white readers when the guns of the Civil War were forever stilled.[37]

Chapter 20.
After the Slaves Were Freed.

William Still made an excellent decision when he hired business agents to handle the sales of *The Underground Rail Road*. If potential buyers lacked the money to buy a book outright, the agents offered them an installment plan. People everywhere wanted to read Mr. Still's records because the Pennsylvania Antislavery Society had commissioned him to publish the events that transpired under his watch at Philadelphia's station2.[1]

Still respected the organization, techniques, and funding strategies employed by the abolitionists who had struggled endlessly to liberate the slaves from the founding of the Pennsylvania Antislavery Society in 1836 until the members foresaw by 1860 the emancipation of the African slaves. When William still sent to William Lloyd Garrison a signed copy of his book, his fellow Underground Railroad agent at Boston sent back to him Mr. Garrison's reply letter dated 7 April 1872 in which he delivered praises for William Still's "voluminous" slave history which he described as "a most important portion of Anti-Slavery history, [which] but for your industry, research, and personal experience and knowledge might nearly all have been lost to posterity."[2]

Mr. Garrison believed that Still's Records kept over a long period of time would furnish facts for readers to relish as a significant part of American history. The colorful captions in The *Underground*

Rail Road 's Table of Contents described exactly, if sometimes humorously, pithy slave interviews Still recorded as follows: "Perry Johnson, of Elkton, Maryland. Eye knocked Out."[3] Joseph Kneeland alias Joseph Hudson."Young Master had a Malignant Spirit."[4] The Arrivals of a Single Month. "Sixty Passengers Came in One Month-Twenty-eight in one Arrival-Great Panic and Indignation Meeting-Interesting Correspondence from Masters and Fugitives."[5] Emanuel T. White. "Would Rather Fight Than Eat."[6] Liberty or death."Jim Bowlegs or Jim Paul."[7] An Irish Girls' devotion To Freedom. "In Love with a slave- Gets Him Off to Canada- Follows Him-Marriage,Etc."[8]

Still's first edition sold out so rapidly that a number of black people who had not purchased copies of Still's first edition urged the author to publish a second edition. William Still concurred in 1878 with a reprint of *The Underground Rail Road* published by The Peoples Publishing Company in Philadelphia. This Preface was directed to a Post Civil War audience of black folks. Living in Philadelphia.

A synopsis of it read as follows: "While the grand little army of abolitionists was waging its untiring warfare for freedom, prior to the rebellion, no agency encouraged them like the heroism of fugitives. The pulse of four million slaves and their desire for freedom were better felt through The Underground Railroad than through any other channel. He praised the contributions of black Underground Railroad agents, and included the heartfelt labors of many a faithful vigilance committee member were best exemplified by these former black abolitionists: Frederick Douglass, Henry Bibb, William Wells Brown, Rev. J.W. Logan, and others [who] gave unmistakable evidence that the race has no more eloquent advocates than its own self-emancipated champions.[9] William Still had this to say to the freedmen, who had been given equal rights with white citizens. Through education and hard work, he saw a better future for his race along these lines: "Well-conducted shops and stores; lands acquired and good farms managed in a manner to compete with any other; valuable books produced and published on interesting and important subjects- these are some of the fruits which the race are expected to exhibit from their newly gained privileges...."[10]

When the second edition of *The Underground Rail Road* had sold out, William Still self published a third edition in 1883. William P. Boyd's biographical sketch of the Still's life appeared in the volume now renamed *Still's Underground Rail Road Records.*[11.] These printings of *The Underground Railroad* remained in the public domain. The Johnson Publishing Company, a publisher of black literature in Chicago reprinted it in the middle of the -twentieth century. The sales the book originally enjoyed soon led to diminished sales. It was reprinted in Medford, New Jersey by Plexus, in 2005.[12]

The years during which the Civil War raged found William Still and his fellow committee members hard at work that winter season of 1864-1865 at the statistical Society on a plan to interest popular platform speakers to deliver speeches at Philadelphia to a paying audience.[13] Still's committee wanted interesting speeches to be preserved for the elevation of the freedmen. Once the data was compiled and printed in condensed form for presentation to Senators, Representatives, and public men who might need it in advocating the cause of universal suffrage, protection of the freedmen, or for the use in originating any measure which might grow out of colored citizenship, or which might tend to establish their rights, people might contribute towards the distribution and dissemination of material with important information for black males interested in learning more about their newly granted right to suffrage.[14]

Hard working and determined black people who showed a deep interest in the preservation of their civil rights, raised $1,260 which was placed in the care of Judge Kelley for safe keeping.[15] William Still was deeply interested in black suffrage. He remained an active agent of the Freedmen's Aid Union and Commission under the leadership of its President, Bishop Simpson. The names of a number of whites formerly involved in the American Antislavery Society, or in subsidiary roles, read like a Who's Who of Prominent men. William Lloyd Garrison (1805-1879), Salmon Portland Chase, (1864-1873), J. Miller McKim (1810-1874), focused on funding in an effort to further future attempts at "furthering the collection of data , from every source, respecting the freedmen." Two well chosen members of the Commission, William Still, and Bishop D. A. Payne were chosen to represent. the needs of the colored race."[16]

Having exchanged his former role as underground railroad agent for his new duty as a Freedmen's Bureau agent, William Still managed to squeeze into his busy schedule a number of philanthropies designed to improve the lot of poor, old people living in The Home For Aged and Infirm Colored Persons then housed in a building was located at 340 South Street in Philadelphia. Still's lucrative coal business made it possible for him to donate generously towards the improvement of the facilities at the home which was established on 28 September 1864. The appreciative Board of Managers elected Mr. Still to serve on the Board on 12 January 1865.[17] At a later time, he became its President. His dedication to this charity was rewarded at a letter date when he became the President of the Board. Moreover, William Still, a life member, made a generous contribution of $100 to the Home.[18.]

Mrs. And Mrs. Still seldom socialized. But every Sunday without fail they went to the Home to visit the old folks some of which had few if any visitors. The Stills either read humorous stories to the old folks, or sang songs that they and their fellow patients loved to hear.[19] Having mastered the art of fund raising, William Still used his experience along these lines to solicit funds[20] with which he produced a program that conditions of their present circumstances, if only for a short period of time. The Constitution and the By-Laws of the Home contain these Sunday entertainments promulgated by William Still.[21]

William Still was gifted as a social reformer. Therefore, when he saw the need for a more modern building to house the more than 150 residents, he approached a few of his abolitionist colleagues for donations for a new Home. Stephen Smith, who had been blessed with wealth accumulated from his prosperous lumberyard, contributed $20,000 towards the $30,000 price of the new building. For those who think that Negroes do not support the less fortunate of their race, let it be known that Smith showed great generosity in this regard. The securities he donated came to more than $28,000, which "together with the estimated value of the lot, made his gift in the amount of $38,000.[22]

William Still was also a prominent businessman given the success of his lucrative coal yards. He willingly contributed to worthy causes. He accepted an offer from the Mercantile Library of Philadelphia to buy a share of its stock offered to him on 10 May 1872.[23] He rallied to another need to help his people when he freely contributed funds towards the purchase of property to house the Colored Soldiers', Sailors' Orphans' Home where he served as a Trustee.[24] Because he loved children, when he was asked to contribute money towards the Home For destitute Children, he immediate responded with a donation.[25] A similar institution in need of funding was The Shelter, which also provided services for boys and girls. The building on 53rd Street near Woodlyn Avenue in Philadelphia that housed these above named charities, was later converted into a training school for youth interested in teacher training.[26] Still was also associated with Storer College at Harpers Ferry founded to honor the slain abolitionist, John Brown.[27]

William Still never forgot the help given him when an employee at the West Penn estate owned by Mrs. Elwyn. He learned to be discerning in what he read. And he learned to master the art of penmanship which helped him to record the fugitive slave stories preserved for posterity. An inveterate reader of books, and magazines which contained interesting articles filled with current ideas, Mr. Still learned to love good writing and those who composed literary works of value.

To his credit, William Still more than met the requirements of the duties expected of the Chairman of the Vigilance Committee at Philadelphia's busy underground railroad. He left for posterity a "study [of] the composition of his notes and letters in the original files of the history of the fugitive slaves arriving via the Underground Railroad."[28] His copy book contained copies of all 900 of the handwritten letters he ever wrote and sent out. [29]

While Still's duties did not require of him the need to record the whereabouts of the funds donated to the Underground Railroad, he decided to keep a financial record of each expense and he did this on his own initiative—a thing which no one else in the office had thought of doing. And just the same way as he gave aid to the fugitive slaves in their struggle for freedom, even so did he give his moral support to the Freedman in his ambitious endeavors."[30]

William Still, who appreciated good prose, had nothing but praise for the literary efforts of his old abolitionist friend, Dr. William Wells brown, the author of *The Black Man.*[31] White groups over time agreed to meet when black writers arrived in their communities to give public readings. It could be said that both Dr. Wells and Mrs. Harper gained significant exposure and praise by whites who heard them read from their books at meeting arranged by William Still.[32]

Still's reputation as an underground railroad agent in Philadelphia awakened in the minds of members of the old Pennsylvania Antislavery Society a respect for his skills they found valuable after the Civil War. When he was asked to contribute money to the establishment of a paper designed to appeal to readers in the North, South, East, and West, he saw the unifying possibilities of such a periodical in dissolving the polarizations that existed before the Civil War. The *Nation,* an independent based on the dissemination of new advances in politics, science, literature, and the arts, needed subscribers to meet the financial requirements stated by its business managers that amounted to $1000 of which William Still donated his share of $1000. His donation tp this mostly white sponsored newspapers removed William Still's contributions to only black programs.[33] The *Nation* was edited by the renowned Edwin Godkin.[34]

William Still's philanthropies drew needy causes to him like a magnet. He wisely chose to support people he felt were worthy of his social and economic help. He had an interest in the political nurturing of the newly freed slaves. Prominent white businessmen sometimes asked to meet with William Still to discuss potential business propositions he might consider worthy. Mr. Thomas Webster presented to him for him an equal number of black and white managers who might be interested in a black bank. Mr. Webster, himself a successful banker. Discussed the handling of shares which he felt would add to the prestige of the colored race.

As was his custom, William Still required time to ponder the proposition. First off, he gathered twenty-five colored men to meet with a group of whites to determine if a committee ought to be formed to make further inquiries into the bank project. Chairman Still held a committee meeting at the home of Stephen Smith to discuss with Mr. John W. Torrey, the president of the Corn Exchange the major premises concerning the bank proposal. Every aspect of banking came up for discussion during the lengthy and exhaustive exploration of banking and the pitfalls associated with this financial plan. Since money was involved, it behooved the individuals assembled who were knowledgeable about the "responsibilities of directorship, the necessary qualities for successful management, the importance of capable and honest clerical assistance, and other intricate details involving training experience, and talent—all of which greatly enlightened and surprised the committee."

The outcome of the committee in the negative, forced William Still to accept the adverse report given by the committee. Although he had hoped for an acceptance of the business plan, that the bank would be highly beneficial to his race, he looked at the data against it and had to conclude that believed he could not at that time find enough trained colored men with sufficient business skills to successfully manage such a project. He reluctantly reported that he thought the scheme was in advance of the talent essential to its success. As a result, he found the plan for a black bank in Philadelphia in substance worthy as to conception, plausible as to argument, but inopportune as to time."[35]

The failure of the proposal for a black bank in Philadelphia was followed by a similar idea that was proposed in other parts of the country. "In Washington, it took the form of the Freedmen's Bank, whose after history and failure confirmed Mr. Still's previous judgment —a judgment he was often rebuked for giving expression to."[36]

Still's capable and logical mind was respected by some, and reviled by others not as discerning. He had a good mind and used reason to support his conclusions. A systematic thinker, William Still applied his methodical thinking style to problems presented to him in his work. His secretarial duties bore the mark of a careful and thoughtful writer who wrote carefully in order not to overly embellish the facts as he saw them.[37] The envelopes of letters he received when in charge of the Vigilance Committee were neatly cut open. He jotted down on one corner of them the name of the sender, date, and in some cases the subject matter. Each of the letters that he received relative to his Address on Voting, etc, ,were bound together with his inscription of the content matter neatly written on the band."[38]

William Still's personality was even and well balanced. Perhaps he kept inside the tensions he surely felt while running off fugitive slaves. As much as he and his wife, Letitia, loved people, they preferred to remain in their home where they entertained family and friends when they were not visiting the old folks at the Home. The Stills chose their friends wisely, preferring those" whose special attainments merited their entrance."[39]

Chapter 21.
An Indivisible nation
After the Civil War.

The humiliation suffered by the South after the Civil war never seemed to end. Although their section was never entirely vanquished by the Yankee armies, their souls were ravished by the Civil War's outcome. Except for the damage done at the battleground at Gettysburg, Pennsylvania, the North was spared the physical damage heaped upon the South. Southerners felt the sting of defeat at the sight of Agents of the Bureau of Refugees, Freedmen, and Abandoned lands, assigned to that region by the U.S. Congress to rescue the refugee freedmen from dire poverty. The Northern carpetbaggers as they were called in the South went into their section to bring medicine, to look after the basic needs of the freed slaves in the area of food, clothing, and shelter. Some arrived to establish schools and colleges, to supervise the supervision of contracts between the former slaves and their employees, and to attend to the management of confiscated or abandoned lands.[1]

Once proud Southerners, after surveying the utter damage and destruction that littered their once proud settled cities and towns, directed their resentment towards the invading armies of hostile Freedmen's Agents some of whom pillaged and plundered with impunity their beloved region. Little wonder, then, that many Southerners hardened their attitudes about the Northerners and refused to accept without a struggle the subjugation of their much loved Way of the South by the entrenchment there of the "Yankee way." While yeoman farmers like their more affluent planters accepted the loss of the Civil War to the Northerners, they could not endure the loss of their slave labor. Although the Confederacy *had* collapsed, and the vast majority of the Confederates *did* accept military defeat of their region, it did not follow that they would readily accept the politics of Lincoln, the economics of [Salmon. P.] Chase, the abolitionist who as chief justice presided over the impeachment of President Andrew Johnson with scrupulous fairness, or the moral principles of [William Lloyd] Garrison, despite the fact that naïve Northerners hoped by 1865 that Virginia would be "regenerated by Northern ideas and free institutions."[2]

After the publication of *The Underground Rail Road* which was widely distributed to an eager readership, William Still traveled to Washington D.C. where he began work as a Freedmen's Agent after his election by prominent Philadelphians to work on the education of the former slaves from the Border states.[3] His years at the Philadelphia Vigilance Committee paved the way for his ability to undertake the duties with former slaves in desperate need of training and educational skills in facilities adapted to their long neglected lives in slavery. A plan proposed at an assembly of freedmen's Agents that met in the nation's Capitol focused on the need for the kind of schools the former slaves needed for the foundation they needed to attain the improvement on "what was being done for the education of 'the freed slaves'"[4]

William Still returned to Philadelphia where he pored over the many letters of congratulation on publishing his underground railroad letters from members of the now defunct Pennsylvania Antislavery Society. Brisk sales of his book that sold at $5 a copy followed in the wake of this adulation from whites and blacks alike. Many freed slaves struggled to pay the hefty price for the volume that featured the heroism displayed by their people who risked their lives to flee from slavery. Other blacks who had come through

Still's station at Philadelphia hurried to buy a copy for their grand children whom they believed should know their history.[5]

Some of the fugitives who found a sanctuary in Canada chose to return to Philadelphia or other Northern cities to settle, while others stayed in Canada. One can only imagine how those whose names were listed in Still's book felt when they read their stories. Mr. G.C. Smith, the assistant Secretary of State at Jackson, Mississippi wrote to William Still with the price of his book enclosed in it for a copy of his "valuable work on The Underground Railroad." Mr. Smith identified himself as a classmate at Oberlin College with his daughter, Caroline Still Wiley, who had taken a post in the Deep South after the war.[6]

William Still was pleased as always to hear from his old friend, Frances Ellen Watkins Harper, who was touring the South to determine the most pressing needs of blacks in that section of the country. She shared with William Still some of her findings on the subject of the educational requirements and the availability of adequate schools needed by black folks by which to realize their needs [7] He was especially pleased with her continued work on behalf of their downtrodden race. And he applauded her diligence as an antislavery speaker, especially for one of her speeches delivered at New Bedford, Massachusetts entitled, "Education and the Elevation of the Colored Race.[8] he really believed her to be one of the more dedicated antislavery speakers who braved the rigors of travel all over the North and even into Canada.[9] She always focused on the "interest of the cause and on matters pertaining to the Negro." Hers was a gift that radiated from her to members in the audience who were pulled into the depths of her heart and the expansiveness of her mind."[10]

Antislavery speakers and writers found common cause with many Pennsylvania Antislavery Society members. The intrinsic strength and some of the beauty connected to antislavery work resulted in permanent friendships. Yet after the Civil War was over and the slaves were emancipated individuals went their separate ways. A letter from Peter Lester,[11] the gentleman who served as a contact man for the election of William Still into the Philadelphia Vigilance in 1847, transferred to Victoria, British Columbia. He wrote to William Still in Philadelphia to congratulate him for his well written book on his Vigilance Committee work, *The Underground Rail Road.* Lester had moved from Philadelphia after the Civil War where he hoped to make a better life for his himself and his family. Others wanted to settle the West where greater opportunities were opening up.

William Still chose to remain in Philadelphia where he took an interest in black male suffrage in 1870.Recalling the earlier episode in the 1850s when the Society had failed to include a revision into the Pennsylvania Constitution to grant to black males the right to vote, the 15th Amendment to the U.S. Constitution in 1870 remedied this problem. His involvement in a Mayoralty election in Philadelphia in 1874 attracted his interest because he saw an opportunity for blacks in the city to gain leverage by voting for the Democratic candidate. Whereas a majority of black men chose to vote the Republican ticket due to their allegiance to the late president Abraham Lincoln's effort to free the slaves in 1865, He tried to convince them to vote their pocketbook rather than to rely on the gratitude they felt for the "Great Emancipator." Called a traitor for lacking the gratitude any black should feel for the president who freed his race from slavery."[12]

True to his own convictions, William Still offered to his people his unpopular opinion that A.K. McClure, the Democrat, "running from the Peoples' Party" would better serve them than the Republican, W.S. Stokely, who took their vote for granted. Still's difference of opinion and his close association with prominent men in Philadelphia who were white infuriated certain disgruntled blacks who lacked his elevated position in the community. They coveted his success as a cola dealership that covered three city blocks, and placed him in close competition with the most competent coal distributors in the city. Some believed that his rise up in the world had removed him from the once strong supporter of black rights in social reforms. A few blacks openly accused him of betraying or selling out his race.[13]

When a handful of disgruntled individuals learned that William Still had been nominated to join the "Coal Fraternity," an elite group of wealthy business leaders who, on occasion, traveled for business and pleasure to places in the coal producing areas, had elected him to serve on the Philadelphia Board of Trade,[14] they threatened to "burn down his coal yards." These threats forced Mr. Still to call in the constables because he feared for his property and even his life.[15] Putting aside his hurt feelings, William Still chose to quell the escalating threat of violence within the colored community at a Liberty Hall meeting. He asked the former Chairman of the Philadelphia General Vigilance Committee, Robert Purvis, to appear on the podium with him when he defended his stand in choosing the Democratic candidate in the last election. The outrage he felt from members of his own race who had accused him of having "turned traitor to their principles." required his defense.

A letter sent to William Still signed by a contingent of twenty "Colored Citizens" dated 2 March 1874, stated their stand, which confirmed a date set for a 5 March 1874 meeting with William Still. Later the meeting was postponed to a 10 March. Meeting at 8 pm to be held at Concert Hall, at which time William Still prepared remarks for his detractors at Liberty Hall, the black section of the city, at which time he detailed a long list of his views on race, loyalty, and on his reasons for voting as he had.[16]

He read from on that assigned date data from a pamphlet he published entitled On Voting and Laboring.[17] Sections of the text taken from Still's fifteen page pamphlet was published in the Philadelphia *Press* on 11 March. Readers were able to form opinions about the conclusions drawn by members of the black race who had attended the earlier Concert Hall meeting when William Still spoke. People read his statement, "I've never 'played politics.'" Now as always, Mr. Still adhered to his devotion to the downtrodden black masses he had always worked to elevate. Actually, he welcomed the opportunity to explain to his people his worldview for them."For me," he averred, "I am simple enough to think that the acquisition of knowledge, the pursuit of business enterprises,, good trades, and comfortable homes, where a more healthy and reputable existence may be secured, are of infinitely greater consequence than to be in any way connected with Politics."

Further, Still cautioned, "If "his people hoped to gain these advantages they ought to forsake 'gratitude and their prosperity to wait' for offices from the Republican Party." Blacks in the audience knew that Still's parents had been slaves. And it was common knowledge that trough hard work and perseverance he had risen above his humble beginnings into the more secure and affluent lifestyle he now enjoyed. It made sense to some in the audience that if they took his advice and aimed their efforts towards the attainment of financial success they sincerely desired for their families, they would gain more than wasting their time and energy to denigrate those very people in their race whom they ought to emulate.[18] William Still was a Presbyterian who relied on a higher power. He asked his people to obey the Commands of Christ to help undo every burden and let the oppressed go free. Moreover, resorted to the adage," Gratitude belonged to God and to those friends of Freedom who endured the greatest sacrifices and sufferings," and "to them who placed their lot in faith, and in the Lord, rather than in a political party that once came to their rescue."[19]

Still continued to defend his choice of the Democratic candidate, Col. McClure, who had helped revise the Pennsylvania Constitution. He decried election frauds, high taxes, etc., and he strenuously fought those who opposed the revision of the Pennsylvania Constitution in the area of including the basic rights due the Freedmen. His talk ended with an address to the "Leading Colored Men," who charged him with "having turned traitor to his race" which he said without a trace of anger in his voice. He simply wanted them to be more productive and to end their destructive attitude and words aimed at him."[20]

Many readers of Still's reprinted article that appeared in the pages of the *Press* delivered a local storm of indignation and comment to the newspaper.[21] Some wrote they believed William Still to be more interested in seeking the means to elevate his race than in bowing at the shrine of politics.[22] These remarks were confirmed by the following events when William S. Stokely, a three time elected Mayor of Philadelphia, met with William Still, and the Rev. Henry Phillips, to discuss the hiring of a black police officers for the first time on the Philadelphia Police Force.[23]

People generally approved of William Still's ideas in his pamphlet, On Voting and Laboring. Letters to the Editor appeared in Philadelphia newspapers both for and against his attitude about voting, but in general, few people doubted William Still's sincerity. His detractors who voiced an opinion that he was bowing to the shrine of politics, came round to the prevailing belief that he was now as before a black leader interested in the elevation of his race. Samuel George King, the democratic candidate, a former member of the Select Council, had a reputation for his "clear judgment, integrity, and spirit of progress [which] gave him a commanding influence which was ever used for the common good."[24] Abolitionists applauded his deference to their ideals. They looked favorably on his Quaker education likely to make him aware of the needs of the black people, even if he now was a member of the Lutheran faith.[25]

Mr. King, when asked by William still and the Rev. Henry Phillips to hire a black policemen to the force, saw no reason not to.[26] When he was elected Mayor of Philadelphia in 1880, Mr. King, promised in his inauguration speech that he was in favor of a non-partisan force.[27] It was reported that the most radical act of Mayor King was the appointment of a three colored men as members of the police force; as previous to his term no colored men had ever worn the uniform of a police man in Philadelphia. raised such a storm of indignation such as no previous Mayor ever encountered; but conscious of the justness of his act, he went on in the even tenor of his way, resting his vindication to time and public opinion."[28]

Chapter 22.
William Still and the Freedmen's Bureau.

William Still was a member of the General Vigilance Committee; but because Robert Purvis was nominated at the head of the list, he was understood to be Chairman of the General Committee. James McKim reported the results of the 2 December election of the reorganized Philadelphia Vigilance Committee in the 9 December 1852 edition of the *Pennsylvania Freeman*. The meeting was called to vote for a new, more effective Vigilance Committee because of the increased influx of fugitives into Philadelphia who were chased in hot pursuit by search agents authorized by the Fugitive Slave law of 1850. On motion Samuel Nickless was appointed chairman, and William Still the secretary.

The meeting was called to form a more structured, active Vigilance Committee to replace the disorganized and scattered efforts performed by the old committee which while adequate to feed, clothe, and shelter the infrequent runaway slaves who arrived in the city, no longer were staffed and organized to deal with the stream of incoming fugitives arriving at this more dangerous period in the Society's history. The 19 member General Vigilance Committee voted Robert Purvis to continue as the Chairman of the general Committee, and Charles Wise was elected to serve as its Treasurer. This election found William Still elected to serve as the Chairman of the Acting Committee, with the following men elected to serve under William Still on this committee: W. Depee, a black man, Passmore Williamson, a white Quaker, and Jacob C. White, another Negro.[1]

William Still's correspondence during his term at the Philadelphia Vigilance Committee acquainted him with British abolitionists before the Civil War. Much of this correspondence was published in his fugitive slave history, *The Underground Rail Road* but some of the letters came from prominent antislavery societies in the United Kingdom that forced him to become knowledgeable with the history of British abolitionism.

Quakers such as Anthony Benezet, The True Champion of the Slave[2] (1713-1784) was known for being the British abolitionist who in the 18th century contributed the most towards ending British slavery and the slave trade. His influence helped shape the minds of future noted abolitionists including William Wilberforce (1759-1833), Granville Sharp (1736-1813), and Thomas Clarkson (1760-1846).[3]

Thomas Clarkson was chosen to serve on The Committee for the Abolition of the African Slave Trade in May 1787. Of the twelve members in this group, nine were Quakers. And it was Clarkson who took the committee to parliament where the issue of slavery was brought to the attention of William Wilberforce [4] who in February 1788 became a leader in the struggle to outlaw the slave trade. When the approval of the Privy Council was called to debate on the present state of the African Slave, Wilberforce, who was deeply influenced by Thomas Clarkson, waged a campaign to end the slave trade in which slaves transported from West Africa to the new World became the crux of the issue of slavery itself. The failing health of Clarkson and Wilberforce who were elected Vice-Presidents' forced them to delegate much of their work to the younger, stronger Thomas Fowell Buxton (1786-1844).[5] Buxton graciously donated funds to found the Buxton settlement in Canada for fugitive slaves to live in freedom from slavery.

A true hearted evangelical, he spent his money to elevate the oppressed including blacks in colonies in the West Indies and to provide a secure home for fugitives during the prolonged period of the emancipation of the slaves. William Still's secretarial duties brought him in contact with other generous British donors to the Philadelphia Vigilance Committee. Towards the end of the Civil War, he received donations from antislavery societies in England, Ireland, and Scotland. Mrs. Anna D. Richardson in England became a regular correspondent to Mr. Still's hard pressed underground railroad.[6]

These facts are mentioned here so that the reader can understand the wide selection of people both white and black who became involved not only in the antislavery movement in the US but most importantly in Philadelphia when William Still served as the station-master at that city before the slaves were freed. Some of the letters he received were included in the pages of *The Underground Rail Road.* Some of the "sheets" he received in the mail, for example were written by an American abolitionist, William Bailey [7] that focused on the destruction of an antislavery printing press in 1858 in Kentucky by a mob infuriated by the John Brown raid at Harpers Ferry.

The section in Still's book apart from his work with fugitive slaves arriving in Philadelphia that dealt with ancillary aspects o the antislavery movement were placed in the back of his book behind the heroism of the runaway African slaves.. He included a paragraph entitled The Persecuted Bereans,[8] an account of the brutal attack against the Christian community by a proslavery mob in Berea, Madison County, Kentucky. The Rev. Thomas G. Fee, who was in charge of the agrarian compound in Kentucky near the Ohio border, where black settlers faced the angry white supremacists who lacked the weapons with which to defend themselves. Forced to flee with his followers into Ohio, Pastor Fee Pastor Fee regretted the destruction of his former saw mill, church, and productive farmlands.

Worth mentioning here is the fact that William Still seldom mentioned Frederick Douglass [9] in his book. The freed mulatto slave from Maryland from spoke on behalf of the antislavery cause in many cities and towns in the Northeast. Douglass traveled frequently to England to confer with white abolitionists. He settled in Massachusetts for a time before he removed to Rochester, New York where he ran a busy underground railroad depot and founded the *North Star,* his antislavery paper. Mrs. Richardson wrote that "Douglass' paper sold for a mere five shillings per annum (with the exception of a penny per month at the door for postage." Mrs. Richardson wrote William Still that her antislavery society contributed funds from time to time to Frederick Douglass to be used to feed and shelter the refugees he took in under his roof.

A seldom mentioned 19th century humanitarian reform was the Free Labor Produce.[10] People in the North boycotted cotton and other slave grown agricultural materials sold by the South. One writer had this to say about the need to boycott materials that helped to encourage the economic growth of Southern planters: We hardly supposed that the most strenuous efforts in this direction would be enough to effect the British market, but we did believe, and believe still, that not only is there a consistency in this preference for free produce, but that this preference is encouraging to the free laborer, and that humanly speaking nothing is more calculated to nerve his hand and heart for vigorous effort. The principle of abstinence from slave produce has been smiled at. But we are sure that it is an honest one, and, as a good old proverb observes, "It takes a great many bushels full of earth to bury a truth."

Martin R. Delany, [11] (1812-1885) a black man involved in the underground railroad, visited Africa in his adult years to determine whether or not cotton could be grown there to fetch a profit as a business run by blacks. Before the Civil War ended and the slaves were freed, Mr. Delany planned a business proposition that used the labor of the freed slaves in East Africa to plant and harvest cotton in sufficient amounts to end cotton growing in the American South. Mrs. Richardson was aware of his attempt to make a business of cotton growing in Africa in order to supply the world with this important commodity. When Delany discussed his plan with members of The African Aid Society in London, he sought financial backing not only to end American slavery, but also to transport the freed slaves back to Africa, their homeland, where they could labor on their own behalf.

Martin Delany's speech, The Black Abolition Papers, was published on 23 October 1860 was read in the City Hall at Glasgow, Scotland. Delany was depicted in its pages as an African American abolitionist and the first proponent of Black Nationalism as an advocate of "Black Israel" in East Africa. The freeborn Delany from Charlestown, West Virginia worked with Frederick Douglass to set up his antislavery newspaper, the *North Star*, in Rochester, New York. His mother took him to Pittsburgh when Delany was a small boy where he learned medicine. His 1859 travel to Liberia where he struggled in vain to set up a new black nation proved unsuccessful, which forced him to return to America where he died of tuberculosis.

William Still in his peak years at the Philadelphia underground railroad depended on donors such as Mrs. Anna D. Richardson for their valuable moral and financial support. He had grown significantly during his tenure at the Philadelphia Vigilance Committee due to his exposure to friends and contributors who shored up his spirits when the lack of money or moral support threatened to break his sometimes sagging spirits when his duties were heaviest. He and Mr. James McKim stood firm during the heaviest use of the "road' from 1852-1857 when the English abolitionists were more clear headed about the realization of the long awaited freedom of the slaves became more evident around 1860.Mrs. Richardson was the writer of the letter on 28 December 1860 to William Still that described the proslavery attack reported by William S. Bailey who had been attacked in Alexandria, Virginia wrote "exposed [him] to the spite and rage of slave holding bullies" because he saw with crystal clarity that bullies were wicked men [who] are generally cowards; and I think would not hesitate to do a base act in the presence of observers.

In one of her frequent letters to William Still, Mrs. Richardson advised that her antislavery agency had donated to Samuel Rhoads, one of the Pennsylvania Antislavery members in Philadelphia "seven pounds for the fugitives, five pounds for thee, and two pounds for the Vigilance Committee." She wrote to him another time about the whereabouts of a party of fugitives who had arrived in London to avoid the peril at hand, and who escaped amid bales of cotton from Charleston, and found work at a local sawmill. She then asked William Still about the possibility of asking your people to emigrate to the African coast, or the West Indies Islands. Mrs. Richardson reported that a colleague, Mr. Fitzgerald at The African Aid Society abhorred colonization, but was considering the proposal of assisting small groups of blacks from America to escape the trials and dangers in their own land for a new life he thought would be a thousand times better for them. She wrote to William Still on 16 March 1860 to praise her brother's wife who was a subject of the book about Peter's life in slavery. She found the story moving and factual simultaneously. She found it exactly the kind of literature on the inhumanity of slavery that would appeal to British readers. She enclosed a small sum of money in the letter from a young Irish girl in Dublin who asked her to send it to America to give to a slave. She regretted that the antislavery society in Ireland lacked the funds to contribute to William Still's committee in this letter.

Her letter to Mr. Still as the Civil War was about to end was dated 10 October 1862. Mrs. Richardson suggested the possibility of severing the North's connection with the South She added hastily that she didn't favor disunion. She deplored the slave catching episode that sent the tragic couple from Georgia to Philadelphia and all the way up to Boston where they found safety in the United Kingdom where she met them face to face and heard their story. Always true to the hunted slave, Mrs. Richardson sent in her next letter to William Still at Philadelphia some money to be used for the stream of fleeing slaves daily arriving at his station. In it she wrote with feeling," If your President had taken the step at first, he is taking it now, what rivers of blood might have been stayed! It is remarkable, how you, as a people, have been preserved to each other, without having your own hands stained with blood.... " But as to expatriation, the very thought of it is foolish. You have been brought to America, not emigrated to it, and who on earth as any possible right to send you away? Some of us are as much displeased with the North, for talking of this, as with the South for holding you in slavery."[12]

William Still and his colleagues welcomed the end of the abolition movement in America when the War ended and freedom came to the African slaves. The political wing of the American Antislavery Society decided rightly to seek a political solution to the question of the extension of slavery into the Western lands acquired in the Mexican War. Abraham Lincoln, the candidate of the free Soil party (1847-1848) opposed this extension of slavery and was swept into the presidency of the US in 1860. The Compromise of 1850 followed in the wake of the twists and turns of various political parties that ended with the victory of President. Lincoln in the 1854 Republican Party [13]

When the guns of the Civil War resolved the issue of reuniting the Union, the issue of the extension of slavery westward erupted into prolonged Congressional debates over the extension of slavery into the territories. The Congress was forced to deal with legislative rights which protected constitutional rights. The issue was not the "necessary-and-proper-clause," which only speaks to the execution of *powers* given the Federal Government. To confuse matters even more were the Civil War Amendments [which] contained clauses empowering Congress to pass laws for the enforcement of their provisions, which the original Constitution, with rare exceptions, did not.[14]

Abolitionists throughout the North focused on the emancipation of the slaves. Once they had attained this objective, members formerly associated with antislavery societies worked to gain civil rights and educational facilities for the freedmen. Because William Still recognized and appreciated the long term antislavery contributions of William Lloyd Garrison, he gave him a reception in his home on 12th street in Philadelphia Many of Garrison's old friends and colleagues traveled from far distant locations to pay tribute to the pioneer abolitionist.[15]

William Still never forgot the words of the esteemed antislavery leader who once said with feeling the following:

> "I am aware that many object to the severity of my language, but is there no cause for severity? I will be as harsh as truth, and as uncompromising as justice. I am in

earnest, I will not equivocate, I will not excuse, I will not retract a single inch, and I will be heard."

The Governor of Massachusetts, John A. Andrew, assumed the responsibility of collecting money for a purse of $50,000 to be given to the ailing old abolitionist, who also lived in Massachusetts. William Still contributed $100 to The Executive Committee of the National Testimonial to William Lloyd Garrison. The Rev, Samuel J. May, Secretary and Assistant Treasurer of the fund, duly recorded Mr. Still's receipt for his donation.[16]

Since William Still had been selected to serve on the Committee of Arrangements for the Centennial in Philadelphia of the American Antislavery Society on 14 April 1874, he sent out invitations to all concerned. Mr. Garrison's letter that said he would not be able to make that difficult travel because of his failing health, also praised his colleagues for having been able to remove the obstacles that had led to the emancipation of the slaves. He then decried the influence of whites in the South and in the Congress who continued to curtail the rights of the freedmen. He wrote that he had always fought against the exclusion of the equal rights agenda he wanted for the freed slaves, William Lloyd Garrison touched upon the exclusion of the "common school" provision which the Massachusetts Senator, Charles Sumner, hoped to find included in the Civil Rights Bill then being debated in the Congress. Apparently Garrison felt it more than Southern Rebeldom could bear and would doubtless lead to many schemes of violence; adding, however, that it indicated progress in the right direction.

His long and moving letter expressed his fear for the future of the emancipated slaves based on his understanding of the Rebel-Democracy which he felt sure would make another attempt to repeat their exclusion at the next session of Congress, perhaps successfully. He had nothing to say about the lamented passage of the Reconstruction Government into the hands of President Grant's Administration, which he stated he hated and maligned, and was also feared, by all the enemies of equality, North and South. The heartfelt letter ended with the hope that all would eventually end well for the "claims of justice and humanity that is our highest attainment."[17]

Friends and Fellow Laborers,, was the title of the document signed by the survivors of the American Antislavery Society. Age had taken its toll on the former members of that national body, save a few who managed to appear at this monumental meeting. Mrs. Lucretia Mott and William Still appeared with a handful of other old timers. A majority of the founders and members of the Society had long since died. Those present at the Centennial continued to proclaim its objective which was the long laboring for the emancipation of the slave, and his elevation to the full liberty and rights of an American citizen, now attained. The Declaration of Sentiments of this Society read as follows:

> That *"all persons of color, who possess the qualifications which are demanded of others, ought to be admitted forthwith to the same enjoyment of the same privileges, and the exercise of the same prerogatives as others,"* its purpose as declared in the 3rd. Article of its Constitution, is *"to elevate the character and condition of the people of color "*and to remove *"public prejudice, that thus may be according to their intellectual and moral worth, share an equality with the whites, of civil and religious privilege."*[18]

The work remaining to be completed for an equitable solution about the place of the Negro in the Post Civil War era in America, became the focus of interest of former abolitionists in the Republican Party in the Congress. The resentment simmering throughout the South over the loss of their slave labor was aimed at the North which left the agrarian society bereft of ever returning back to its former glory. The South instituted in the Reconstruction Era what came to be known as the Black Codes, a set of social mores designed to keep the Negro in his place. When word about a series of atrocities against the freedmen reached the Radical Republican wing in the Congress, former abolitionists shuddered at the thought of these barbaric Codes. Wendell Phillips declared," Now is the critical time (since) the rebellion has not ceased, it has only changed its weapons. Once it fought; now it intrigues; once it followed Lee in arms; now it follows President Johnson in guile and chicanery."[19]

This sordid treatment of former slaves was met with disgust and anger by Northerners who witnessed the denigrating treatment devised to keep the Negro in his place. Although President Grant's more moderate view of this dastardly treatment heaped upon innocent black folk in the South, Horace Greeley, editor of the New York Tribune, and E.L.Godkin, editor of the *Nation,* denounced the "Confederate form of Reconstruction' in his widely circulated magazine. The helpless freedmen had no recourse but to continue to be controlled by their former slave masters despite the law mandated by the US Congress enacted on their behalf.[20]

The Northerners who abhorred such treatment of the freed slaves, did all they could to hasten the progress of the former bonds men who thirsted for equal treatment now that they were freed of their chains. Rutherford B. Hayes, when inaugurated President of the US on 7 March 1877, refused to improve the lives of millions of black folk in the South. Blacks were denied a peaceful and smoothly orchestrated future, when the Reconstruction Era ended with "No final solution of the problem created by the war and its aftermath."[21.]

Chapter 23.
A Kinsman Redeemer and Women's Rights.

When the Civil War was over, William Still focused his energies on soliciting money for the education of the freed slaves in Philadelphia. He began to think of himself these days as a social reformer and civil rights advocate.. He knew about the rights given the freed slaves in the post Civil war Amendments to the US Constitution with the promise of the right of due process of law (habeas corpus), equal protection under the law, and other rights taken for granted by American citizens at the time.[1.] Working out of his home at 107 North Fifth Street, Mr. Still received letters from local and distant black educational institutions who were concerned about the upward mobility of needy blacks student.[2]

He became involved in cataloging the Society's large collection of papers and books they promised to donate to the Pennsylvania Historical Society, except for the volumes of the *National Antislavery Standard* which they had already promised to the Philadelphia Library.[3]

Much of the success of the 14 April 1875 Centennial of the American Antislavery Society was due to the hard and dedicated efforts made by William Still, the Chairman of the Committee on Arrangements. His work at the Centennial of the Pennsylvania

Society for Promoting the Abolition of Slavery, for the relief of Free Negroes Unlawfully Held in Bondage; and for Improving the Condition of the African Race, formed in April 1775, came from his heart. His people once held in perpetual bondage were emancipated black folks free forever of the chains of bondage. W.H. Furness, D.D. gave the Invocation at Concert Hall in Philadelphia which was followed by the Vice-president of the United States, Henry Wilson's Commemorative oration. Only a few of the noblest abolitionists appeared at the gala. They included Frederick Douglass, Lucretia Mott and her husband, James, Robert Purvis, and Abby Kelly. They bemoaned the inability of William Lloyd Garrison to make the arduous trip to Philadelphia to sit with them on the platform.[4] The Titular head of the militant form of American abolitionism sent his regards to his colleagues for their victory against the inhumanity of slavery in the American Union in the last ten years. [5]

Requests from educational institutions poured into William Still's mail. His position as an agent of the Freedmen's Bureau placed William Still in the position of the contact man in charge of answering queries from black schools and colleges. Lincoln University's Financial Secretary, Mr. E. Webb, according to the Minutes of the Society, applied for and was given $100 for this purpose.[6] When the Society learned that Vice-President Henry Wilson had died, a Minute on his life and death were written into the Records.[7] A meeting on its 12 December 1878 meeting was called to discuss a major commitment of the Society. Members decided to pay close and immediate attention to the monumental task of organizing its books and records. The Acting Committee of the Board of Education, composed of William J. Buck and William Still, began to collect the papers accumulated from the very beginning of the Pennsylvania Antislavery Society which they promised to the Pennsylvania Historical Society.[8]

William Still's reputation attracted prominence wherever he went. A group of white bankers approached him with a proposal to establish a black owned and operated bank in Philadelphia. Before he made a decision, he consulted a committee he formed to investigate the idea. After the lapse of sufficient time, the committee members met at Stephen Smith's house to confer John

W. Torrey, the President of the Corn Exchange. They discussed the issues connected with management, hiring, and training of reliable clerical staff, duties and responsibilities expected of its Treasurer, duties to be undertaken by a Bank Director, and other areas common to staffing less high level staff.

As Chairman of the Banking Committee, William Still, after considering the issues at hand, concluded that "the scheme was in advance of the talent essential to its success." He added that it was "in substance worthy as to the conception, plausible as to its argument, but inopportune as to time." [9]

Other cities were also approached about the feasibility of founding black banks. The Freedmen's Bank founded in Washington, D.C, operated for a short period of time before it failed due to the poor executive ability of properly trained bank officials, which, in hindsight, was inevitable, given the lack of formally trained officials. William Still was the operator of one of the city's most successful coal distribution enterprises. He learned by experience to use his common sense and innate business skills to anticipate and to deal with business problems before they got out of hand. The D.C. bank failed because of a poorly trained work force. His recognition in advance of the difficulties prevented the founding of a black bank in Philadelphia, but placed him in harm's way by how own people who resented his logic and common sense method for dealing with business matters.[10.11.]

Still's clerical skills were also first rate. He organized the letters he received while the Executive Secretary of the Philadelphia Vigilance Committee in a methodically assembled letter collection system that facilitated their retrieval. The clerical system he initiated was not only practical but also innovative. He dated the envelopes and marked their corners with important information about their contents. The names of the sender appeared visibly on the envelopes which he bound into separate bundles based on the date and the contents of the letters in them. He even made a separate pile for the correspondence he received about his pamphlet, An Address on Voting and Laboring.[12]

Another of William Still's contributions was his compilation of products made by black folks in Philadelphia he thought worthy of appearing before the world class audience who assembled at the Exhibition Hall to celebrate the Centennial of the Founding of the City of Philadelphia in 1876. In this way, William Still made sure that visitors were able to see on display some of the achievements produced by some of the thirty-thousand colored citizens of Philadelphia in mechanical science, literature, and by proofs of many of their other achievements." [13] Still's history of fugitive slaves in Philadelphia, *The Underground Rail Road* was displayed in various colored bindings artfully arranged under a heavy glass case.[14] Visitors from every corner of the globe clustered together in awe of the arts and industries produced for the display by talented Negroes." [15]

William Still was responsible for the renovation of the defunct Institute for Colored Youth school house which now became known as Liberty Hall.[16] The committee formed to transform an old site into a modern meeting hall in the black community. Mr. Still, now as in the past, poured his own money into the project which was completed in time for the induction into the Philadelphia Police Force of the city's first black policemen.[17]

The Women's Rights Movement emerged high on the list of the 19th century humanitarian reforms espoused by The Great Awakening, the series of religious revivals that swept over the American colonies which although battered by bitter doctrinal disputes , also resulted in missionary work for the Indians, and the founding of schools for minority students. The Women's question, or more properly, the Women's Rights Movement, affected the American Antislavery Society. When William Lloyd Garrison proposed that Abby Kelley, a capable antislavery member of his Massachusetts Society, serve on the Business Committee of the national Body, his request was refused out of hand.

In 1840, a schism within the American Antislavery Society involved politics and the woman's question. In fact, the Garrison-Kelley matter erupted when the Weld-Tappan political wing focused less on the technique of moral suasion held by the Boston group and more on a political solution to slavery, the real issue of the Society. Women had for long been relegated to a second place in American life. Frances Ellen Watkins Harper, in 1835 delivered talks on women's rights all over the North. Sarah Moore, (1792-1873) and Angelina Emily Grimke, (1805-1879), sisters who left their South Carolina home to advocate abolitionism and women's rights in the North.[18]

They were called for their efforts "Carolina's High-Souled Women," too stubborn to end their crusade for women's rights". They met with favor at the Massachusetts Antislavery Society where William Lloyd Garrison encouraged them to meet in the "promiscuous assemblies" that crammed meeting halls in the Boston area. He arranged speaking tours for them in remote areas in Massachusetts where audiences waited to hear them speak on behalf of the feminism they espoused openly on platforms. The Rev. Samuel J. May and John Greenleaf Whittier, the Philadelphia Quaker poet did not see eye to eye with William Lloyd Garrison's sponsoring of Legislative hearings in Boston that approved of an address of Angelina Grimke at the Society's Boston headquarters.[19]

Women associated with the antislavery movement rightly resented the provision in the 15th Amendment to the US Constitution when the right to vote was given black men and ignored suffrage rights to women. Theodore Dwight Weld, (1803-1985) the disciple of Charles G. Finney, an evangelical Christian, and one of the founders of the American Antislavery Society, worked to select the agents to head the national body formed the following year. One of the most dedicated agents himself, Weld, edited *The Emancipator,* authored *Slavery As It Is,* and married Angelina Grimke all in 1839. It was said that the pages of his treatise on Southern slavery rivaled in its impact against the hated institution Mrs. Harriet Beecher Stowe's world famous, *Uncle Tom's Cabin.*[20] Weld's searing expose of slavery detailed in graphic terms the cruelty endured by slaves every minute of their waking days. Sample chapter headings were Cruelties,"[21] "Floggings under Punishments, "[22] "The Privation of the Slaves Which Included their inadequate Clothing,"[23] and "Their Dwellings",[24] shouted to northerners the unending desperation driven by the peculiar institution.[25]

The Tappan-Weld political faction represented the schism in the American Antislavery Society in 1840 which left William Lloyd Garrison's seemingly softer moral suasion agenda incapable of liberating the slaves straight away. [26] A newly elected president of the American Antislavery Society, Isaac T. Hopper, moved into its headquarters on Nassau Street near Beekman.[27]

James McKim, however, failed to understand the truculence in the character of his revered friend, William Lloyd Garrison, when he broke with his fellow abolitionists over the political schism within their ranks. His letter to the Rev. Samuel J. May in 1843 in his capacity of Corresponding Secretary of the Pennsylvania Antislavery Society rebuked the stand taken by Mr. Garrison who opposed the founding of the Liberty Party as the official offshoot of the main body's antislavery position.[28] Garrison's idealism was nowhere wing of the Society, as questionable. Garrison stood firm in his support of the "domestic sphere" which some women's rights advocated as a kind of slavery. Thinking women opting for equal rights insisted on opportunities for women taken for granted in male dominated professions, included the right to own property, and the respect due them on an equal par with men.[29]

The Rev. Samuel J. May's November 1845 speech at Syracuse, New York entitled *The Rights and Conditions of Women,* cited the following areas he believed to be worthy of consideration in an equal rights program for women: The right to attend institutions of higher learning, the right to own and keep property, and to have control of their earnings, if any, gained from employment outside the home, and the self respect commonly accorded to men. Rev. May commented that these were the same rights already given women in 16th century England by men.[30]

Wendell Phillips in Tract No. 2, given at the Worcester, Massachusetts meeting on 15, 16 October 1852 contained material incorporated into the Massachusetts Constitution on Womens' Rights. He outlined the following solution to the problem as follows:

"Women must no longer rely on men to protect them; women must be enfranchised; women deserve equal rights with men; any self respecting social reformer not in favor of equal rights for women were imposters; women in America must be given the right to use her God given talents and intellect; women were entitled to their civil rights; women deserved freedom of choice, provided she has the aptitudes, and ability to pursue higher education; women with domestic duties should not be denied her professional rights because of her household duties; and the illusion made to other unmet social reforms affecting the freedom of the lower classes; improvement in penal legislation, in the press, in thought, etc.[31]

Wendell Phillips believed that the key to advancement of women was education. His premise was based upon his belief that if the mind of a woman was amenable to intellectual growth and development then it followed that she required similar intellectual stimulation from texts supplied to help her discipline her mind. Lacking such material, he believed that even a gifted woman's mind would not develop to its highest potential. He believed this neglect to be a sin and a crime.[32] Horace Mann, the innovative Massachusetts educator believed that if girls were to receive an education equivalent to a boy's, they would need an implemented curriculum. He founded the nation's first Normal school for training women teachers because he found such training vital to the instruction given to young women.

Loyal feminists generally attended talks on Women's Rights. Abby Kelley, who was married to Stephen Foster, an abolitionist active in the New England Antislavery Society, sent her regrets in a letter to the Worcester Conference that outlined a few of her ideas on the subject of the education of women. She strongly favored the concepts espoused by Horace Mann. However, she faulted the scanty education provided girls at finishing schools and ladies' seminaries. She believed that women able to endure the rigors of classical studies were capable of learning Latin, Greek, mathematics, and science on a par with men. Sadly, no men's colleges that would accept female students on this level existed at that time. Mrs. Foster praised Mount Holyoke College at South Hadley, Massachusetts, for having a curriculum equal to the most rigorous found in the best colleges for men in the country.[33]

Harriet Martineau, an English visitor to the United States on a regular basis, sent a letter dated 6 October 1851 to the Women's Rights conference she could not attend. A committed feminist, she mentioned some of the basic rights she hoped to see realized on behalf of women: women's suffrage, property rights, civil rights, equality with men, etc.:

"Fewer women would become mothers if they had an education, or if they were educated to the extent of being entitled to a political professional career life on a par with men."[34]

Dr.Harriott Kezia Hunt's letter was read in her absence at the 1852 Conference on Women's Rights. It began with a warning to women who were refused admission to all male medical schools not to be discouraged when they were ignored. She was refused by the Harvard Medical School when she asked to be seated with male students only at lectures. Her feelings had been hurt when she found herself placed in the same capacity as" idiots, drunkards, felons, and minors" because of her gender. She implored those women interested in the study of medicine to matriculate, as he had been forced to do, at those colleges that accepted female students. She wrote that she earned her M.D. degree at the Female medical College at Boston, although even now she still could not vote.[35]

Mrs. Angelina Grimke Weld, who now lived in New York City, wrote to the Rev. Samuel J. May a letter she asked him to read at the Women's Rights Convention he planned to hold at Syracuse, New York. He read in the letter from Angelina Grimke Weld, dated 25 August 1852 the following: "The despotism of slavery was at its ebb, and [therefore] the energy used to destroy it ought to be directed towards helping the morally diseased wherever it existed."[36]

Mrs. Elizabeth Cady Stanton, Susan B. Anthony, and Mrs. Lucretia Mott founded the Women's Rights Movement at Seneca Falls, New York, in 1848. When the Second Women's Rights Convention was held at Worcester, Massachusetts, in 1850, Mrs. Stanton was proud to say that a guarantee that women would be entitled to equal rights was revised into the New York State Constitution for the first time. She continued her efforts to advance for women equal rights in education and women's suffrage. Mrs. Mott opted less for women's suffrage in favor of the Women's

Temperance Association and the daughters of Temperance movement.[37]

Mrs. Stanton bemoaned the position of women in American society who "remained half developed, [while] wives were degraded creatures subjected to the tyranny of their husbands." Her advice to these unfortunate women was to refuse to pay taxes on any property she might own to a state government unless she was allowed to play an active role in its activities. She favored the education of children in co-educational schools because the girls would partake of the best teaching tools given the boys. Finally, she advised women to boycott the clergy until they discontinued their practice of forcing her to act like a heathen savage.[38]

Chapter 24.
The Women's Rights Movement and Women in Medicine.

William Still's Preface in his second printing in 1878 of *The Underground Rail Road,* had this to say about his background in a self emancipated slave family:

"Like millions of my race, my mother and my father were born slaves, but were not contented to live and die so. My father purchased himself in early manhood by hard toil. Mother saw no way for herself and her children to escape the horrors of bondage but to escape but by flight. Bravely with her four little ones, with firm faith in God and an ardent desire to be free, she forsook the prison-house and succeeded, through the aid of my father, to reach a free state...." [1]

He looked Janus-faced back to slavery and forward to life in freedom for his race. When he served his race as the station-master at Philadelphia, he marveled at the heroism of his downtrodden people and their love of liberty hardly compared to any other mass exodus in the history of the world. William Still grieved with his people who struggled against the odds to find better lives in freedom in the North. He tried to console his bedraggled brethren staring vainly towards the Promised Land with these words:

"...in this country, no small exertion will have to be put forth before the blessings of freedom and knowledge can be fairly enjoyed by this people; and until colored men manage by dint of hard work, acquisition to enter the ranks of skilled industry, very little substantial respect will be shown them, even with the ballot-box and musket in their hands. Well-conducted shops and stores; lands acquired and good farms managed in a manner to compete with any other ; valuable books produced and published on interesting and important subjects – these are some of the fruits which the race are expected to exhibit from their newly gained privileges."[2]

A presidential veto ended the Act of 1866, the law responsible for the administration of the lands confiscated after the Civil War from the Southern planters. The equitable distribution of confiscated lands was no more. The Way of the South was forced to bow down to the Yankee North with respect to the abdication of their lands and the slave labor needed to maintain the planter's honor and survival.[3]

Radical Republicans in the US Congress worked hard to enact in the Congress the 15th Amendment to the US Constitution in 1870.They foresaw the need to counteract the re-enslavement of the former slaves who had only the skills needed to work the soil. Now that black males could vote, many former planters and other Southerners averted their eyes from members of the Ku Klux Klan whose headquarters in Tennessee did for the planters what the agents at the northern vigilance committees did for the abolitionists in the North. Aging Republican abolitionists tried hard to rescue former slaves from the precarious position in which they were forced to live and work in the South. Wendell Phillips, the Massachusetts orator, warned northern freedmen in his short article entitled To the Freedmen! In which he urged the hapless Negroes "to learn to read and write to qualify for the vote soon to vote to come to them." [4]

Border state and Upper South freedmen took advantage of the various educational institutions established as day, night, Sunday, industrial schools, colleges, and vocational and training schools open to their participation in the Reconstruction Era. Howard

University, in Washington, D.C.; Hampton Institute, In Hampton, Virginia; Atlanta University, in Georgia; and Fisk University in Nashville, Tennessee, began the process of providing opportunities for black men, women, and children, to learn trades, vocations, and even professions to prepare them for employment as citizens of the country into which they now moved and lived.[5]

The children born to William and Letitia were certainly more prepared for higher education than the masses of poor black young people crowding the streets and the black community in Philadelphia. Their four college age children were Caroline Virginia, (1848-1919), William Wilberforce, (1854-1919), Robert George (1861-1900), and Frances Ellen, (1857-1944). Caroline, the oldest child, was born on 1 November 1848. She entered Oberlin College, in Oberlin, Ohio, in its Preparatory Course, in 1864 when only fifteen. In 1868, she graduated in 1868 with a diploma in the Literary Course. While a student, she had the honor of presiding over the Ladies' Literary Society, and was the only female in a class of forty-five.[6] Her younger sister, Frances Ellen, who also attended the preparatory course at Oberlin, left the college in 1875 after only a year in to begin a career in teaching grade school black children in Philadelphia.[7]

Oberlin College was founded by evangelical Christians in 1833. William Still wanted his daughters to attend Oberlin because of the good reputation of its second President, the Presbyterian minister and evangelist, Charles Grandison Finney, (1792-1875). He taught (at Oberlin College, (1837-1875), and served as its president (1851-1865).He was responsible for the matriculation at Oberlin of African American students on a regular basis, and in 1835 established a co-educational system of education at Oberlin College in the town of Oberlin, Ohio, known as a key underground railroad depot some referred to as "the town that started the Civil War."[8]

Both of the sons of William and Letitia Still attended Lincoln University in nearby West Chester, Pennsylvania. William Wilberforce, and his younger brother, Robert George, both graduated from this African American college before entering into the practice of law in Philadelphia. Robert George Still became a journalist, and then ran as a print shop business on Pine at 11th

Street in Philadelphia.[9] William Wilberforce who graduated in 1874 continued to practice law in Philadelphia. [10]

Lincoln University was first named Ashmun Institute for a religious leader and social reformer, Jehudi Ashmun. John Miller Dickey, a Presbyterian minister and his Quaker wife, Sarah Emlen Cresson, when the first founded the school, focused on the curricula for African American student. African studies dominated the framework of the future Lincoln University which in 1866 took the name Lincoln University in honor of the slain Abraham Lincoln. "This became the first institution founded anywhere in the world to provide a higher education in the arts and sciences for youths of African descent."[11]

It stands to reason that the children of William Still, the famous underground railroad conductor would easily find for his children some of the best black educational facilities. Considering the fact that few freedmen or their offspring were sufficiently prepared to meet the qualifications for matriculation at good colleges, the vestiges of slavery prevented even bright young people from being able to compete in this difficult market. Caroline Still grew up on the Underground Railroad. She attended the Raspberry Alley School, run by upscale Quakers, before she attended Mrs. Henry Gordon's private school. Caroline Still's secondary school was the Institute for Colored Youth.

Miss Still returned to her native city where she taught at her old high school. In 1869 when she began her teaching career, she married Edward A. Wiley, a former student at Oberlin. Their short lived but happy marriage lasted until his untimely death in 1874. Her mourning ended with a decision to study medicine which Mrs. Wiley believed would help her to provide medical services to the many sick and poor black women and children in Philadelphia. She applied to the Medical Department at Howard University in Washington, D.C. for a place in the class of 1875-76; and was accepted as a medical student whose tuition she helped defray by teaching elocution and free hand drawing to university students.[12]

Major General Otis Howard, a white man who graduated from Bowdoin College in Maine, and in 1854 from West Point, founded

Howard University from his own cash reserves. Usually the US Government Treasury provided the funds for the establishment of the black colleges in the Border States and the Upper South. But these post-Civil War black educational institutions were considered reparations for the blacks who fought on the side of the North in the Civil War. In 1865, Mr. Howard accepted the post of Commissioner for the Bureau of Refugees, Freedmen, and Abandoned Mines, also known as the Freedmen's Bureau in 1865 despite the amputation of his right arm. At that same time, he incorporated into the privately owned Howard University, the Department of Theology, and the Department of Seminary training for freedmen interested in missionary work in Africa or in the American South,.

The Normal and Theological Institute, founded for the training of teachers was important enough to warrant the expansion of this field of study into a regular university for black students under the name of Howard University which was incorporated under a charter on 12 March1867, by the 39th Congress, into law by President Andrew Johnson. The Medical Department of Howard University , began to teach its first student body on 5 November 1867 that consisted of nine students who attended class 9 November of that year. Dr. Augusta, a black physician who had earned her M.D. in 1856 at the Trinity Medical College in Toronto, officiated over the sub-divided, mixed race class, with the help of a faculty of five. For the next hundred years, Howard Medical School in Washington, D.C., and the Meharry Medical College at Fisk University, in Nashville, Tennessee, trained in medicine the vast majority of the black physicians in America.[13]

Caroline Still Wiley chose to return to her home city of Philadelphia because she missed her family. The Catalogue for the Twenty-Eighth Annual Announcement of the Woman's Medical College of Pennsylvania, which had accepted her as a medical student, was prepared by Rachel L. Bodley, A.M., the dean who had printed in it the names of the students matriculated in the 1876-77 winter term. Also outlined in that catalogue were the rigorous Requirements for Graduation Also listed as prerequisites for an M.D. degree, the female students were required to have been "engaged in the study of medicine for three years- the year commencing in March, or the Spring term, and during at least two years of that time, must have been either the private pupil of a respectable practitioner of medicine, or the Special student of the College."The candidate must have attended two courses of lectures on the following subjects:

> Chemistry and Toxicology.
> Anatomy. Physiology and Hygiene.
> Principles and Practice of Medicine.
> Principles and Practice of Surgery.
> Obstetrics and Diseases of Women.[14]

The Women's medical College of Pennsylvania was the first medical college for women in the United States. According to Guliema Fell Alsop, a graduate, whose book about the school referenced it as having represented a real and unique contribution to the study of medical education in the United States.[15] Emily Dunning Barringer's excellent summary of the Woman's Medical College encapsulated the history of the school from its inception, all the way up to the turn of the 19th century when women doctors were everywhere the object of discrimination by male physicians,[16] who supported the prejudices of many people in society who could not accept the idea that females could compete with male doctors who had the endurance needed for this line of work.

If women faced the moral obliquity of their detractors, blacks found themselves in an inferior position because of their color. From the time of their arrival in the New World, Africans, snatched from the cultural restraints of their own cultural comforts such as language and religion, differed from the situation faced by slaves brought into Europe from other homelands. The slaves who were brought to the Roman Empire, i.e. according to the British historian, Arnold J. Toynbee, wrote [17] "the Egyptian, Syrian, and Anatolian slave-immigrants [who] found consolation in the religion they had brought with them; the Africans turned for consolation to the hereditary religion of their masters." He also had this to say: "... for the American convert to Christianity does not, of course, really owe his conversion to the ministrations of a plantation-gang overseer with a Bible in one hand and a whip in the other. He mentioned John G. Fee, the leader of the black community in Kentucky that was ousted from their community by a horde of horse riding slave masters out of maliciousness and spite for God fearing men and women."

Quakers, in general, believed in and practiced equal rights for women. A Quaker physician, Dr. Bartholemew Fussell, who sheltered fugitives in his underground railroad depot near Philadelphia, revealed by his words and actions that he "believed in women as only a thoroughly good man can, and from early youth, he had been impressed with her peculiar fitness for the practice of medicine." True to his word, as early as 1840, he held medical classes for women in his home. Since women were refused the right to study medicine in the male colleges, many learned medicine as apprentices Dr. Fussell helped found the Women's medical College on North College Avenue in 1850 though he played no part in the formation of the school's curriculum.[18]

The Female Medical College of Pennsylvania (1850-1867), became known as The Woman's Medical College of Pennsylvania (1867-1970), and was finally known as The Medical College of Pennsylvania (1970-1995). The WMP merged in 1993 with the Drexel University College of Medicine. It merged to its present form-the Hahnemann School of Medicine of Allegheny University in Health Science, the largest private medical school in the country.

The discrimination against women doctors and black women doctors, in particular, raged in the middle of the 19th century. For that reason, a goodly portion of the antislavery societies were sympathetic to the problems faced by those so afflicted. Some women found solace in the study of medicine. Some male physicians were sympathetic to the plight of women and lent their medical schools a hand with their curriculum. Drexel University College of Medicine evolved into The Medical School of Drexel University in Philadelphia, where it became consolidated with two venerable medical schools: the Women's Medical College, the first of its kind in the nation, and the first college of homeopathy, Hahemann University (HU 1848-1869); Hahnemann Medical College and Hospital (1869-1982); Hahnemann University (1982-1993).,The Medical College of Pennsylvania (MCP) that began (1850-1867) as the Female medical College of Pennsylvania; the Woman's medical College of Pennsylvania (1867-1970); Medical College of Pennsylvania (1970-1993); Drexel University College of medicine: (1993-1980),MCP Hahnemann School of Medicine (merger of HU and MCPP); (2002- present), and Drexel University College of medicine.[19]

Homeopathy was prevalent in the 19th century medical colleges for men and women. Simply put, it was defined as a system of medical practice based on its treatment of diseases by the administration of minute doses of a remedy that would in a healthy person produce symptoms similar to those of a disease. American medical practitioners were hesitant to accept homeopathy as a treatment of choice in their professions. Many had a universal fear of the idea that "like cures like". Homeopathic physicians were eyed with suspicion by the doctors who earned their M.D. degree at regular medical colleges because its use replaced or counterbalance their healing plan and would surely delay the action they expected in the care of disease.[20]

"Both the Female medical College of Pennsylvania, and the Homeopathic Medical College of Pennsylvania were founded on progressive principles and innovations which have remained a hallmark of both institutions for over 150 years...."[21]

Quakers in Philadelphia championed liberty. Time was to prove to them that diverse elements were eventually interwoven with abolitionism, homeopathy, women in medicine, women's liberation, and the acceptance of women doctors in a formerly male dominated profession. The first woman to earn an M.D. degree at the Geneva College in the Finger Lakes region of upstate, New York, Elizabeth Blackwell, earlier had apprenticed to Dr. Fussell in Philadelphia early on. She had applied to numerous male medical colleges and had been summarily refused because of her gender. On 11 March 1850, the Pennsylvania Legislature passed an act to incorporate the Female Medical College of Pennsylvania, the first regular medical school for training women doctors in the United States. Only the most determined women entered the profession of medicine. Many were talented in medicine and science and were determined to work hard at their new careers in the male dominated profession of medicine in the US.[22]

Like the most militant abolitionists in the Pennsylvania Antislavery Society in 1834, women. Interested in studying medicine generally came from upper echelon homes. Lee .Crumpler M.D., the first black woman doctor, began her career as a nurse in Massachusetts before she graduated from the Female Medical College in Boston, in March 1846. Rebecca J. Cole M.D. (Women's medical College of Pennsylvania, 1867) was the first African American to earn this degree at the Woman's medical College and the second of her race to earn an M.D. degree in the United States. She worked under Dr. Elizabeth Blackwell for fifty years to implement a social service program formed to lift black and white poor women in need from the thrall of poverty and vice.

The following black women doctors also earned their degrees in this order: Susan Smith McKinney (Homeopathic, New York Medical College and Hospital for Women) 1870; Sarah Merinda Loguen Fraser (Syracuse University College of Medicine 1876), was the daughter of a Bishop and an important Underground Railroad station keeper at Syracuse; Verina Morton Harris Jones (Woman's medical College of Pennsylvania), 1888); Lulu (Louise) Fleming, M.D. (Woman's medical College of Pennsylvania), 1895; and others of their race.[23]

Caroline Virginia Still Wiley, earned her M.D. degree at The Woman's Medical College of Pennsylvania in 1878.She represented women who came from financially secure families in Philadelphia. Had they not been given the social and economic advantages they enjoyed, one might wonder how they could have achieved the status of being a woman physician in those days. Many of these pioneer black women doctors took it for granted that they would use their medical skills to help the downtrodden blacks in the city of Philadelphia. Some came from homes where education represented an escape from menial work such as domestics. Others learned nursing, or in a few cases, medicine. Whites refused to hire them as sales clerks, elevator operators, or typists.

White and black women doctors alike found it difficult to secure suitable work in medicine after having spent time and money to train for the profession. James Miranda Barry (1795-1865), a woman doctor in male disguise; Dorothea Lynde Dix(1802- 1887) a champion of humane treatment of the mentally ill, and the founder of the Pennsylvania Hospital for the Insane at Harrisburg; Ann Preston, (1813-1872), a pioneer woman doctor who devoted her life to medical education for women; Harriott Kezia Hunt (1805-1875), widely known as the first woman doctor, taught school beginning in 1827, and later was prevented from sitting in on lectures with the male medical students at the Harvard Medical School by a vote of the male student body itself. She was later awarded an Honorary Doctor of Medicine by the newly founded Female College of Pennsylvania; Hannah E. Myers Longshore (1819-1901), became the first faculty member of an American medical school; Elizabeth Blackwell (1821-1910), the first woman ever to graduate with a regular medical degree anywhere in the modern world had earlier been rejected by the Harvard Medical School, and several others, before being admitted in 1847 to the Geneva College of Medicine in Geneva, New York. She founded the New York Infirmary for Women and Children, and later instituted a program to train women physicians, one of whom, Marie Zakrewska, founded the New England Hospital for Women and Children in Boston in 1862, with its highly accredited internship program in the diseases of women and children many considered the celebrated bedside training in practical medicine coveted by women physicians who felt it necessary to gain the hands on training available to women doctors in need of practical experience before returning to their home cities to establish their medical practices.[24]

William Still's daughter, Caroline Still Wiley, M.D. majored in the diseases of women and children in medical school. As many did, she applied to the new England Hospital for Women and Children in the Roxbury area of Boston, to serve for one year an internship focusing on their area of medical expertise known all over for its excellent quality of training. She was upset and mortified when her application was refused because of her race. The Board of Physicians stated that because they feared the Southern doctors would walk out and leave the patients without necessary medical care, they had no other option but to refuse her application.[25]

Chapter 25.
The Decline of the Abolitionist Influence and the Emergence of Jim Crow Segregation.

The historian, David Potter, wrote "The Negro of the northern states of course escaped chattel servitude, but did not escape segregation or discrimination, and [but] he enjoyed few civil rights. North of Maryland, free negroes were disenfranchised in all the free states except the four of upper New England; in no state before 1860 were they permitted to serve on juries; everywhere they were either segregated in public schools or excluded from public schools altogether, except in parts of Massachusetts after 1845; they were segregated in residence and employment, and occupied the bottom levels of income; and at least four states- Ohio, Indiana, Illinois, and Oregon- adopted laws to prohibit or exclude Negroes from coming within their borders."[1]

While not at all providing excuses for the stand taken by the majority of whites in the Post Civil War era, the consensus belief was that the uncivilized African had no previous schooling in the importance of maintaining the basic ideas of Western Christendom. European settlers were readily welcomed to settle the American West because they were raised to understand and to appreciate

Western Christendom. Their hard working culture made them naturals to settle the prairies and to tame the wilderness. Newly delivered from their chains, the mass of black people in America after the Civil War lacked even the basic determinants of citizenship. Unable to compete with the semi literate European peasants, they compared more to the Native Americans herded onto reservations than their white brethren, who were able to hold down menial jobs in the cities and towns.

The stigma of color prejudice did not overlook the lives of the Still children, despite their father's prominence in Philadelphia. Caroline Still Wiley M.D. sent to the New England Hospital for Women and Children an application for a year's internship to gain clinical practice in the diseases for which the hospital had gained a wide reputation. Instead of receiving a welcome she was informed by mail that the Board of Directors at the hospital, mostly Southern that they would walk out of their duties on the wards if a colored doctor was accepted there as an interne. William Still complained to the racial prejudice that prevented his daughter from acceptance at the New England Hospital. Men of prominence and means once associated with the abolitionist met with surgeons who did the operations on female patients at the hospital removed the proscription against William Still's daughter.

Since even the most important female doctors at the hospital could not in good conscience prevent their patients from being helped by these surgeons, they capitulated and allowed Dr. Caroline Still Wylie begin her internship in the fall of 1878 Not only did Dr. Wylie perform well on the obstetrical and gynecological wards, she delivered babies who were named for her by their grateful mothers. Her gentle manners, and her excellent professional care were duly noted and recorded in the hospital Minutes.[2] She was listed in the Annual Report of the New England Hospital for Women and Children for the year ending in December 1879 as Rebecca Wiley from Philadelphia, Pennsylvania[3]

The 1896 Supreme Court decision, Plessy v. Ferguson, that mandated for black people in America a separate but equal status, upheld the State of Louisiana's right to segregate its railway coaches. The 14th Amendment to the United states Constitution clarified the political aspects inherent in the lives of the former slaves, but failed to clarify the future social role of the freed Negroes on the verge of moving into the wider society. of American life. After 1896, race became everything in America. Dr. Wiley's application for an internship at the New England Hospital for Women and Children had no box to check on the subject of race. However, future applications printed boxes for applicants to check on the matter of race.

The Minutes of the New England Hospital for Women and Children reveal a similar incident at the turn of the 19th century. Dr. Melissa Thompson's internship application failed to indicate her race. When she appeared at the hospital for an interview, her race was apparent. Emily F. Pope, the Executive Secretary at the New England Hospital, wrote with feeling the perplexed state of the white doctors, some of whom were from the South, when they were forced to refuse her application. Some threatened to walk off the wards if the black doctor joined their staff. Staff who interviewed the black physician included a group of Southern doctors who threatened to walk off the wards if the black doctor was accepted. The Folder in Negro Women Internes, in the Collection of the New England Hospital for Women and Children at Smith College, referenced the earlier incident concerning Dr. Wiley who was alluded to in the Minutes as: "our first colored interne [who] was received in 1878",'...we were afraid of trouble with patients, but the Directors were eager to have her accepted , so it was done. We were at those times a small Institution. All the patients except the maternity were under one roof, and the Resident Physician there had charge of all the patients. Although Dr. Wiley cared for them and her babies, on the maternity Ward, the staff found it necessary to be careful of the choice of the patients under the care of the Colored Interne, although she got along fairly well, the woman being fairly tasteful..."[4]

Nora Nercessian's"*Against All Odds: The Legacy of Students of Students of African Descent at Harvard Medical School Before Affirmative Action 1850-1968*, wrote in her book about the difficulties encountered black students tried to matriculate at the Harvard Medical School in Boston. Dr. James Thomas Still, the eldest son of James Still of Medford, New Jersey, entered HMS in 1867,[and] was the third African American to graduate in 1871 from the Medical School. Women who applied to sit in on lectures at that prestigious medical school were refused. A Faculty manuscript, dated December 13-26, 1850 addressed "the question of admitting a woman and three African American men resulted in a furor by the students which forced Harriott Kezia, before she became Mrs. Hunt, to withdraw her application to pacify the outcries of students, who did, however, rail less loudly at the continuation of the three black males -Martin Robison Delany, Isaac Humphrey Snowden, and Daniel Laing, Jr., admitted to lectures at the winter term. The debates regarding these two issues remain in the Minutes. The three candidates admitted to the Harvard Medical School as regular students after the Civil War, were Edwin C.J.T. Howard and Thomas Graham Dorsey, and Robert Tanner Freeman, a Dental School student in 1869, all of whom earned their degrees.[5]

James Thomas Still, M.D. (Harv.), 1871, was listed in the Alumni Rolls in the Catalogue of the Harvard Medical School, Vol,2.,1855-1871.[6] Thomas Frances Harrington, M.D. in his *Harvard Medical School: A* History, *Narrative, and Documentary* (1792-1905, (N.Y. 1905), also listed in Vol. 3.No. 2002, James Thomas Still, M.D. b. July 12, 1840, Medford, New Jersey; d. June 22, 1895, Boston; practiced, Boston; member School Board (1875-1878); surg. 2nd ,Mass. Volunteer Militia (1871-187).[7]

Medical education at the renowned University of Pennsylvania Medical College, the first organized institution in this country dedicated to teaching medicine, began in 1765 when John Fothergill, a physician from London, recommended that the American medical practitioners, Morgan and Shippen become certified as men well qualified to teach; and added that both " will not only be useful to the province in their employment, but if suitably countenanced by the legislature, will be able to exert a school of physic among you that may draw students from various parts of America and the West Indies." Morgan's correct idea lead to the founding of the Harvard Medical School twenty years later, when he wrote to John Warren, "Medicine is a science as important in its object as it is difficult in the acquisition."[and] "It is very extensive in its researches, and presupposes the knowledge of many other sciences, and the cultivation of it requires no small abilities, and demands of those who engage in the arduous pursuit an enlarged and benevolent mind."[8]

"The purpose of the first medical schools in America was merely to supplement the existing apprenticeship method of instruction, and not in any sense to set up a new method of instruction. Therefore men aimed at the concentration of this extra school instruction into the shortest time, four months, which became the standard for the new schools then rapidly springing into existence," according to Henry Beecher, M.D., and Marc Altschuler .[8] students hoping to qualify for a slot at the best medical colleges in the early days needed a college degree as a requisite. Even those so qualified had to pass an examination in Latin, mathematics, and Natural and Experimental Philosophy. In 1792, The University of Pennsylvania ended their requirements for a knowledge of Greek and a thesis prepared in Latin. Soon it was not mandatory to know Natural Philosophy, Natural History, and Botany. Pennsylvania also abolished the M.B. degree at once instead of placing the student on a three year probation period of practice between the two degrees. Under these influences the first thirty years suffered to cause the Bachelor's Degree to be abandoned by all schools, and the length of the annual college term to be shortened one third."[9]

When James T. Still matriculated as a student, tuition payments were made directly to the professors at the Harvard Medical School, and not to the Treasury of the College. His father's attention to his son's entrance requirements were more than met through excellent tutoring. Moreover, his character references and good morals were attested to in the entrance requirements for medical students in that day. Nevertheless, he faced an uphill battle to keep abreast of the newest techniques based on the most advanced medical sciences taken from the curricula of European medical colleges. in Europe. James Thomas Still received his M.D. degree from the Harvard Medical School in Boston, Massachusetts in 1871.

Dr. Still was a student under the presidency of Professor Eliot who introduced the innovative curriculum at the Harvard Medical School based on the rigors of the germ theory, and the use of the microscope, which allowed student doctors to study the cause of the infections they had never before been able to investigate. Other scientific and technological advances were inculcated into the teaching program at Harvard gleaned from some of the most progressive ideas then all the rage in Europe.

Resident physicians gained valuable clinical experience at the Massachusetts General Hospital then adjacent to North Grove Street site of the Medical School since 1847.The first Medical School at Harvard University was housed at Harvard Hall in Cambridge, Massachusetts, where lectures were first given in the basement rooms. Associated with the world's development of medicine, either as a creator or a challenger.[10] In 1783, it moved to Holden Chapel, Cambridge, where classes began after the Medical School had been outfitted. The School next moved to 49 Marlborough Street, Boston (now 400 Washington St.) in 1810. In 1816, it moved to Mason Street, the first building constructed specifically for this purpose. In 1883, Harvard Medical School moved to 688 Boylston Street, Boston, its expected new home meant to last into perpetuity, which actually lasted only for twenty-three years. The Harvard Medical School presently is built into a marble quadrangle on Longwood Avenue, which was dedicated on 25, 26 September 1906, and opened for classes on 27 September that same year.[10]

Dr. James Still treated black patients in the Roxbury and Dorchester sections of Boston. The need to improve the lives of the less fortunate members of his race, came to young Dr. Still as a second nature Inclined to aid the poor, neglected black people in the Boston area, Dr. Still admitted his patients to the Massachusetts General Hospital where he was first a resident physician, and later a staff physician.[11]

His herbalist physician, "Dr. " James Still, had established at this time a flourishing patent medicine business in Burlington County, New Jersey. Most of his patients lived in Medford Township, Buddtown, Red Lion, Lumberton, Vincenttown, and Eayrestown. The backwoods area through which Jim Still rolled in his horse-drawn wagon stopped at homes and farms also located in Smithville, Pemberton, and Birmingham, a village built in the revolutionary War with its 1800 Bolton& James Iron Forge. He treated patients at Lumberton, a shoe manufactory town near Indian Mills, where his father used to buy the childrens' shoes. Some of his patients lived as far out into the county as the farm lands near Rancocas Creek.[12]

The old timers waited for the arrival of Still's fancy Rockaway wagon in places too small to appear on the county maps. He eased the pain and suffering of people who lived deep in the Pines. Friendship, Chairville, Hampton Gate, Indian Mills, that later was called Shamong James Still's medicines were arranged in the drawers of a chest with pills, potions, elixers, and essences compounded with the help of his wife, Henrietta. The sale of his medicines quickly left his medicine drawers empty. For the first time, he needed to hire help to gather botanical specimens needed for his wife to distill their healing factions in the still she tended at the wood burning stove in back of the house. James still used the distillate to compound into a variety of syrups, sudorific drops, emetic powders, and cough balsams derived from such common plants as skunk cabbage pleurisy root, Virginia snakeroot, etc.[13]

Recently emancipated freed slaves scarcely hoped to attain the success of James still, or of his family members who had achieved a semblance of economic security The roadblocks that impeded their progress was anticipated by the ageing Radical Republicans in the Congress who strived to help them move into the place in society mandated by the Civil War Amendments. Black males could vote, but were blocked from the use of the ballot in the South by The Ku Klux Klan, a Tennnessee vigilante organization founded by resentful Southerners to deny to blacks in their region the rights enacted on their behalf in the 1870s.

Southern Negroes were resigned to their pre1870s place mandated by the South. The Civil Rights Act of 1871, also called The Ku Klux Klan Act, was passed in February 1871. The following year, Lt. Governor Pinckney Benton Dewart Pinchback, a black man from Louisiana served for only 1 month of his term as the Governor of Louisiana-from December 1872 to January 1873. He was the first ever African American to hold that position. Seven blacks were elected to the 43rd Congress. However, the U.S. Supreme Court in the Slaughterhouse Cases ruled that the "due process" clause of the 14th Amendment protected national, not state, citizenship.

The Federal Government was forced during this tumultuous Post Civil War era to send troops to Vicksburg, Mississippi in January of 1875 to protect African Americans about to vote. On 1 March 1875, the Congress of the United States passed the Civil Rights Act. A black man, Blanche Kelso Bruce (Republican) of Mississippi was the first African American to begin and serve a full six year term when he took his seat in the U.S. Congress on 3 March 1875. In the summer of 1876, riots erupted against blacks who tried to cast their votes in South Carolina, an incident that pressured President Grant to restore order by sending in Federal troops. A positive asset to blacks in Nashville, Tennessee, was the establishment of Meharry Medical College on 13 October 1876 by the Freedmen's Aid Society of the Methodist Church. In 1877 there were three black members of the 45th Congress; and Frederick Douglass became the U.S. Marshal for the District of Columbia. In 1879, and about six thousand African Americans left Louisiana and Mississippi counties along the Mississippi River for Kansas in what became known as the Exodus. [14]

William Still, an invited guest at the early May 1879 Conference held at Fisk University, in Nashville, Tennessee, delivered a speech, Opportunities and Capabilities of Educated Negroes. He stated: "Long before the advent of Emancipation, and ever since, the attitude of our people in this country has absorbed no small share of my study. I have looked upon their condition with intense interest, feeling to be fully identified with them, however regarded."His was a heartfelt speech on the topic of the status of the Negro since Emancipation.[15]

William Still revealed in his presentation an impassioned plea for the training and education he believed vitally important for the advancement of the freedmen if they were to gain the skills needed for social and economic power he felt was long overdue. Placing himself on the same level of his less fortunate brethren, Mr. Still allowed that millions of former slaves were liberated from bondage only fifteen years ago. Unprepared for the requirements of citizenship in the modern 19th century, the bleak future of the majority, left them, very poor, without land, without education, without homes, without protection, universally proscribed, and wholly dependent. Still urged the negroes to take the first trembling steps in pursuit of their manhood.

He presented himself as a mature black man who was an advocate for social improvement with a voice. He believed that individuals must learn to crawl before they walk. He spoke from his authority provide him by the Freedmen's Bureau. He allowed that the former slaves lacked a stable roof over their heads to keep out the heat of the day and the cold of the night, nor schooling to open his eyes to fraud, and not place to lay his head now that freedom had delivered him from the shackles of slavery. Those in the South who ignored the impoverished blacks in their areas, who were living as pathetic, impoverished humans and who showed them no concern for their survival, were, in Still's view, heartless.

William Still deplored those individuals with the power to alleviate the suffering of the destitute black people ought to open their eyes to the poor person without a penny to his name facing starvation for the want of food, and who had no home to shield them from the heat and cold He referred to those who having been freed, moved to faraway places in search of a better life. His heart went out to the unfortunate members of his race left behind in the South he characterized as "needing a shelter or employment, or a piece of land to till, or to purchase, or a store to buy his provisions, clothing, medicine, or what not; a physician to attend him when sick, a lawyer to defend him when in trouble, a scribbler to write him a receipt or an agreement, or a conveyance to draw him up a deed, the only sources to apply to in the ninety-nine cases out of a hundred were those from under whose yoke he had been delivered."[16]

William Still placed the hope of his race on their acquisition of education. He saw education as the path of enlightenment needed by the freedmen to enlighten their benighted minds. He believed that the illiterate former slaves required the tools and skills required to lead them into better, more productive lives. Still had much to say about the Freedmen's Bureau which had worked hard to address the enormity of the task facing the recently liberated slaves in the area of eliminating their pressing and wretched conditions, despite the mistakes earlier by some of the Bureau agents. Still focused on the mistakes made by Agents who believed that the problem of race was resolved once the freedmen had been given the right to vote. William Still, however, knew that the problems surrounding the freedmen would be filled with hardships and trials not easily eliminated from their lives. Yet, he praised their early efforts at rising above their troubles. He urged the former slaves to work hard while remembering that other groups such as immigrants also faced staggering odds when they first arrived in this land of opportunity He realized the hard road ahead for those freedmen whose poor understanding of the value of labor would hold them back from the economic progress they truly desired. Black males used to cotton picking and heavy labor needed job training to exist as new citizens in the North. Education would replace the slave mindset over time to make the freedmen competitive with white workers unaccustomed to the barbarism of slavery.[17]

Chapter 26. Opportunities and Capabilities of Educated Negroes.

William Still's speech at Fisk University, Opportunities and Capabilities of Educated Negroes[1] was an argument on behalf of the future of the freedmen who he believes would one day realize the improved lives they so sorely needed. After all, they had only just been emancipated for a little more than fifteen years. He cautioned whites who believed that blacks were backward socially and intellectually because of their innately inferior natures, when the truth of the matter lay in their lack of opportunity to leave slavery behind. He alluded to the Darwinian Theory of Evolution, then prevalent in some academic circles, which confirmed this prejudiced idea about blacks. William Still insisted in his talk that once given opportunities and education, black people would be capable of competing on an equal par with whites.

Still's many intellectual achievements had prepared his mind to contend with the black dilemma without resorting to high flown rhetoric which black orators resorted to in order to impress their audiences with their learned skills at public speaking skills. He looked down upon the liberating airs of Black Nationalism as a solution for the rapid rise into society of his formerly enslaved race. William Still relied on his methodical approach to problem solving based on past performance and future benefits to be derived thereon. He felt a duel responsibility to the Freedmen's Bureau and to the deeply felt allegiance to their improvement born of his family tradition for freedom, to advise the freedmen to the best of experience and ability to listen to his ideas.

Black Education was the key needed by the freedmen to open the door to freedom that was locked closed by the hard and paternalistic hand of the Southern planters and their sympathetic yeoman. Since the majority of freedmen remained in their home land in the South after the Civil War, William Still was constrained to offer them advice to cope with the problems of those unprepared to feed, clothe, and shelter themselves and their families. Left landless, uneducated, without homes of their own, bereft of an authority to hear their complaints, his people lacked the courage and the means to step beyond their infancy into the manhood they longed to find and embrace.

William Still shuddered at the unyielding mass of freed slaves who continued to live in the South where they were forced to count their pennies to survive. Deserted by the U.S. Army when the troops were withdrawn, the small farmer stood in fear of unscrupulous Southerners ready to pounce upon them in lieu of the hated Northern white man who had laid waste to the Way of the South during the Civil War. When it came time to harvest his small crop, the black farmer who had with difficulty worked his small piece of land, lacked the money to pay for a physician when he fell sick, or a lawyer when he was in legal trouble, scrounged a living sufficient enough to buy food and other necessities no longer furnished them when slaves. The freedmen in the South hungered for education. Still said in his speech, that the former slaves praised the contributions of the "goodly number of noble hearted and liberty loving men and women in the North who were ready and willing to brave the perils of the South to help satisfy this thirst and hunger, [which was] abundant cause for trusting that the race will in due time be uplifted."

The Pennsylvania Antislavery Society in Philadelphia and the Freedmen's Aid and Union Bureau, taught William Still the rules of organizational procedures. He disagreed with them, however, even in the face of their boundless help and support given the freedmen, that it would take fifteen or twenty years to remedy the problems facing them as they advanced towards freedom.

Few could anticipate the unscrupulous acts some white Southerners perpetrated upon the small black farmers in rural and small town settings. Nevertheless, a sizeable group of these dedicated Christian men and women continued relentlessly to contribute endless hours of their time, substantiated by donations of their money to establish black schools and colleges in the South. Responsible whites in the South, on the other hand, tried hard to provide for those freed slaves choosing to remain in the South, the means to become gainfully employed. Education made it possible for former slaves to become aware of his rights to implement his financial station, in many ways. Once he had the necessary training, the freedmen could provide for himself and his family and to get property and a house. In other words, freedmen recognized the importance of thrift and integrity, major character traits sure to evolve from training and education. William Still, while he recognized some of the faults exhibited by workers at the freedmen's Bureau in the South, he said he felt certain that the U.S. Government did all it could to extirpate the corruption that was the product of political infiltration into its Agency.[2]

Another area with some disappointment attached to it was the 15th Amendment which granted the ballot to black males. Here too, many Negroes lacked the maturity of thought needed to choose the best possible candidate interested in the improvement of their race. Primarily in the South, blacks were impeded in the use of the ballot due to the violence of small groups of white Southerners who prevented the execution of this right to frightened former slaves. Not surprisingly, many black people were relegated to lives of endless poverty.[3] Northern whites also faced failure when they proposed the establishment of black banks in several major cities. Even when the Freedmen's Bank was established for the black community located in Washington, D.C., poor management and dishonest practices resulted in its failure. At this juncture, Mr. Still restated his belief that slavery had for long left the freedmen with benighted minds. Lacking judgment in many areas of expertise, it was clear that once educated to assume responsibility for positions in their community, the Negro would be expected to remedy what he lacked and to aspire to peace, order, and prosperity, as was experienced by those new to the country now living and working in comfortable circumstances all over the country.[4]

Getting down to the facts of the situation, William Still thought it wise to base the freedmen's new life on the bedrock of the old. Since the slaves had learned skills when they were slaves, he suggested that the freedmen ought to improve upon the skills they already knew when they were free. The point was to build upon this bedrock of expertise where he had little or no competition from other competitors in the South. Already able to perform these labors, the former slave had it within his power to convert his labor into paid employment. However, the former slave needed the skills to evaluate the value of his labor. The acquisition of business skills would add to his being able to keep accounts concerning his labor in a more businesslike manner. Business courses would acquaint the worker with a clear and businesslike way the exact amount of money he spent in the pursuit of his labor and the ability to anticipate the capital needed for him to finish the project he had in mind. Now determined to make a success of his business plan, the freedman would then be forced to determine whether or not the project he had enough money to complete his projected plan. If he had to buy a deed, this required careful thought and planning to avoid involvement in a fraudulent legal document or agreement which might result in a loss of the little money he already had on hand. Bookkeeping skills would prevent the purchase of goods or supplies already listed in his account book. William Still believed that the data in his books were facts the worker could rely on, if faithfully kept, which could ensure the amount of capital needed to carry him until the harvest of his crop.[5]

William Still spoke about the emigration of freedmen from the South to the newly acquired Western territories where a myriad of skills were desperately needed. But he cautioned them about leaving their homes for an unknown section of the country unless they carefully read maps and located specific locations on globes where he felt he could find slots for his skills. Only after the potential emigrant felt certain enough to leave his old home in the South to seek better opportunities in the West should former slaves pull up stakes and make the change. William Still warned those about to leave the South to master some of the needed skills open to emigrants to the western areas. These were some of the employment openings in dire need of trained workers:"the art of animal husbandry, mechanics, keeping stores, trading, and all kinds of industrial labor, unless they were [willing and able] to rough it in the woods, in log cabins- to begin labor by cutting down and clearing up the forest under great difficulties".

William Still chose business as a vocation which he suggested to every colored man. Having succeeded in business himself, he offered this line of work to his people who were so inclined, because it could relieve the unskilled worker from the lowliest levels of labor where the income was less lucrative. Blacks had gained the reputation for being unable to rise above the ordinary lower callings as laborers due to a lack of education. Mr. Still spoke in opposition to this claim by providing data he complied which he hoped would answer some of the queries he had earlier presented to freedmen still living in the South: "How they were getting on, was their increased education making it possible for them to buy and live in more comfortable homes, what percentage were getting into business and the type of business they were undertaking, were their marriages more stable,&"[6]

Frances Ellen Watkins Harper also worked for the betterment of the freedmen, especially in the Post-war South. She traveled extensively throughout the South before and after the Reconstruction Era. The data she wrote to William still in a letter substantiated the impressions William Still already had learned about the poor black farmers forced to eke out an existence from the soil in The South. Mrs. Harper visited small black settlements throughout the South to interview former slaves living and working in remote areas in former slave holding sections of that region. Not all of her data were hopelessly negative. Mrs. Harper quoted the words of a former slave, Mr. Montgomery, who had established a thriving business with hundreds of transactions which netted a hundred thousand dollars. Other enterprising Negroes who conquered early hardships and many difficulties pooled with family members their energies and talents in successful businesses that eventually benefited them all. They raised fences, tilled hundreds of acres of farmlands, and produced on their own initiative about 107 bales of cotton.[7]

Since not all freedmen had the drive and good fortune to make new lives with capital derived from their hard work and planning, William Still included the names of the men and women, black and white, who were willing and able to provide their advice to the needy on ways to improve the capital-using skills they already possessed. Much remained to be accomplished in the areas of farming, trades, stores, and literary pursuits requiring the application of brainwork on the part of the freedmen. Because education was to be the fulcrum needed to tip the scales in favor of black progress, William Still concluded that "we shall do little towards breaking down the color line or towards conquering the prejudices which now proscribe our sons and daughters who are fitted by education and character to fill stations in life other than menial ones." William Stressed the adage,"Knowledge is power," which he pressured his people to understand by reading the Book of proverbs." Moreover, "he also counseled, them never to forget another volume, entitled the "Pursuit of knowledge under difficulties."

An admirer of good books, Mr. Still advised his people to learn to read with appreciation books of value and to avoid the cheap books filled by yellow journalism, popular in those days. He urged them to select volumes whose contents were designed to develop their minds and hearts in order to advance morally, mentally, and financially. Education would provide the skills of discernment in the choice of literature necessary to elevate their once benighted minds as slaves from the doldrums into more practical modes of thought. Slavery had consigned many black people to a negative way of thinking which the former slave accepted as his normal way of thinking, and hence behaving. Education was the magic wand that opened the mind to business, oratory, or science.

To illustrate his point, William Still mentioned a few of the former slaves turned writers and underground railroad agents whose talents in these areas represented outstanding contributions to their people once they shook the dust of slavery from their shoes. Frederick Douglass, now the Honored Marshal of Washington D.C., the highly intellectual Rev. Samuel R. Ward, who dispelled a mob of angry citizens in New York City which not even the police could control, Henry Bibb, J.W. Loguen, and scores of other brave runaway slaves who served the antislavery cause before the Civil War. They gave evidence of the untapped genius of black folk in need of education before being able to make significant contributions in various capacities to their country and their people. Clearly, Mr. Still lamented, "Our condition is very lowly, and in many respects sad. And there are no signs discernible to my mind that we are likely to have our status improved very soon, either through politics or the liberal bestowal of land, money, or the preferential treatment for any positions by the Government. Hence, we have nowhere to look but to self-reliance and to God."[8]

"True, we are not friendless," William Still opined, about the current status of freedmen currently living in the South. The credit he gave to the worthwhile contributions of white Christians for the improvement of black people after the Civil War was well received. Yet he hastened to impress upon the black race the importance of self- reliance, instead of succumbing to self pity for his bleak condition. Having outlined some of the difficulties associated with the solution of Southern freedmen to emigrate to the West, Still felt it more prudent for him to make the best of his present condition in the South by the aid of education and job training to better his lot where he was now living. Many schools and colleges established for the rectification of this problem were established by the American Missionary Society in the South after the Civil War. A total of thirty-seven schools, colleges, and universities were founded there in all; seven of which were listed as regularly chartered institutions.

Hampton Normal and Agricultural Institute, Hampton, Virginia; Berea College, Berea, Kentucky; Fisk University, Nashville, Tennessee; Atlanta University, Atlanta, Georgia; Talladega College, Talladega, Alabama; Tougaloo University, Tougaloo, Mississippi; and Straight University, New Orleans, Louisiana. Also founded by the Methodists, Presbyterian, Protestant, and Quaker religious denominations were not as well known but of equal value and importance as educational institutions for black advancement. Other denominations including Congregational, Methodist, Presbyterian, and Baptist sects founded and operated theological schools for the seminary education needed for future black ministers of God. Duly noted were two black colleges in the North-Wilberforce University, at Xenia, Ohio, and Lincoln University, at Oxford, Chester County, Pennsylvania. Lincoln's early president, Rev. D.A. Payne, a president of Lincoln University, founded by the African Methodist Episcopal Church, where William Still's elder son, William Wilberforce, (before the matriculation of his younger son, Robert George was of age),and two nephews graduated from the well respected black college.[9]

Wilberforce University, was named for William Wilberforce, the British statesman and humanitarian, who secured the passage of a bill in 1807 to abolish the slave trade in the British Empire. The all black college taught algebra, arithmetic, geometry, grammar, composition, music, etc., by dedicated black professors whose alumni represented the finest black students that could be found anywhere in the North.

In conclusion, Still's arguments for education as a means to sharpen the mind of black people was born out in a letter he carried from the President of Lincoln University, Rev. J.N. Rendall, D.D., at Philadelphia. The educator urged those with the power to administer the topic of the education of colored students, opened with his dedication to the promise to give to these students every advantage the teachers, themselves, possessed. The aim to quicken the minds of black people in need of career preparation in society where "churches are to be established and administered; the principles of domestic economy are to be applied, and industry to be encouraged. It will not answer to make the foundations of these widest interests narrow. These precious interests must be entrusted to the hands of men who have the advantage of a liberal culture in the world's experience, as it is given in history and in scientific discovery. Above all, they ought to be imbued with the principles of Christian morality."[10]

The development of the body of William Still's presentation was skillfully arranged to awaken the audience to make in his own mind a comparison between the advances colored men were making over their fifteen or twenty year emancipation period from slavery, while giving due appreciation and thankfulness to the work done on their behalf by good hearted whites and blacks anxious to bridge the gap between the opportunities available in slavery and the advances achieved in freedom. Education was the capstone that stabilized the foot bridge leading from darkness into the light. In other words, William Still opted "to renew our efforts to advance education and true, and undefiled religion; to promote more economy, more union; more regard for morality, more willingness to work out and extend a helping hand to the 'million' who are of the most lowly and degraded."

He relied on Scripture with a Biblical quotation, "He that reapeth receives the wages!" "In the morning sow thy seed, and in the evening withhold not thine hand." He ended with a word of warning to black people, "The race is not to the swift, nor the battle to the strong, but to them that endure in the end!" [11]

Chapter 27.
Contributions of the Still Family to their Fellow Blacks.

Levin and Charity Still, a full sixty years before the slaves were emancipated, that responsibility came with liberty. The Still children passed along this helpful concept to their children, who taught it to theirs. Caroline Virginia Wiley, M.D., as soon as she returned to Philadelphia from Boston in 1879, set up a medical practice for poor women and children in its most degraded section. Frances Ellen Still taught poor blacks in the public schools of Philadelphia

James Still's self published autobiography with the distinguished Philadelphia publishing house, Lippincott in 1877, titled *Early Recollections and Life of Dr. James* Still.[1] was written with the hope that " this book may be a stimulus to some poor, dejected fellow-man, who almost hopelessly, sits down and folds his arms and says, 'I know nothing and can do nothing." He alluded to the Biblical story of David and Goliath in his Introduction to show to downhearted blacks that a boy with a slingshot could topple a giant with a sword. How he wished that Negroes aspiring to become doctors would persevere against the odds against them in this pursuit! He used as an example of his self taught medical skill the treatment he provided for those with high fevers. Beginning with a diagnosis of the malady, he tried various cures in order to find the correct medicine which directed the use of the home remedy sure to stay the course of the fever. He stressed the efficacy of his medicines "I think best or safest to use in practice for the benefit of suffering humanity."[1]

James wrote about his long year as a purveyor of home remedies in the pages of his 274 page autobiography in which he outlined the incredible hardships he and his newly self emancipated parents were forced to endure in Indian Mills, New Jersey. Dr. Still remarked about the results of the dire poverty, racial prejudice, and privations he was forced to endure because money and education were practically non-existent. He had nothing but good to say about his parents for raising their children to work hard, help those in need, and to believe in Scriptures.

James had much to say about the Philadelphia Centennial Exhibition in 1876. His daily visits to experience the displays that filled the Exhibition Hall put him in close proximity with people all over the world. He rubbed elbows with visitors from as far away as Argentina, Great Britain, New Zealand, Victoria, New South Wales, The Bahamas, The Bermudas, Queenland, Tasmania, Canada, France, Germany, Austria, Switzerland, Belgium, the Netherlands, Denmark, Sweden, Norway, Italy, Egypt, and too many other foreign lands for him to remember. [2]

The enormity of the exhibitions staggered his imagination. James who had early curbed this faculty in order to discipline his child's mind for the medical practice he felt was his calling. James seemed mellowed by his experiences which had earlier daunted him when he penned his memoir. He wrote with feeling about the effect the Philadelphia Centennial celebration had on him in his mature years as follows:"No child then living would likely be alive to witness the next one in a hundred years. The world is not our home, and should we be possessors of all that we have seen with our eyes, with all its charms and glittering show, we are admonished that we must leave for other spheres of which we have not yet made the acquaintance; a country where I hope our eyes will not tire of seeing, or our bodies be wearied; a land where the inhabitant shall no more say, 'I am sick.'" [3]

The black community in Boston depended on the excellent medical care given them, often free of charge, by Dr. James still, in Boston. When Dr. Still ran for a seat on the Boston School Committee in the General election of 1875 in Boston, he received a plurality of votes from the mostly black Ward 9, in Roxbury and Dorchester for a three year term from1875-1878. The search he immediately made was for a black teacher which he found qualified to teach in the Boston Public Schools.

As was the custom for his fellow graduates of the Harvard Medical School, Dr. Still served in the Massachusetts Volunteer Militia (MVM) as a surgeon under Major Lewis Gaul from 1871-1874.[4]

Dr. Still juggled a career of medicine with the education of young people throughout his career. Much the same as was the career of his uncle, William Still, he became an advocate for the less fortunate members of his race. He used his position on the Boston School Board to advocate education as an important facet of upward mobility for blacks everywhere in the country. 1870s Boston was populated with an influx of European immigrants whose children swelled the rolls of the public school system. Black families were forced to compete with these similarly neglected school children from substandard neighborhoods that comprised the Boston area. White parents naturally wanted for their children the best possible public school education. That was one of their reasons for leaving the Old World for the New. [5] Dr. Still worked to provide better schools for all of the city's children whether black or white.[6]

The Boston School Board faced at that juncture a series of problems that stood in dire need of repair. Dr. Still and his colleagues faced an uphill struggle to deliver to the students the best education they could possibly implement. Some of the problems began with members of the School Board who tried to do their best but didn't always achieve their intended objective. Try as they might, no significant progress was made by the hard working if inefficient School Committee members. The problems inherent in education during this interim were due to the rapidly growing influx of immigrants whose needs required a more sophisticated approach to overcome the inertia in the pre1870s. Much like the previous unscientific approach to medicine in the early 1870s, the process of educating a mass of incoming students with differing needs and capacities found no ready solution. The need for a more modern curriculum became obvious if an improvement in education in the Boston Public Schools was to comply with its growing student body. Sadly, however, it was not until 1906 that the diverse needs were adequately met by the Boston School Board which resulted in a glowing metamorphosis of a widely scattered school system into one of the best public school systems found anywhere in the United States.

The Harvard Medical School under the competent direction of Dean Eliot had in 1871 not only improved drastically its medical curriculum, but had inculcated in its course work the most modern scientific laboratories and innovations used in the most progressive European medical colleges. The Louis Pasteur's germ theory predated the future discovery and use of antibiotics. Another clinical innovation was modern anesthesia. Harvard Medical School adapted the theory and implementation of techniques in the area of sepsis and antisepsis, newer surgical techniques, wound healing advances, and other scientific methods used in clinical settings, all of which heralded in a discerning new approach to modern medicine in the United States.

When Dr. Still began his service on the Boston School Board in 1876, he was but one of an at-large group of twenty-five. This enlarged body was nominated to serve on a general ticket which was less likely to seek nomination from political motives as was previously the case. They were able to attend to their legislative duties under a set of possibilities heretofore not formally known before on the Board. The teachers they nominated for appointment to the school system were forced to meet more stringent qualifications than before. Every facet of education for public school students was examined and re-examined with a fine tooth comb by those elected to assess the areas of curricula, physical fitness, knowledge of arts or handicrafts if such skills were part of the curriculum to be taught to the students qualified to prepare to enter the master's class in the high schools. This scrutiny of teachers who were well trained in subjects to be taught the students, elevated the Boston Public Schools to first place when compared to the more advanced scrutiny given to the matter in the Western schools.[7]

In 1877, the problem faced by the Boston Public Schools this problem of implementing a systematic "graduation of our primary and grammar Schools, but there the system ended. There was no adjustment of the relative classes of the grammar and the high schools. Five new high schools, each different in many respects from every other, appeared." By limiting the advanced course to the English and the Girls' High School, open to pupils who had completed the three year course in any of the high schools, the Board saw the savings that would be made when it came to purchasing apparatus. This would enable the schools to supply specialties in some of the most important departments of high school education. And it would require a complete revision of the three year prep course, and render necessary a uniform course of study. Now the Girls' High School students would be prepared to enter college on a par with the Girls' Latin School pupils.[8]

The 1878 Boston School Committee Report began with a glowing report that "the changes made since the 1875 reorganization of the School Committee have proved themselves salutary. Before the reorganization of the Board, the election of members of the School Committee were confined to wards. Under that system the nominations made in party caucuses in the several wards of the city, and nomination by the party dominant in one ward, was equivalent to an election." Further, it stated that "The majority of votes of but a single ward was necessary to elect a member of the Board. Now the election is by a General ticket, each candidate's name being brought to the consideration of all voters throughout the city. The nominations are more cautiously made, the merits of the candidates being carefully weighed by a sub-committee, and by the same nomination conventions which nominate the mayor or alternates, In this way, the local ward feeling heretofore, too prominent in the conducting of our schools, is suppressed, no member of a ward represents the whole city."[9]

The Supreme Judicial Court of the Commonwealth wrote: "The School Committee [is] an independent body entrusted by law with large and important powers and duties; the Legislature have imposed on the School Committee the duty of seeing to it that the public schools are in a condition and of the character best calculated to advance the improvement and promote the good of the pupils."[10]

Dr. Still turned his energies at the completion of his duties on the School Board in 1878. Married at the time with a family, Dr. Still continued to reside in the Beacon Hill area of Boston in order to be near to the Massachusetts general Hospital where he served on the staff of physicians. When he was a medical student, he lived during his student boards with his peers at 13 Phillips Street. After he earned his M.D. degree, he became a house doctor at the hospital for a few years.[11]

Dr. Still, and his wife, Elizabeth, a Philadelphia native, had several children in quick succession. Their firstborn was James Harrison Still, in 1876 when the family lived on North Anderson Street near Massachusetts General Hospital. Next came Henrietta, on 10 March 1877.[12] Israel, T., was born the next year. Wendell Phillips managed to survive after several of his siblings died in their infance.[13]

He was enormously proud of his Uncle William Still's magisterial fugitive slave history, *The Underground Railroad,* which highlighted the suffering of the fugitives who faced terrors their progeny never experienced. Some were moving up in life oblivious to their hard pressed past in slavery.[14] Dr. Still made it one of his life's work to acquaint young people from the podiums of black churches stories about their past in slavery. He chose to do this to remind young people of their heroic past at a time when many of them were drenched in the hopelessness of their own despairing lives.[15]

Their present day emancipated legal status put them in mind of a new set of obstacles to surmount which differed from those faced by their forebears before freedom came. For that reason, The preface in the 1878 reprint of William Still's *Underground Rail Road* contained a message to freed slaves intended to smooth their transition from slavery into independence. He offered in its pages the following snippets of sober advice mean to help them improve their lot "by dint of hard acquisition to enter the ranks of skilled industry, which if they failed to do so, the former slaves would enjoy very little substantial respect will be shown them, even with the ballot-box and the musket in their hands." Further, he urged them "to strive for the attainment of high moral standards now that most had learned to use with wisdom the proper use of the ballot in order to advance politically in the face of the present, negative, public sentiment which generally excluded their race. He opened his preface with opened with a sketch of his own parents' hair raising escape from slavery which he hoped would forever remind the freedmen that their own relatives made similar choices which "gave testimony for thousands and tens of thousands as no other work can do."[16]

William Still witnessed the upward mobility of a segment of the black community from the downcast Lombard Street into more affluent neighborhoods such as North West Philadelphia. it occurred to him that he might be able to facilitate their social and economic unmet needs by programs opened Mr. Still's eyes to the unmet social and economic needs in this new location. William Still, a member of the Central Presbyterian Church in Philadelphia thought that West Philadelphia with only a Methodist Mission might benefit from a Presbyterian Mission He took his idea to the Elders of his church.[17] A committee, headed by Dr. John Reeve, and assisted by Elders Still and Robert Jones, was formed to organize a Presbyterian Mission. The committee met in rooms at Milton Hall, at 1914 Fairmount Street in North Philadelphia on 6 January 1878.

The committee discussed the matters concerned with the establishment of a Mission Sabbath School to be named the Gloucester Presbyterian Mission after the Gloucester Presbyterian Church, William Still's church. The above mentioned Executive Committee agreed to serve as officers and teachers at the Mission's Executive Committee.[18] William Still who continued his duties as an Elder at the Gloucester Presbyterian Church also served as the Superintendant of the Mission's Sabbath School.[19]

Inevitably, problems arose associated with fund raising and the involvement of prominent men required to underwrite the project that had its fair quota of unanticipated difficulties from its very inception. William Still and his fellow workers on the project persevered until the Berean Presbyterian Church was established on 19th and South College Avenue in North Philadelphia. The committee solicited and received funds for the founding of the Berean Vocational Training School which adjoined the church for the purpose of proving the motivation and training needed by black youth in search of the skills needed for meaningful work.

A problem facing new arrivals to West Philadelphia was housing. Blacks with small income found it difficult to afford the rent required by landlords who owned the nicer apartments in the North side. Because black workers lacked the income to rent nice apartments in the better sections, they were forced to live in substandard rental units in the slums.[20] William Still became aware of the problem which he felt could be alleviated by the founding of a credit union where black laborers could save each week to save for a down payment on a home which they could affords to buy.

William Still investigated the steps needed for him and others to form a building and Loan Association for black workers interested in home ownership.[21] Mr. John Magill, who had previously shown an interest in the improvement and general welfare of the colored people, contributed funds to establish a business plan which required several years to implement Eventually, the Berean Savings and Loan Association was fully incorporated in 1888. William Still became its first elected President.[22] Black workers applauded the opportunity to save money to eventually own a nice home in North Philadelphia. The following statement by Mr. John H. Glower, one of the Building and Loan founders, in 1910, had this to say about the success of the project initiated by William Still:

"There have been purchased through the Association since its organization, in 1888 Two hundred and fifty homes for its stockholders, at an average valuation of $1,800, making the entire valuation of the homes owned now by the stockholders, to be $450,000. ... These two hundred and fifty homes are now for the most part excellently located on good streets, and it is quite possible that not one of them would have been purchased by these families had it not been for the assistance they received from the association."[23]

Blacks continued to do business with The Berean Loan Association in North Philadelphia into the 1930s. Alberta S. Norwood, about this same time, was a student at the University of Pennsylvania who was working towards a MA based on the life and times of William Still. She consulted Frances Ellen Still, the sole surviving child of William and Letitia Still, about her father's illustrious career, to be entitled "Negro Welfare Work in Philadelphia Especially as illustrated by the career of William Still 1775-1930.'[24]

A 23 February 2005 article by the University of Arizona's English Department's Professor Joe Lockhard, "William Still and Philadelphia's African American Underground," was read at the English Department of Temple University in Philadelphia. Professor Lockhard reported that as William still matured, he enlarged his already significant social reform agenda into a series of important contributions to the freedmen in North Philadelphia as the 19th century waned. One of his citations was from a book written by one of William Still's family members.[25]

William Still's contributions included the founding of the first black YMCA in Philadelphia. This met the need for young black men to have a safe place to meet and congregate for the enjoyment of extracurricular activities and social clubs which prohibited membership to black youth. The desperately needed funds for the Y were provided to William still by white men who were in a position to donate funds to establish this black focused social club. The Rev. Henry Phillips was elected to be responsible for meetings held at Association Hall at 15th and Chestnut Streets for YWCA business. Around 1880, a securely implemented black YMCA was founded in a building it owned.[26]

Before this became a fact, the "Y" faced the usual difficulties inherent in black organizations due to transient leadership and diminishing funds. Although well trained Negroes took the helm of the organization with some success, they were forced to relinquish control of its leadership when called away for personal and professional reasons. Rudderless betimes, Rev. Phillips was forced because of his heavy work load at his church to relinquish his leadership role at the YMCA. Candidate after candidate officiated until it became obvious that stable leadership was needed if the organization was to survive. The lack of funding by the businessmen who had been more than generous along these lines, William Still used his social power to interest white philanthropists into process of reinvigorating the black YMCA into a more secure position. A site at 1724 Christian street was donated to provide a place for the most destitute black youth to congregate in a secure social environment where they were free to develop their mental, moral, and physical skills. [27]

Chapter 28. Church and Community: The Berean Experience.

Arnold Toynbee, in *A Study of History,* compared the "plantation-slaves of Roman Italy [who were largely drawn from an ancient and deeply cultivated Oriental population] whose children might be expected to cling to their cultural heritage, whereas the African Negro slaves ancestral religion was no more fit than any other element in their culture to hold its own against the overwhelming superiority of their white masters." Moreover the oriental slaves in Roman history "had nowhere else to look, outside their own native religious heritage, for religious consolation, since their Roman masters were living in a spiritual vacuum. Armed with their own cultural religious strengths, these slaves were more able to survive the onslaught of Roman dominance while in the Western case " the spiritual treasure as well as the worldly wealth and power, has lain in the hands of the slave-driving minority."[1]

The slave-driver had problems with reaching the heart of the slave. Yet Christians were able to transfer their religion to the American Negro many of whom willingly converted to Christianity before, during and after the Civil War. Many black slaves were able to accept a religious conversion from men such as John G. Fee, whose Kentucky antislavery enclave was a success despite the late incursion of "plantation gang overseers whip in hand who destroyed the community of black, later known as "he persecuted Bereans, put to flight from the State of Kentucky and sent in flight for religious safety in the free State of Ohio.[2]

William Still knew well the story of the invasion into John G. Fee's settlement in Kentucky where blacks were living a self sufficient and Christian life under his guidance. The innocent Christians when forced by the mob of proslavery agitators had to abandon the farmlands they had so carefully worked as an antislavery community in Kentucky. John G. Fee, the white antislavery white leader of the community publicized the details of the Christian community of African farmers which became known as the suffering Bereans in their new Ohio community.

The Rev. Matthew Anderson, D.D. presided as the Pastor of the Berean Presbyterian Church on 1926 North College Avenue in Northwestern Pennsylvania. A thorough search of potential African American ministers resulted in the procurement of Rev. Anderson (1848-1928). He proved to be not only brilliant at his clerical chores but also an energetic young Pastor who left his former parish at the Lombard Street Gloucester Mission.

Caroline Still Wiley, M.D. married the Rev. Matthew Anderson 0n 17 August 1880. This talented couple pooled their talents, training, and dedication to the church to produce together a religious and social uplift service so fruitful and unique over time that it became known as a "Church and Community: The Berean Experience."[3] William Still in his later days was pleased to see the emergence of productive labor on behalf of the less fortunate members of their race eagerly embraced. He was especially proud of the contributions being made in the black community by his daughter, Caroline Still Anderson, M.D., who embraced church service in conjunction with her professional skills.

Dr. Anderson had cared for women and children in the worst areas in the black community even while a medical student. She established a Dispensary adjoining her husband's church while she served as the City District Physician in Philadelphia. Unwilling to let go to naught her literary skills she had learned as an Oberlin College student, Dr. Anderson volunteered to teach grammar to illiterate young blacks in the Berean Manual Training and Industrial School. When she was given the responsibility of serving as the Head of the English Department, she also assumed the responsibility soon afterwards as the Assistant Principal. Her foray into social service resulted in the formation of the first black YWCA in Philadelphia for the social and extracurricular advancement of young colored girls and women to enjoy. [4]

Barraged with racial and sexist prejudice, Dr. Anderson persevered in her duties while raising a family. Yet she managed while being a wife and mother to serve as the Treasure of the Women's Medical Society in Philadelphia, and the a member of the Board of the Home for Aged and Infirm Colored People of Philadelphia.[5] Dr. Caroline Anderson had the highest respect for her multitalented father, William Still. He was known throughout the black community in Philadelphia for his underground railroad contributions and especially for his book, *The Underground Rail Road*[6] As a member of one of Philadelphia's Representative families, she became one of the city's pioneer black women doctors.[7]

Rev. Anderson, a respected Presbyterian Pastor at the Berean Presbyterian Church, ably led the church from its twenty-six member congregation in November 1884 to its one-hundred and one member church in 1893 that included a Sabbath School of one-hundred eighty eight young people. The Centennial Anniversary of the Berean Church held at its new location at Broad and Diamond Streets reported a membership of six-hundred and thirty-two.[8]

The establishment of the Berean Church and The Berean Training School was financed by white benefactors in Philadelphia. After the Government had met its obligations to the banking community which had received the species payment, or payment in gold or silver not in paper money, to settle debts incurred in the Civil War, it provided funds to train black youth for more than menial employment. These courses were given to inspire and motivate young people to improve their lot. William Still used his considerable influence with prominent businessmen to facilitate the more difficult early phases of education that sometimes sidetracked students until large sums of federal money were appropriated to fund this growing program. This basic educational plan required assiduous toil to get moving a curriculum especially designed to implement the problem of preparing blacks for good jobs. In the 1890s, The Berean Manual Training and Industrial School, was prepared "to meet the educational and vocational needs of the young colored men and women" of Philadelphia.[9]

The Berean Manual Training and Industrial School described briefly its program in a 1916 pamphlet: "The training, of the head, heart of young men and women for the practical requirements of everyday life." Competitive courses were made available to those young blacks interested in following the rules outlined in the Berean Institute whose classes were open to those students seeking preparation for employment in specialized business and technological areas of expertise. For instance, wood working and hair dressing were morphed into upgraded skills such as furniture making and beauty culture. The expansion of industrial offices required the skills of book keepers, secretaries, and typists trained in stenography, court reporting, and in business practices.[10]

Dr. Anderson served as the President of the Berean W.C.T.U- the Women's Christian Temperance Union in Philadelphia.[11] Her long list of accomplishments appear in *Co-Laborers in the Work of the Lord: Nineteenth century Black Women Physicians, 1835-1920,* in the section, *"Send Us a Lady Physician" Women Doctors in America,"* (New York: W.W. Norton, 1985).[12]

In February 1985,The Samuel Paley Endowment Fund at Temple University, displayed a collection of letters, memorabilia, and artefacts designed to present to the public the Helen Anderson (Still) Waller Papers, which included letters, etc., commemorating the Still family of Burlington County, New Jersey, and Philadelphia. Case I-II, titled Still Family, displayed a letter from William Still to his daughter, Caroline, in her youth. His sage, fatherly advice reminded her to:"open your mind and strengthen your purposes."[13]

Included in the Case marked Still Family is a remark by William's brother, James, about the newer generation of freedmen in and around the Philadelphia area which had become the home of many blacks fresh up from the South in search of better opportunities. He voiced a concern that his people whom he believed to be innately talented, had, in his view, an obligation to offer to their less endowed brethren a helping hand whenever they saw the need.[1] Case III, titled the Anderson Still Family, contained a collection of memorabilia. A portion of an unsigned letter dated 12 March 1874, sent to Caroline Still with poignantly described events describing a "spectacular crowd assembled in Washington D.C. at the burial of Massachusetts Senator Charles Sumner, an eminent antislavery laborer: ...A crowd of person both white and colored were assembled in the street about his house anxiously awaiting news from the house." [15]

Rev. Matthew and Dr. Anderson made certain that their sons had the opportunity to get a good education. Their two sons, William D., and Daniel B., Anderson attended both the College and the Seminary at Lincoln University. Daniel was a student in the class of 1891 at the College, and in 1894,at the Seminary which prepared him for the Presbyterian ministry at Plainfield, New Jersey in 1918. William D. attended the College in 1876, and ex class of 1885 Seminary. He became a teacher at Augusta, Georgia in 1918.[16]

Their daughters, Helen Vera (1882-1953), Maude (188?-1916), attended Cushing Academy in Ashburnham, Massachusetts, a private, mixed gender , elite boarding school that enrolled black and white students.[17] Cushing Academy reported that a fire in the Alumnae Department had unfortunately destroyed some of their records in the 1890s.The family mourned the loss of Maude who died of appendicitis in Philadelphia in 1916.[18] Little data about sister Margaret was readily available from the research.

Cushing Academy prepared Helen Vera, the eldest Anderson daughter, a General Studies student, for enrollment at the Conservatory at Oberlin College in 1906. Instead of a career in music, she married John Edward Waller after she had earned her degree in Domestic Science at Temple University in 1913. They traveled to the Panama Canal Zone, when her husband agreed to manage the Cristobel Silver House, a country club of sorts for U.S. Government employees in the Canal Zone. Mrs. Waller kept busy with many interests while her husband was employed at the Panama

Canal Zone. She lead a group of young West Indian women in the West Indian Girls' Reserve and taught at the Sabbath School at the Presbyterian Church The budding character of Helen Anderson is evident by an entry into her diary in 1904 when she was twenty-two: "I am going to try…To keep before me the beautiful words of 'Onward and Upward.' To strive to live a noble life'…."[19] When John Waller retired after his thirty year commission in the Canal Zone, he and his wife returned to Philadelphia to live in William Still's family home in Philadelphia. They entertained a distant relative in their 12th Street wood frame home in 1953 with the genteel kindness and family solidarity that was the hallmark of the Still family.[20]

The reader deserves history of some of the old Still heads, if only in a desultory manner. Oral history is notoriously unreliable here as in other oral family histories, therefore, is a partial list of those Stills closest to Levin and Charity still for wont of sufficient space to include recent additions. Beginning with the progenitors of the Still family are listed Levin Steel (17?-1842), and his wife, Sidney Steel (?-1857), who changed their names to Levin and Charity Still in Burlington County, New Jersey, ca. 1805. [21]

Their Maryland-born children were Ann (1798-?),who either died or was sold away; Levin (1799-1836?), sold to a Kentucky brickyard owner before being bequeathed to a kinsman in Alabama where he died from excessive floggings, Peter (1801-1868), who bought his freedom in 1850 in Alabama, lived, worked , and is buried in Burlington, New Jersey, his son, Peter Still is probably buried in a grave in the Odd Fellows Burial Ground, also in Burlington, New Jersey, Mahalah (1803-?); Kitturah, or Kitty(1805-?), fugitives from Maryland who later settled in Indian Mills, New Jersey. Samuel, the first freeborn Still (1807-1875), is buried in the Jacob's Chapel Cemetery in Mount Laurel, New Jersey, Mary (1808-?), Hannah (1810-?), James (1812-1882), James is interred with his wife, Henrietta, his infant granddaughter, Henrietta Lucy (b. 1897-d. 1897), and James' daughter, Angelina, (1844-1896) Isaac (1814-?), John Nelson (1815-?), Charles (1817-?), Joseph (1819-1841), were also born to Levin and Charity still in Shamong, New Jersey, and are probably buried at the old homestead along with Levin and

Charity Still, their parents.William (1821-1902), is interred in his final burial site in the Eden Cemetery with his wife, Letitia (1825-1906), and daughter, Frances Ellen (1857-1943), in Upper Darby, Pennsylvania.[22]

The daughter of James and Angelina Still, Beulah (1838-1839), is buried in her father, James Still's grave site in the Jacob's Chapel Cemetery .with her father's second wife, Henrietta Thomas (1814-1888). James Still's seven children were as follows: Beulah (1838-1839); James Thomas (1840-1895), interred near Boston, Massachusetts, Eliza Ann (b.?-d.?), Angelina (1844-1896), William (1858-?), Joseph C.(b.?-1930), Emmaretta (1859-1929), and Lucretia (1854-1930).[23]

Emmaretta Still married Jacob Smith (1849-1931), the writer's maternal grandparents. Their older daughter, Mabel Smith Khan (1898-1960), her mother, is interred in Boston, Massachusetts near her sister, Bertha Smith (1900-1978?).Their brother, James (1901-1983), is entombed next his parent's gravesite in the old Colemantown Negro Cemetery, now called the Jacob's Chapel burial grounds at the A.M.E. Church in Mt. Laurel, New Jersey. Jacob Smith came from the Roanoke, Virginia clan of "Free Colored People" sometimes called the Melungeons,[24]

Jacob Smith, a mixed-blood Scots-Irish, Indian, and Angolan non-slave Negro had a family of children before his marriage to Emmaretta Still. They were Joseph, Will, and Alvin, and a sister, Lydie, who also lived in West Philadelphia. They had another brother, Joseph, who lived in Mount Holly, New Jersey. These were the children born to Jacob Smith by a previous marriage Emmaretta Still Smith's oldest daughter, Mabel Smith Khan, married the writer's father, Fazil Ameir Khan, an Orthodox Mohammedan from India's old North-West Frontier Province, now Pakistan. Bertha Smith, the writer's aunt farmed land in Medford, New Jersey, following the death of her parents, Emmaretta and Jacob Smith in the late 1920s and early 1930s.[25]

Cousin George Moses (b.?-1959, and his wife, Cousin Rose (b.?-1974) lived in West Philadelphia. Cousin George was one of three children born to Eliza Ann, and her husband, John Moses (?-?), together had three children-Beulah (?-?), Cummings (?-1970), and

George. The childless George and Rose Moses were fond of their niece, Eunice, the daughter of Cummings Moses were childless, but helped raise brother Cummings Moses' daughter, Eunice (1950?-1970?), whose mother was Annie Tomlinson (?-?), a mulatto. woman from the Medford, New Jersey area. Beulah Offit, George's sister (?-?), had two children, Althea (b.?-d. 1985), and Bob (b.?-d.?), who were last heard of living in the Trenton, New Jersey area.[26]

Frank W.H. Convery, a journalist at the *Mt. Holly New* Jersey *Herald,* wrote an article on Thursday, 11 January 1962 in which he gathered "from sawyers, farmers, gas station attendants, and dairy men from Colemanton where "Doc" Still was buried, from Moorestown, Buddtown, Lumberton, as far as Indian Mills and Mount Laurel Township where he had practiced medicine," information for a three part article he intended to write on the life of Dr. James Still. The following excerpt is taken from the second of these articles:[27]

"Doctor Still had spent a good part of his life practicing medicine in Medford, New Jersey, a town in Burlington, New Jersey. He left three sons and four daughters- James, Joseph, and William. Angelina, Eliza Ann, Emmaretta, and Lucretia." When his will was read shortly after his death, his wife, Henrietta, was to receive "$19,921, the bulk of the estate. His two sons, James, and William, who were chosen to execute his estate, made sure that their mother also received $300 a year for the rest of her life. Provisions were made for his sons to $1.75 for the rest of his life "Dr." Still James bequeathed to his younger brother, Charles Wesley Still, for as long as he remained single, the sum of $1.75 a week for the rest of his life"

Mention was made in Mr. Covery's article about Dr. James Thomas Still,M.D., James Still's Harvard educated son, who was born on 12 July 1840 in Medford, New Jersey, and who lived at the time of his father's death at 166 Cambridge Street, Boston, Massachusetts, where he had a large medical practical practice. Dr. Still's second oldest son, Joseph C. Still, who also had developed a skill at herbal medicine much the same as his father had, bought a house shortly after his father's death on a large plot of land in

Mt. Holly where he began a medical "practice" soon to rival his father's.

Margery Cridland's Historical Sketch [28] in *Early Recollections and Life of Dr. James Still*, a Facsimile Edition, (Medford, New Jersey: Medford Historical Society (1971), contains several interesting family related excerpts. She outlined the trials endured by young James Still in his fruitless quest to gain a "regular" medical education. The location of the office next the home of "Dr." James Still, "remains on Church Road just East of the Mt. Holly Road (Route 541); a historical marker denotes the site of the residence, which his daughter, Lucretia inhabited until it was demolished in 1930.[29] Also in this Historical Sketch is a biographical sketch of Dr. "B" whom James Still mentioned in his memoir, (see pp. 91-94, 111, 143, 177.) in which he referred to the University of Pennsylvania trained physician whose medical practice in Vincenttown, Burlington County, often conflicted with that practiced by James Still.[30]

Stephen O'Keefe's feature article, Doctor of the Pines Philosophy Could Heal Today's Racial Ills appeared in the Camden-Courier Post, (20 May 1971), with quotes from James Still's text (p.228)," It has long been my opinion that the colored people as a race have much to blame in themselves for their present condition."[31] Lester King, M.D., JAMA (April 1972), had this praise for James Still's memoir: "For the Social Historian the book presents vividly the Picture of Poverty in Rural New Jersey."[32]

Chapter 29. Social Reforms of James T.Still, M.D. In Education, Health Care, and Economics.

Dr. Still's interest in the education of black churches took him to the black churches where they congregated with their family Sundays. He spoke not only as an interested individual with the credentials of a School Committee Member who had the authority to awaken the black youth to greater aspirations. with respect to their future lives. As an educated man, he realized the value of a professional degree which he had enjoyed due to his father's hard work and frugality. He came of age at the end of the abolitionist movement when white men of means supervised the future of the freed slaves. He also came from the younger generation of freedmen in the last decades of the 19th century who no longer relied upon upper echelon whites in various antislavery societies whose organizational abilities resulted in the emancipation of the African slaves in America.

Dr. Still became a father figure for young black males whose own fathers lacked the energy to overcome the present racial proscription forced upon the African race. Dr. Still was acquainted with the social structure of the black community before Emancipation came. His activist speeches were designed to shake from apathy the black youth who lacked the means and motivation to push for higher education, especially if they possessed the determination to matriculate in the white, prestigious colleges where they would be able to compete financially on a higher level of life for the good of their future family lifestyles.

Dr. Still's awareness of the segregated pattern of racial division that deprived the minds, hearts, and souls of black men while not ignored, was addressed in a pamphlet he wrote that dealt with the condition that plagued black males more than it hindered the advancement of black females. The following publication was entitled thusly:

"Don't Tell White Folks,"
Or
Light Out of darkness.

Uncle Sam's reverie!

Also published under this title,

What Shall Be Done

With the

Pickininnies?

A Humorous Lecture,

By

James T. Still, M.D.[1]

This Dedication was written by Dr. James T. Still:

"To the numerous Lovers of truth And of Humanity-Many Who Have Lived and Acted, and Many Who Still Live and Act For The Good Of Mankind-And To The Many

Earnest Aspirants And Workers For Truly Manly Positions Among Men In Their Native land, Yet Are Sidetracked and Crushed Universally. Is This Picture of serious Truth Dedicated, By A Lover Of Truth."[2]
The Author.

His Preface reads as follows:

"It is to assist in giving light to many who are striving to solve, what some have chosen to call a problem, that I submit these facts for the people. To the people, about this particular people. I seek to injure no one. I desire to strengthen the weak, at the expense of a picture of some erring. In doing this I am aware of my doom. The world's history has taught me to know the penalty awaiting new exponents of the truth, who are lovers of their neighbors.

Those who chose to read this simple statement of mine, need not, I prefer them not to believe my words, until they have investigated and learned the facts: until they find out the whole truth.

Be as fair as I have been fair, and we will agree in a common fairness."

James T. Still.
82 West Cedar Street, Boston, Mass.
December 1882.[3]

Dr. Still realized the seriousness of his address though he coached his words in humor. His solution on behalf of the poor African when thrown overboard through the "middle passage, and "his cries still reechoing uttered while in servile bondage so many long years under the lash and beneath oppressive toil, and the boastful attitude of his , *not yet* to forget his low estate, and the man to remember who was the originator of the Negro among us."[4]

He recognized that this nation was established under the principle of the brotherhood of man whose democratic government, and the United states Constitution, which were also founded upon a belief in God, the ruler of mankind and in the natural and inalienable rights of man, [which resulted here in the establishment of] a government, under God, by the people, of the people, for the people...."[5]

He had nothing but praise for the founding fathers for their wonderful plan which, sadly, met with a number of unanticipated national problems and unlimited criticisms, which Dr. Still thought "no more serious questions than some concerning the American Negro." He alluded to the impartial and well informed observers o his time began with this question, "Now, who are the people of these United States? To-day, under God, are they only the people of our country who came here for liberty and freedom, and blotted out the Indians, save a handful, and forced the negro here for their personal gain?" [6]

Dr. Still argued that the negro, who might have been a natural tiller of the soil, had bled and sweated, unrequited for so many years, deserved merits today. sweated, unrequited, so many years, though he has always proved his loyalty, ought to be given the merits he had earned these days. None will deny his perilous condition through years of bondage! And few are so low- minded as to deny the emancipation to have been a blessing to this country. There are multitudes of colored people, called leaders, who boast of "Our wonderful improvement since freedom came."

Referring to the progress made by his race in the last twenty-five years, Dr. Still wrote,"...the achievements and accomplishments, claimed by himself and many friends, have been over-stated. Yet, if the truth be told, he thought these advances which friends and sympathizers provided to blacks in that time frame, now view the negro as less fit for the advances they had earlier thought best for him. "Are these fears entertained from proper investigation into the true merits of this newly enfranchised race?" asked Dr. Still, referring to these specifics:

"Most blacks exaggerated their wealth," wrote Dr. Still. He provided some observations about his race that were telling. Yet he faced their unmet needs and came to certain conclusion about their real interests, their "standards of manliness, fitness and probity, disposition and ability for acquisitiveness, in true education, the faculty for acquiring specific knowledge and practical accomplishments, that demonstrate a brain in man, in the Negro" have, in my view, been, "for very obvious reasons, hidden, ill-appreciated and excluded, by members of his own race, and by, probably, most white people."[7]

Continuing, Dr. Still described his view of the near anarchy that prevailed upon the businesses undertaken when the "negro came into freedom. Corruption was rampant when the black man was forced to act as, not a man, nor a citizen, "but a thing." He referred , of course, to the period of freedom for the slaves that followed the Civil War when black men had only a few opportunities to use the education they got at the black colleges, and universities set up for them to advance their cause. No wonder then, they became muscular "haw-bucks, lean and slender dudes and sports."

Still called black education "taught by attenuated, superannuated, and feeble minded teachers, in these arenas where they are huddled together like so many bovines and pigmies with minds naturally clouded and stupid, where they have no eminence to ascend, no superiors to emulate or to learn from-nothing but the same noxious pabulum to subsist upon-the same atmosphere of ignorance to be inhaled over and over again, for a short two weeks, when they are turned out upon the race as colored Christianity to colored people only."[8]

He praised the reorganized curriculum at the Boston School Committee which allowed a student to work at the top of his bent regardless of his race, creed, or color. He realized that the mass of black youth lived nowhere near the New England area where such fine public schools existed to provide the basics of education upon which they would be able to enter good first rate colleges. This left the mass of aspiring youth deficient in a good grammar school education sorely needed to qualify for entrance into Yale, Harvard, etc. Still's colorful description of black leaders who revealed an envy, contempt, and jealousy of these top flight white institutions of higher learning went like this: "...These lords of the golden-slipper religion, [and has caused them] to repudiate, to ignore, to condemn, every young man among us who fits himself outside their domination."[9]

He minced no words when he concluded:" The masses of colored people do not desire this state of things. They as a whole are a liberty-loving people, but lack proper *leading men and public teachers.*" [10]

Humor softened his message at this point in his speech when he berated the black preachers: "In short, while not all of my people agree with me that the days of the Rev. B.A. Doing-good, D.D. A.P.E., Professor of Infallible, Hallelujah, true-colored-saving-religion, with his compeer, the Hon. Ego-Venerator-Self-Lauder Seize-'r Opportunity-For-Self-Prominence, are numbers?"[11]

Dr. Still was born free, and had no real acquaintance with slavery except at the second hand. He excused the behavior of former slaves who had been conditioned to the horrors of slavery, although he focused more on their Post Civil war era problems, the residue of their previous, and intimate association with slavery. If they could rise above the sub-standard education offered the freedmen in the segregated black colleges, vocational schools, and universities built to train them for menial work, they would be able to provide the kind of decent living they could only imagine for their place outside the ghetto where their color had forced their families to reside. The trades open to Negroes in the North included the barber's profession, and the janitor and the messenger's callings. Dr. Still 's query begged for an answer "if it was not more feasible for the 'wise, 'race-loving negro to form race-respecting leagues' to protect the pickininnies from these blizzards of race-destruction, which are more deadly than the combined evils of southern tyrants?"

He pleaded with whites and blacks alike to "Reform for the good of the people."[12]

Dr. James Still was consulted for his opinion on the role of black journalists by Mr. I. Garland Penn, the editor of the *Afro-American Press.* Dr. James Still admitted that he had scant knowledge about this new field, but offered his view that carefully selected Negroes able to rise above the reputation of some of his race who had succumbed to the fascinating, contagious fever of imitation, rivalry, and emulation, could conceivably use their integrity to help their people. He summed up his opinion by saying that well trained black journalists could bring to the reader the volumes of these compositions which he believes could contribute to a better understanding between the races.[13]

He mentioned the envy, jealousy, and strife reflected by many of the pioneer journalists, but allowed that some progress had been made to correct this failing. He found journalism to be an exciting area for gifted black journalists who might bring to the negro press a good name provided they adhered strictly to good business practices. His graduation from the Harvard Medical School placed him in a hard won, prestigious position in the black community. He wanted for black newspaper and magazine writers a similar pride in their training and professional skills. In order to gain the respect they deserved, he focused on these virtues, "originality, accuracy, truthfulness, promptness,[and] manly independence."[14]

Dr. James T. Still, M.D. (Harv.), 1871 died on 22 June 1895 of meningitis and otitis media when fifty-four and eleven months. At the time of his death, he and his wife, Elizabeth, and their children lived at 27 North Anderson Street.[15] Dr. Still was buried in one of the family burial plots purchased in 1881 at the Cedar Grove Cemetery in the Dorchester section of Boston, Massachusetts. He was buried in grave site no. Twelve, in Range H. in the Oak Hill Section near the interred children named John, Hannah, and Benjamin.[16]

Mrs. Still who had moved to 15 Mount Vernon Street on Beacon Hill filed a petition for the guardianship of her two minor children. At that time, James Harrison Still and Eliza Still had reached their majority.[17] The 11 March 1897 petition also asked the Suffolk County Probate Court for permission to administer her husband's estate, and to be named as the Guardian of Israel Thomas Still, William Wendell Phillips Still, Mary Elizabeth Still, and Charity Still.[17]

The court allowed her to emancipate Israel, born, in 1878, to live with his childless uncle, Joseph C. Still, who ran a successful medical practice in Mount Holly, New Jersey. Israel Still's adoption was approved by the Suffolk Superior Court.[18]

Mrs. Still was allotted for the care of her minor children, a yearly sum of $86 and twenty-five cents. Since the inventory of her husband's estate amounted to little cash outside of household items and furniture, his widow was forced to subsist on very little income.[19] The Administrator's Affidavit she filed on 13 April 1897 stated that she had put an ad in the *Boston Traveler* to begin on 27 March 1897. Her husband left little in the way of earthly wealth, but much in social reforms he initiated on behalf of his less fortunate race. Further, his devoted wife, Elizabeth cared for their minor children, Charity, Mary E., and Wendell Phillips.[20]

Chapter 30.
Will We Ever Be Free?

The Specie Payment Resumption Act (on 14 January 1875, ch.15, 18 Stat.296) that provided for the redemption of United States paper currency, commonly known as greenbacks, into gold, beginning in 1879, diverted the government from focusing on the implementation of the Civil Rights Act of 1866. The Eastern financial community used money allotted to the Act, instead, to allow the Treasury Secretary to manipulate the nation's money supply This tactic served as a divisive economic issue to detract people from the approaching presidential election of 1876.[1]

Mrs. Elizabeth Cady Stanton, the Women's Rights activist, voiced her opinion on species payments and the redemption of the U.S. paper money by the banks, she referred to as "the vices of men in politics." She spoke out at the Woman's Suffrage Convention held in Washington, D.C. in 1868, on "the positive influence women could have on Society" when free from the annoying interference of men on their rights.[2]

Ian Haney Lopez, wrote in his book in his book, ***White By Law The Legal Construction of Race,***(New York: New York University Press , 2006), under the chapter on Birthright Citizenship, "The U.S. Constitution as ratified did not define the citizenry, probably because it was assumed that the English common law rule of *jus soli* would continue."[3] Under *jus soli*, citizenship accrues to all "born" within a nation's jurisdiction. Because this nation did not "Fully encompass racial minorities" in its first hundred years or more, the word "all" is qualified. "The importance of the Dred Scott decision" is based on this precedent.[4]

William Still decried this decision of the Supreme Court because he understood the meaning of the phrase to be "the black man has no rights the white man is bound to respect." Judge Taney, the Chief Justice of the Supreme Court in 1857 when this momentous decision about the freedom of a black slave named Scott who had sued for his freedom in the federal courts, was that Scott and all blacks, free or enslaved, "were not and never could be citizens because they were a subordinate and inferior class of beings." This decision that sided with the slave holding South also infuriated many in the North. It tore apart the already splintered nation, and some even blamed it for the hastening of the Civil War.

After the War ended, the Civil Rights Act of 1866 invalidated the Dred Scott decision. It stated that "all citizens born ...in the United States, and not subject to any foreign power, excluding Indians not taxed, are declared to be citizens of the United States."[5] Mr. Lopez continues" "*jus soli* subsequently became part of the organized law of the land in the form of the Fourteenth Amendment "All persons born or naturalized in the United States in the United States, and subject to the jurisdiction thereof, are citizens of the United States and of the state wherein they reside."[6]

Questions arose, despite the careful wording used in the 14th Amendment to the U.S. Constitution,-"though in keeping with the words of the 1866 Act-some racial minorities remained outside the bounds of *jus soli* even after its constitutional enactment." Areas still in question concerned the children born to noncitizen parents in the United States as well as the status of Native Americans.[7] In 1898, the Supreme Court decided that in the former case, that native born children of aliens were considered birthright citizens of the United States though "barred by race from acquiring citizenship." Citizenship rights for Native Americans answered in the negative in 1884 because it was stated that Indians owed allegiance to their tribe, and therefore, "did acquire citizenship upon birth".[8]

About this time, a number of books were published by white abolitionists anxious to memorialize their considerable contributions to the antislavery movement. The passage of time following the Civil war placed the emancipation of the slaves in a far different historical perspective than the period in the nation's history when the underground railroad hummed. Yet the reminiscences published by aged abolitionists garbled their activities with fading memories that shrouded the true story of their exploits.

William Still reportedly said that he never expected his early fugitive slave histories to be published during his lifetime. The records he kept of his activities when elected the Chairman of the Acting sub-committee of the Philadelphia Vigilance Committee beginning in 1852, were part and parcel of his obligations. He entered into the pages of his documented fugitive slave history, *The Underground Rail Road*, all of the material he had compiled from the inception of his term of service at the Pennsylvania Antislavery Society in 1847.

The Underground Rail Road first published in 1872, was reprinted in 1878. The third printing in 1883 contained A Biographical Sketch of William Still: His Life Work to This Time, by James P. Boyd.[9]

Slavery in America existed before the ratification of the 1789 U.S. Constitution in Philadelphia, Pennsylvania. Slaves learned via a grapevine that the Quakers, of members of the Religious Society of Friends, sheltered fugitives from slavery when they arrived within the borders of the State of Pennsylvania, when they were pursued by slave owners or their agents. Who were sent there to take them back to the South. Actually, there existed no highly organized underground railroad for about the 75 years before emancipation came, though slaves were helped to run away from slavery by individuals with kind hearts. Some of these whites, and at times, blacks, daily risked life, limb, and civic respect for what they considered personal moral integrity."[10]

The Fugitive Slave law of 1850 was passed to punish those who were prosecuted for their part in this clandestine, illegal activity. Between 1850 and the Emancipation Proclamation on 22 September 1862, thousands of volunteers transported as many as75000 slaves over the U.S. border into Canada, but not without the dire consequences, that sometimes followed. Thousands of vigilantes either ran off slaves or contributed funds to finance the work. The U.S. marines were sent to Berk's County, in south eastern Pennsylvania along the Schuylkill River, to restore order. One of their citizens was apprehended and jailed for treason. A hundred years later on 2 December 1859, John Brown, a white abolitionist, was found guilty of a similar charge and hanged.

Wilbur H. Siebert, an Associate professor of History at Ohio State University, at Columbus, Ohio, researched the entire underground railroad in the U.S. East of the Mississippi in *The Underground Railroad* (1889).[11] He defined the Underground Railroad in a 1923 article, entitled "The Underground Railroad in Michigan, Detroit Historical Monthly 1:10 (March 1923)" as " a vast network of secret routes over which fugitive slaves were passed along chiefly in the nighttime, from Southern States to Canada during a prolonged period before the Civil War."[12]

Professor W.H. Siebert addressed a letter to Frederick Douglass, who ran a depot at Rochester, New York State; and he sent another letter to William Still, the station-master at the hub of the south eastern Pennsylvania Underground Railroad, Station 2. Professor Siebert queried these men about the logistics they used in the slave delivery system that ran from their depots to Canada west before the Civil War.

Mr. Douglass' reply to Professor Siebert's letter from Columbus, Ohio, dated 27 March 1893, began with his own slave escape from the South in 1838. He mentioned the various stops in New Bedford and Lynn, Massachusetts, through which he had traveled before he settled in Rochester, New York. This was his summary of his work: His underground railroad depot sheltered "as many as eleven fugitives under my roof at one time." While he verified that William Still's place in Philadelphia as the hub of the underground railroad where slaves were dispatched North and into Canada, he stated that these "passengers" from Philadelphia took "trains" through the extensive New York network of depots of Albany, Syracuse, Rochester, and eventually those settlements in Canada."

Capable black conductors received and sheltered fugitives sent by William Still into their New York depots. They were David Ruggles, Mr. Gibbs, and Stephen Myers at Albany, then to J.W. Loguen at Syracuse, then to Frederick Douglass at Rochester, and finally to Hiram Wilson, at St. Catharines in Canada West. Before he ended, his letter, Mr. Douglass mentioned "a book called *The Underground Railroad*," written by Mr. Still" which for reasons best known to Mr. Still did not include his biographical sketch with the other conductors in the back of his book. Douglass wrote that "because I, in my power, permitted a criticism of his conduct in taking from the fugitives who passed through his hands, what was thought wrong. I see that he has omitted my name in his book, as one of the Conductors on the Underground Railroad."[13]

Notice that Mr. Douglass did not specify the exact comment he attributed to William Still, who had long since become accustomed to slurs and slights from a few disgruntled members of his race. William Still had a gift for getting along with his peers, black and white. Therefore, he made allowances for a few differences of opinion h that circulated from time to time from the mouths of resentful black people he had met in the line of duty.

Dr. Siebert also mailed letters to a series of agents connected with the Underground Railroad. A well respected historical scholar, Professor Siebert simply wanted the facts about the romantic underground railroad for posterity. William Still's 18 November 1893 letter to Professor Wilbur Siebert was later incorporated into "The Underground Railroad in Pennsylvania," Vol. 3, now in the Ohio Historical Society, at Columbus, Ohio. He stated in it that the Pennsylvania Underground Railroad was responsible for the only recorded data because it was here that he kept the only records of the "U.G.R.R," the code Mr. Still used to refer to in letters he wrote to agents about this secret operation. He also wrote," many names and places on the way, never were secured, as there seemed to be no good reason for such exactness; while I preserved so much as I did, I never dreamed that my records could ever be published in my day."[14]

Professor Siebert culled data from the many sources he researched; and he compiled the most reliable data in his definitive work, *From Slavery To Freedom* (New York: Macmillan, 1998)."[15] He concluded that William Still's 1872 publication, *The Underground Railroad,* was written by a black man who was " at first a Negro clerk in the Philadelphia Anti-Slavery Society, but later virtually central director of the movement in southeast Pennsylvania." Still's book faced unfair criticism from some quarters, however. Instead of praising the untutored black farm boy from the New Jersey backwoods for his superlative presentation, some said that his organization of the voluminous data left much to be desired. Other faulted him for placing the Good Samaritan, Seth Concklin, at the beginning of his fugitive slave history to commemorate his failed attempt to rescue his brother, Peter's family from Alabama slavery. Still others rued the absence of an index for the 780 page history of fugitive slaves.

Some of his descriptive language is humorous, though always carefully encoded. Deeper into the book he records his correspondence with white antislavery agents and other concerned citizens who contributed to the movement in diverse ways. And finally, he published biographical sketches of some of the most active underground railroad conductors towards the end of the book, not because their contributions were inconsequential, but more because he wanted to honor the harried runaway slaves up front because they were the subject of his exposition.[16]

Robert C. Smedley's *History of the Underground Railroad in Chester and the Neighboring Counties of Pennsylvania,* Lancaster, Pennsylvania: published by the Office of the Journal, 1883, was read with interest by William Still. Dr. Smedley, of West Chester, Pennsylvania, near Philadelphia, first intended to write a single newspaper article about the movement in West Chester, but became engrossed in stories oldsters and their descendants revealed to him as associates of the Underground Railroad. He died before he had finished with the preparation of his data into book form. Two of his friends had promised him that they would edit his data which they published in 1883.[17]

Larry Gara, author of *The Liberty Line: The Legend of the Underground Railroad* (Lexington, Kentucky: University of Kentucky Press, 1961),[18] also agreed that William Still's *The*

Underground Rail Road was "the only authentic history of this phase of antislavery work then being published."[18]

The letterhead on Still's stationary used to reply to a letter from Mr. S.L. Cratty, in Bellaire, Ohio, is given here. It begins with words describing his 1883 reprint of *The Underground Railroad,* under which is written 244 Twelfth Street, Philadelphia, and the date of the letter, 27 March 1885.

Just Out,

The new and Revised Edition

of the

Underground Railroad.

By William Still.

With A Life of The Author.

"The only book that fully explains the secret work of the **U.G.R.R.**, a thrilling

and important chapter in the history of the United States."

William still sent to Mr. Cratty, one of his several business agents for his book, the autograph he requested in his last letter to the author. Mr. Still wrote in his reply to Mr. Cratty, "To be enrolled with the letters of some of the noblest and bravest abolitionists who had labored so earnestly and successfully before the Rebellion to abolish American Slavery, is before me, and is awakening many interesting reminiscences I can assure you," wrote Still.[19] He also enclosed with it a pamphlet from the "The Commemoration of the Fiftieth Anniversary of the Organization of the American Anti-Slavery Society, which I am sure you would be pleased to have."[20]

Time had taken its toll on William Still, who asked his daughter, Frances Ellen to respond to a letter from Grace Anna Lewis on 7 January 1893. Miss Still described her father's palsy of his hand that prevented him from writing as legibly as before. She mentioned the well attended, gala Reception her father had for William Lloyd

Garrison, in his house, and other matters of interest he thought important to an old abolitionist friend. Miss Still wrote that her seventy-five year old father's failing health mandated the sale of his coal business. She mentioned his praise about the Home for the Aged & Infirm Colored Persons where he once served as Vice-President for quite a number of years, and then as President for more years.

William Still also served as Chairman of Principle Committees at "this glorious Institution [which] has never brought me any financial reward, it has nevertheless brought me a great "[deal] of satisfaction & happiness because of the benefits & blessings it has brought to so many of the poor I have been laboring for." He said he wanted to make a speech and to have a holiday celebration for some of the lonely, old people. His daughter, Dr. Anderson, promised to read from some pages from *The Underground Railroad* to the elders who might still remember those days now fading quickly into the past." His handwriting revealed a signature that was barely legible.[21]

Barraged with correspondence, William Still replied to them as soon as he could. One, using the same letterhead he had earlier had printed to advertise his *Underground Railroad Records,* William Still wrote to Mr. J.E. Bruce at 409 5th Street, N.E. Washington, D.C., on 1 August 1893. He began with a statement that on the 30th ult., Garrigues brothers, Booksellers forwarded Bruce's letter to him for a copy of "Mrs. Harper's book (called *Iola Leroy* he wished to have sent to "a Mrs. Dabney at 1626 5th Street, Washington, D.C" Still blamed his busy schedule for the delay to Mr. Bruce's letter, and then praised Mrs. Harper's book for "there is much in it that is calculated to do great benefit to the race."

He recommended that Mrs. Harper's work might be better served if she had an agent to increase its circulation. He thought, too, that an agent might better promote his book. His businesslike talents prompted him to offer to reduce the price of the edition entitled, *Still's Underground Rail Road Records* from its current $4.50 price down to $3.50. Still closed with this advice:"I see that Johnson & Bruce are engaged in a big work on the race line & and I wish you much success. There is considerable effort being put forth just now to advance knowledge among the people of our race,[which is] good! [22]

Afterword. The Passing of William Still and the Underground Railroad.

Civil rights are the rights protecting a person against arbitrary or discriminatory treatment The U.S. Constitution guarantees the freedom of religion, speech, and the Press, freedom of assembly, and rights of due process of law (e.g. habeus corpuss and equal protection under the law). After the Civil war, efforts to extend civil rights to blacks were only in part realized by the 14th and 15th constitutional amendments. In the 20th century, the black civil rights movement, led by the National Association for the Advancement of Colored People, The national Urban League, Martin Luther King, Jr., and others, was instrumental in securing legislation, notably the civil rights acts of 1964 and 1968, and the voting rights act of 1965 which prohibited discrimination in public accommodations, schools, and employment, and voting for reasons of color, race, and religion, or national origin.

Woman Suffrage was achieved in the U.S. under the 19th amendment, prohibiting discrimination on grounds of sex , but the amendment failed to obtain the necessary ratification of thirty-eight states by July 1982.(No footnote is made of this citation found in *The Concise Columbia Encylopedia,* 2nd, ed.,(N.Y.: Columbia University Press, 1989), p. 169.

The era of the Underground Railroad has faded from memory and sight with the knowledge of the Civil Rights Act of the 1860s. The failed attempts made in the 1860s by the Congressional radical Republicans were realized fully in the 1960s. The 19th Amendment to the U.S. Constitution provided in 1920 to women the right to vote in state and federal elections. Harvard Medical School accepted women as regular students for the first time in 1945. And Rosa Lee Parks (1913-2005), an American civil rights activist born in Tuskegee, Alabama, refused to give up her seat to a white man on a Montgomery, Alabama bus in 1955.She was said to have started the civil rights movement in the U.S. Few people, black or white, know that almost a century earlier, William Still's eight year campaign against the proscribed seating of black riders on the Philadelphia street cars ended with the right of black riders to be seated where they chose on the city street cars.

William Still was commended by the Philadelphia Presbytery in Philadelphia for his long time effort to improve the lives of the freedmen in that city. He was honored by an invitation to represent his church in Philadelphia in 1885 at the Presbyterian General Assembly at Cincinnati.[1] In 1888,The Dallas Texas Trinity Historical Society invited Mr. Still there to accept a commendation at Dallas for his Underground Railroad work.[2] His 14 January 1888 letter explained his reason for declining the generous offer due to "sickness in the family and his many duties in connection with the charitable work; prevented him from making the trip to Dallas."[3]

William Still's life was forever inextricably intertwined with his beloved Pennsylvania Antislavery Society at Philadelphia he worked tirelessly in many committees even after the Society only sporadically after the slaves were freed. He was especially devoted to his role in the Board of Education and the Acting Committee[4] A list of Still's accomplishments appears towards the end of the M.A. thesis which appears in the Foreword of this project. Ms. Alberta S. Norwood's Master of Arts thesis was accepted in 1931 by the University of Pennsylvania, entitled, Negro Welfare Work in Philadelphia, especially as Illustrated by the Career of William Still 1775-1930.[5]

Letters from underground railroad conductors continued to be sent to William Still even in his declining years. Booker T.

Washington wrote him in 1888 with praises for his devotion to the Pennsylvania Abolition Society. Mr. Washington gave praises to the antislavery society for its work relating to the elevation of the Negroes, who appreciated their brave, generous, unselfish contributions for the betterment of the black race. Booker T. Washington, the Marshal at Washington, D.C., wrote to William Still about his wife's illness that had prevented his appearance at the Twenty-Five Year celebration of the Pennsylvania Society's contributions to black education. William Still received many such letters people connected in various ways with the antislavery movement and the freedmen's cause after emancipation.[7.]

Education for the freedmen was the focus of William Still's efforts until he died. The Superintendant of the Franklin Reformatory in Philadelphia wrote to William Still on 18 March 1889 to seek advice to give to the warden who was concerned about educating black youth in his institution.[8] Definitive data based on the contributions of William still can be found at the Pennsylvania Anti-Slavery Society Minutes-1847-1916.[9]

The Pennsylvania Society for promoting the Abolition of Slavery, the relief of Free negroes Unlawfully Held in Bondage, and for Improving the Condition of the African Race was the heading on the letter a committee signed and sent to the president of the United states, William McKinley which bemoaned the lynching of black people in some Southern states.[10] It stated, in part, "...We ask a hearing in behalf of the hundreds if Negroes who have lately suffered violence, outrage, and 'lynching' in North and South Carolina, Texas, Arkansas, and other States during thy administration, and to earnestly direct they direct and energetic efforts for the suppression of these outrages against our fellow citizens who deserve protection under the law, not only because they are victims of persecution on account of their color, but because they are fellow men...."

William still was elected to serve as the Vice-President of the Pennsylvania Society consecutively from 1887 until 1895. On 26 December 1895 he was elected to serve as President of the Pennsylvania Society.[11]

The Minutes-1847-1916 note that on 25 April 1901, William Still was forced to resign due to his increasingly disabled condition.[12] William Still died in his Philadelphia home on 14 July 1902.[13] His grieving wife, Letitia Still followed him in death in 1906. The Memorial Park gravesite where the remains of William and Letitia Still were first interred, were relocated from their plot in Memorial park to their present grave in the Eden cemetery. When Frances Ellen Still died in 1944, she was buried with her parents at the Eden cemetery on Springfield Road in Collongsdale, Pennsylvania. The writer visited the Eden Cemetery in Upper Darby, Pennsylvania outside of Philadelphia.

William Still's many accomplishments are listed in a variety of reference books. His biographical sketch appeared in the 1897-1902 edition of the Marquis Who Was Who in America.[14] His biography also appeared in The Dictionary of American Negro Biography,.1935-1936.[15] And again, in *The Journal of Pennsylvania History,* (Philadelphia: The Pennsylvania Historical Society, 1961).[16]

The Rev. Matthew Anderson, and his wife, Dr. Caroline Still Anderson, are also interred in the Colostine section of the Eden Cemetery. Eden cemetery, not far distant from the gravesites of their daughters, Margret Anderson, and her oldest sister, sister, Helen Waller, and her husband, JohnWaller. John. Linn Washington, of The *Daily News,* had also earlier located the final burial site of William Still on 20 February 20 1987.

The Still family that began as slaves on a Maryland cornfield migrated first to the New Jersey Pines of Burlington County, New Jersey, where their freeborn children were born. James and Samuel remained in New Jersey to live and work. William found his forte in Philadelphia. James' son settled in Boston, Massachusetts, the present home of the family historian, and various northern cities and towns have become the home of the Still family members at the present time and into the future The Medford, New Jersey. Historical Society has recently proclaimed the office of "Dr." James Still, on Church Road, in Medford Township, in Burlington County, New Jersey, to be preserved in the New Jersey Register of Historic Sites as well as in the National Register of Historic sites.[17]

End Notes.

Chapter 1.

1. David P. Currie, *The Constitution and the Congress* Descent into the Maelstrom *1829-1861,* (Chicago: University of Chicago Press, 2005). Preface, ix. Hereafter, Currie, T*he Constitution and the Congress.*
2. Ibid.
3 William Still, *The Underground Rail Road,* (Philadelphia; Porter & Coates, 1872).4
4. Currie, *The Constitution and the Congress;* Appendix C. pp.287-301
5. Ibid; pp.3-36; 135-185.
6. William Still, *The Underground Rail Road,* P.37. Reprint edition. James Still, *Early Recollections and Life of Dr. James Still* 1812-1885, (Medford, NJ: The Medford Historical Society, 1972). Ist edition self published by James Still, (Philadelphia :Lippincott, 1877). Hereafter James Still, *Early Recollections and Life.*
7. Ibid; pp.37-38.
8. Ibid.
9. Kate Pickard, Camillus, NY, letters 1850-1856, Peter Still, Burlington, NJ. Peter Still Papers, Rutgers.'
10. Ibid.

11. Still, William, The Underground Rail Road, pp.37-38.
12. Alberta S. Norwood, Negro Welfare Work in Philadelphia Especially as Illustrated by the Career of William Still 1775-1931. Accepted in partial fulfillment of a MA degree ,Philadelphia : University of Pennsylvania, 1931); Recollections of Miss Frances Ellen Still; William Still, *The UGRR .iiv-v.*
13. Ibid; p.3. Manuscript History of the Pennsylvania Society for Promoting the Abolition of Slavery, etc; Book 1, 5. Hereafter Manuscript History. Pennsylvania Historical Society, Philadelphia; Sources and Bibliography of the Alberta S. Norwood MA. p.190.
14. Ibid; Manuscript Collection Belonging to the Pennsylvania Society, etc; Vol.1, p. 21. Hereafter, Manuscript Collection.
15. Ibid; Manuscript History, Book 1, 5.
16. Ibid.
17. Ibid; Needles, Edward, p.4. An Historical Memoir of the Pennsylvania Society for Promoting the Abolition of Slavery, etc. 108. Printed Sources and Bibliography, Philadelphia, 1848. p..191. Hereafter, An Historical Memoir.
18. Ibid; p.15. Manuscript History, Book 1, 8.
19. Ibid; Book1, 15.
20. Ibid; p.5.
21. Ibid; p.5; Needles, An Historical Memoir, p.29; Manuscript History, Book 1,17, 18.
22. Ibid; p.8.
23. Ibid; p.40. *Constitution in the Congress. Fugitive Slaves,* pp. 183-185.
24. Ibid
25. bid.

Chapter 2.

1. Ghosts of By-Gone Glories Haunt Quiet Lanes and Memories of Bastow's Old-Timers. http://www.nj pinebarrens .com; First published in the *Newark Star Ledger,* June 22, 1947 Reprinted with permission, Transcribed by Ben Ruset. Ghost Towns, written by Henry Charlton Beck; An Introduction to the New Jersey Pine Barrens, by Ben Ruset. http:// www.nj pinebarrens.

com/content/view/15/48/; and www.NJ Pine Barrens.com. http://en. Wikipedia.org/wiki/ Pine Barrens (New Jersey.

2. James Still, Early Recollections and Life, pp. 13-33.
3. Ibid; pp. 16-18; 72-75.
4. Catalogue Of the children of Levin and Charity Still, 1798-1821, Peter Still Papers, Rutgers.
5. Alberta S. Norwood, Negro Welfare Work in Philadelphia, etc., p. 21. Still, William, The Underground Railroad, vi ; p.22. ibid; p.22; ix; ibid.
6. James Still, *Early Recollections and Lfe.* pp. 54-62; pp. 63-7.
7. Ibid; pp. 63-67.
8. Alberta S. Norwood, Negro Welfare Work in Philadelphia, pp. 22-3. William Still, The Underground Railroad, xvii.
9. Ibid; pp. 23-4.xviii.
10. Ibid; p. 25.ix; Personal records of William Still in MS.

Chapter 3.

1. Alberta S. Norwood, Negro Welfare Work, in Philadelphia, p.22, Still,William *The Underground Rail Road,* ix.
2. Benjamin Quarles, *Black Abolitionists* (New York: De Capo Press, (1969).P. 86.
3. *The* Life of Charles B. Ray, The Journal of Negro History: Vol. 4 (Oct. 1919), pp. 361-371. See also I Garland Penn, *The African Press,* pp. pp.32-47.in possession of the Ray family. http:///links.jstor.org/sici=0022-2992 (1919100 4% 3A 4%C361%AtloCBR%3E2.0....4/30/2007JSTOR.
4. Alberta S. Norwood, Negro Welfare Work, pp 3-4; Manuscript History, Book 1,5.
5. Ibid; An Historical memoir, 29; Manuscript History, Book 1. 17,18.
6. Quarles, *Black Abolitionists* pp. 9-10.
7. Alberta S. Norwood, Negro Work in Philadelphia, etc., p. 8, Needles, An Historical Memoir, 40; Manuscript History, Book 1, 99.
8. Ibid; pp. 8-9; Needles, An Historical Memoir, p.41.
9. Ibid; p.9, Manuscript Collection, Vol.3, 293.
10. Ibid; Needles, An Historical Memoir, 40.

11. Quarles, *Black Abolitionists*, pp.12-13.
12. Currie, *The Constitution and the Congress*, pp.39-41.
13. Quarles, *Black Abolitionists*, pp.221-23.
14. *Currie, The Constitution and the Congress.* Article IV of the U.S. Constitution. Appendix C. pp.293-294.
15. Ibid; pp.6-10.
16. Alberta S. Norwood, Negro Welfare Work in Philadelphia, etc., pp.16-17; Manuscript History, Book 2. pp. 239-240.

Chapter 4.

1. Alberta S. Norwood, Negro Welfare Work etc; p. 3. Manuscript History belonging to the Pennsylvania Society, etc., Vol. 1, 21.
2. Currie, The Constitution and the Congress.p.183.
3. Ibid; pp. 184-185.
4. Judith Bentley, *"Dear Friend," Thomas Garrett and William Still" Collaborators on the Underground Railroad*, (New York: Dutton, 1997), p.29.
5. Alberta S. Norwood, Negro Welfare Work in Philadelphia, etc., pp.22-23. Still, William, The Underground Railroad, XVII.
6. William Still, *The Underground Rail Road*, p.711.
7. Ibid; pp.735-40.
8. Benjamin Quarles, *Black Abolitionists*, p.55.
9. Ibid; pp. 143-144; 144-145.
10. Currie, The Constitution and the Congress. p. 183.
11. William Still, *The Underground Rail Road.* Pp. 623-641.
12. Wilbur H. Siebert, *Directory of the Names of Underground Railroad Operators.*
13. William Still, *The Underground Rail Road.* pp. 611-612.
14. Ibid; pp.665-679.
15. Quarles, *Black Abolitionists*, pp.68-74.
16. Ibid.
17. William Still, *The Underground Rail Road.* pp 698-710.
18. Ibid. pp. 740-745.

19. Alberta S. Norwood, Negro Welfare Work in Philadelphia, etc; pp.5-6; Needles, An Historical Memoir, 37; Manuscript History, Book 1, 58; Manuscript Collection, Vol. 2, 41.
20. Ibid; p.7; Manuscript History, Book 1, 86.
21. Ibid; p.87.
22. Ibid; p.8. Needles, An Historical Memoir. 40.
23. Benjamin Quarles, *Black Abolitionists,* pp. 51-52.
24. William Still, *The Underground Rail Road.* pp. 680-688.
25. Currie, *The Constitution and the Congress,* pp. 4-5.

Chapter 5.

1. Quarles, *Black Abolitionists,* pp.51-52.
2. Ibid; p. 55
3 Ibid; pp. 154-155.
4. Alberta S. Norwood, Negro Welfare Work in Philadelphia, etc; p.28. Manuscript History, Book 3, 279.
5 Ibid
6 Ibid; p.29. *Public Ledger,* Philadelphia, 14 December 1902. Recollections of a Tumultuous Period, as described by Isaac H. Clothier.
7. Ibid; *North American and United States Gazette,* 4 April 1859.
8. Ibid; An Antislavery Repository in the Home for the Aged and Infirm.
9. Ibid; pp. 29-30. Manuscript History, Book 3, 281.
10. Currie, *The Constitution and* The *Congress.*pp.184-85.
11. Samuel J. May, Jr., *The Antislavery Conflict* (Miami, Florida: Mnemosyne Publishing Co.,1969). 1st. printing, in the Negro Collection. P.345.
12. Currie, The Constitution and the Congress, p.346.
13. Ibid; p.347.
14. William Still, *The Underground Railroad.* pp. 343-348.
15. Currie, *The Constitution and the Congress.* pp. 165-178.
16. Ibid; p.185.

Chapter 6.

1. Alberta S. Norwood, Negro Welfare Work in Philadelphia, etc., p.13. Manuscript History, Book 3; 270.
2. Ibid; p. 16. 271.
3. William Still, *The Underground Railroad,* pp.23-4.
4. William Still, Philadelphia, 7 August 1850, to James O. Cousins, Cincinnati. The Peter Still Papers.
5. James Still, *Early recollections and Life,* pp. 105-07.
6. William Still, *The Underground Rail Road,* pp. 24-6.
7. Ibid; pp. 26-8.
8. Ibid; pp. 28-9.
9. Ibid; pp. 29-30.
10. A Slave Family's Struggle for Freedom, Kenneth R. Johnson, 1978; pp. 1-9. (Used here by permission of the author.) http://www.rootsweb.com/~alcober/aa-struggle.htm.
11. William Still, *The Underground Rail Road,* pp.30-2.
12. Ibid; pp. 32-4.
13. Ibid; pp. 34-5.
14. Ibid; pp 659-65.
15. Ibid; pp. 36-7.

Chapter 7.

1. Samuel Dubois Cook Understanding Negro History, "A Paradox," 36-39. *Journal of Negro History,* XLV, No.4 (October 1960). 219-240. P.39.
2. Ibid; 35-6. Walter Rauschenbush, "The Christianizing of the Social Order". (New York, 1912), 418.
3. Ibid; "The Negro Effort," 293-240. Larry Gara, *The Liberty Line: The Legend of the Underground Railroad,* Lexington, Kentucky: University of Kentucky Press),1961
4. Ibid; Chapter viii.
5. Alberta S. Norwood, Negro Welfare Work, etc., p.11; Turner, F.J. The Frontier in American History, 201.
6. Ibid.
7. Samuel Dubois Cook, Understanding Negro History. "On Turner, Beard, and Slavery," Staugh to Lynde, pp.106-07.

Journal of Negro History, XL, xiii No. 4. (October 1963), 235-240.

8. Ibid; Introduction to Frederick Jackson Turner, United States, 1830- 1845: *The Nation and Its Sections,* [New York, 1935], p. vii.
9. Herman Beltz, editor, *The Webster-Hayne Debate on the nature of the Union: Selected Documents,* (Indianapolis): Liberty Fund, Inc;) 2000. The American People vi. 478. Agreement of the North to let It Alone; ibid 178.
10. Loranzo Sears, *Wendell Phillips, Orator and Agitator,* (New York: Benjamin Blom,) 1909. 120; Reissued, 1967.
11. Alberta S. Norwood, Negro Welfare Work in Philadelphia, etc., p. 17. Manuscript History, Book 2, 239-40.
12. Samuel Dubois Cook, Understanding Negro History, 138-39. "The Abolitionist Dilemma: The Antislavery Movement and the Northern Negro." William Ellery Channing, "The African Character," John A. Collins, editor, The Antislavery Picknick: A Collection of Speeches, Poems, Dialogues, and Songs, (Boston 1842. P.56-8.).
13. (The Life and Times of Frederick Douglass 1884). P.269-70.
14. Ibid; Martin R. Delany, "The Condition, Elevation, Emigration, and Destiny of the Colored people of the United States, (Philadelphia, 1852), p.10-24; p. 25-7
15. Ibid; Elizur Wright, Jr., to W.L. Garrison, 30 June 1834. Garrison Papers, Boston Public Library, and the Wright Papers (Library of Congress). A New Bedford, Massachusetts abolitionist wrote in 1837 "It is hardly desirable that there should be a colored school established , for the public schools are all open, and black children are all on terms of the most perfect equality." Deborah Weston to Maria (Weston) Chapman, April 1837. The Weston Papers, (Boston Public Library).
16. Ibid; p. 152. The Triumph of Equal School Rights in Boston. *Proceedings of the Presentation Meeting Held in Boston,* 17 December 1855., including addresses by John T. Hilton, William C. Nell, Charles W. Slack, Wendell Phillips, William Lloyd Garrison, Charles Lenox Remond, (Boston, 1856).

17. Larry Gara, *The Liberty Line; Legend of the Underground Railroad* (Lexington, Kentucky: University of Kentucky Press,) 1961, p.105, *Journal of the Vigilance Committee* 1852-57, Pennsylvania Historical Society; Still and the Underground Railroad, passim.
18. Samuel J. May, Jr., *Some* Reminiscences *of the Antislavery Conflict, hereafter Some Reminiscences, etc.*(Miami, Florida: Mnemosyne Publishing Co) in the Fisk University Library, Negro Collection; p.135. "Pacification and Agitation".
19. Samuel J. May, Jr., *Some Reminiscences,* etc. pp. 345- 49.
20. Ibid.
21. Ibid; The Underground Railroad, pp. 296-7.
22. William Still, *The Underground Railroad,* pp. 348-9.
23. Ibid; pp. 611-12.
24. Judith Bentley, *"Dear Friend" Thomas Garrett and William Still Collaborators on The Underground Railroad,*(New York:Dutton,1997), p.30.
25. Benjamin Quarles, *Black Abolitionists,* Chapter 2, "Sowers of the Word".
26. IIbid.

Chapter 8.

1. William Still, *The Underground Rail Road,* p.348.
2. Ibid; pp. 347-53.
3. Ibid; pp. 252-357.
4. Ibid; p.362.
5. Ibid; pp. 368-70.
6. Ibid; pp. 370-74.
7. Ibid; pp. 374-77.
8. Ibid; p. 374.
9. Alberta S. Norwood, Negro Welfare Work in Philadelphia, etc. p. 71 Appendix 14; Still. William, The Underground Railroad, xxx. Appendix 14; William Wells Brown, Cambridge Port, Massachusetts, 10 July 1863, Letter to William Still, Philadelphia.
10. Ibid; pp.71-72. Still, William, The Underground Railroad, p.755-80.

Chapter 9.

1. William Still, Philadelphia, 10 May 1852, to Peter Still, Burlington, New Jersey. Peter Still Papers 1852-1855.Receipt Book held by Dr. Joseph Parish, Burlington, New Jersey.
2. Lewis Thornton, Esq., Tuscumbia, Alabama, 19 August 1852, to Richard E. Ely, [? Address]. Ibid.
3. William Still, Philadelphia, 12 October 1852, to Peter Still, Burlington, New Jersey. Ibid
4. Mrs. Kate E.R. Pickard, Camillus, Onandega County, New York, to the Rev. Samuel J. May, Syracuse, New York. Ibid.
5. Dr. Joseph Parish, Burlington, New Jersey, 5 October 1852, to John Parish, Philadelphia. Ibid.
6. Judge E.E. Boudinot, Burlington, New Jersey, 6 November 1852, to Peter Still, Burlington, New Jersey. Ibid.
7. Mary A. Buckingham, Burlington, New Jersey,[undated], to Peter Still, Burlington, New Jersey. Ibid.
8. Cortlandt Van Rensselar, Burlington, New Jersey, 6 November 1852, to Peter Still, Burlington, New Jersey. Ibid.
9. H.B. Stowe, [? Address], 10 November 1852, to Peter Still, Burlington, New Jersey. Ibid.
10. William Still, *The Underground Rail Road,* pp. 610-11.
11. Ibid; pp.611-12.
12. William Still, Philadelphia, 18 December 1852, to Peter Still, Burlington, New Jersey. Ibid.
13. Mrs. B. Bronson, Andover, [? Massachusetts], 25 December 1852, to Peter Still, Burlington, New Jersey. Ibid.

Chapter 10.

1. Mrs. Kate E.R. Pickard, hereafter, Mrs. Pickard, Camillus, New York, 29 January 1853, to Peter Still, unknown address in Boston, Mass. Peter Still Papers.
2. Writer's Name (illegible), Letter of introduction given to Peter Still, 31 January 1853, Boston, Mass. Peter Still Papers.
3. Joseph Parish, Burlington, New Jersey, Record of funds donated to the freedom of the Alabama family of Peter Still, 1852-54;ibid.

4. Mrs. Pickard, 21 March 1853, to Peter Still, address unknown in the Boston area; ibid.
5. T.L. King, Boston, 28 March 1853. Letter of introduction to Peter Still, ibid.
6. William Still, Philadelphia Antislavery Office, 29 April 1853, to E. Gray Loring, Esq., Boston; ibid.
7. William Lloyd Garrison, Boston, 31 May 1853, to Samuel J. May, Syracuse, New York. The May-Garrison Papers, Boston Public Library.
8. Samuel J. May 27 July 1853. Letter of introduction for Peter Still. Ibid.
9. William Still, Philadelphia Antislavery office, 9 November 1853, to Peter Still, address unknown in the Boston area; ibid.
10. Morris L. Hallowell, Florence, Alabama, 19 September 1854, to Charles L. Gurley, New London, Connecticut; Ibid.
11. Mrs. Pickard, Camillus, New York, 24 April 1854, to Peter Still, address unknown in Boston; Ibid.
12. John L. Simpson, Florence, Alabama, to Morris L. Hallowell, Florence, Alabama; ibid.
13. Mrs. Pickard, Camillus, New York, 22 January 1855, to Peter Still, Burlington, New Jersey, correspondence re the proposed ms, *The Kidnapped and the Ransomed.*; ibid.
14. Rev. Samuel J. May, Syracuse, New York, 9 March 1855, to Peter Still, Burlington, New Jersey; ibid.
15. Ibid; 27 April 1855.
16. Mrs. Pickard, Camillus, New York, [?]1855, to William Still, Philadelphia [?]; ibid.
17 W.J. Baxter, re William Handy, Franklin County, Tuscumbia, Alabama, 25 June 1855, to Peter Still, Burlington, New Jersey; ibid.
18 Mrs. Pickard, Camillus, New York, 28 September 1855, to Peter Still, Burlington, New Jersey; ibid.
19. Alberta S. Norwood, Negro Welfare Work in Philadelphia, etc., p.31; Appendix 1.
20 Ibid; Still, William, Underground Railroad, xxv.
21 Ibid; xxvi.

Chapter 11.

1. Currie, *The Constitution and the Congress,* pp.196-200.
2. William Still, *The Underground Rail Road,* pp.86-7.
3. *The Case of Passmore Williamson,*
4. http://www.librarycompany.org/Jane Johnson/habeascorpus.html.
5. *Opinion of Judge Kane on the Suggestion of Jane Johnson.* http://www.library company.org/Jane Johnson/judgekane.html.
6. William Still, *The Underground Rail Road* . pp. 87-91.
7. *Narrative in the facts in the case of Passmore Williamson. http://www.librarycompany.org/janejohnson/narrative.html.*
8. William Still, *The Underground Rail Road,* p.93.
9. Ibid; pp. 91-93.
10. Ibid; pp. 649-54.
11. Ibid; pp.93-96.
12. Ibid; p.96.
13. Ibid; pp. 721-23.
14. Ibid; pp. 95-7.
15. Ibid; pp. 585-86. Rev. N. R. Johnston, Topsham, Vermont, 1 September 1955, to William Still, Philadelphia; http://www.history.org/beavercounty/Be...cation/Geneva College/GenevaBeg MSP85. html;Beginnings of Geneva College. Milestones, Vol.10, No. 2-Spring, 1985. Boston Public Library.

Chapter 12

1. Samuel J. May, Syracuse, New York, 9 March 1855, to Peter Still, Burlington, New Jersey.
2. Mrs. Pickard, Camillus, New York, 23 June 1856, to Peter Still, ibid.
3. Ibid; 9 May 1856.
4. Ibid.
5. James Still, *Early recollections and Life,* pp. 105-09.
6. Ibid; p. 90.
7. Ibid; pp. 93-5.

8. Currie, *The Constitution and the Congress,* pp. 13, 48, 150, 171, 201, 203-9, 205-8.
9. Norwood, Negro Welfare Work in Philadelphia, etc., pp. 57-8; A Brief Narrative of the Struggle for the Rights of Colored people of Philadelphia in the City Railroad Cars, and a Defense of William Still, pp. 7, 8, 9; Still, William, The Underground Railroad, LI, LIII; *The Philadelphia Press,* 15 December 1863. Printed Sources, Norwood, Negro Welfare Work in Philadelphia, etc., p. 191.
10. James McKim, Philadelphia, 22 November 1852, to David Lee Child, Boston, Massachusetts. The David Lee Child Papers, Boston Public Library.
11. Journal of the Vigilance Committee, Station 2, Philadelphia 1852-1857, Reel 32. William Still Papers, The Pennsylvania Society for promoting the Abolition of Slavery, etc., 1775-1787. The Pennsylvania Historical Society, Philadelphia, Pennsylvania
12. William Still, *The Underground Rail Road,* p. 296.
13. Ibid; pp. 296- 99.
14. Negro Welfare Work in Philadelphia, etc., pp. 70-1. Ledger in possession of Miss Frances Ellen Still.
15. Ibid; Appendices 3A, B, C, D, E, F.
16. Ibid; Still, William, The Underground Railroad, x xviii.

Chapter 13

1. Arnold Toynbee, *A Study of History An Abridgement of Volume VII-X,* by D.C. Somervell, (New York: Oxford University press, 1957). P. 318.
2. Ibid; pp. 396- 97.
3. Benjamin Quarles, *Black Abolitionists* (New York: Da Capo Press, Inc., 1969). P.59.
4. Ibid.
5. John F. HumeThe Abolitionists- Full Text Free Book (Part1/4) 7/22/2007.
6. Quarles, *Black Abolitionists,* pp. 61-2.

7. Norwood, Negro Welfare Work in Philadelphia, etc., p. 71; W. Wells Brown, Cambridge Port, Massachusetts, 10 July 1863, to William Still, Philadelphia, p. 71. Appendix 14.
8. Quarles, *Black Abolitionists,* pp. 66-7.
9. Ibid; p. 68.
10. Ibid; pp. 68-9.
11. Ibid; p. 56.
12. Ibid; pp. 72-3.
13. Ibid; p. 70.
14. Ibid; p. 82.
15. Ibid; p. 71.
16. Ibid; p. 33.
17. Ibid; p. 32.
18. Ibid; pp. 87-9.
19. Ibid; pp. 218—19.
20. William Still, *The Underground Rail Road,* pp. 680-88.
21. Ibid; p. 680.
22. Ibid;
23. Ibid; pp. 688-90.
24. Ibid; pp. 694-98.
25. Ibid; pp. 691-95.
26. Ibid; p. 693.
27. Ibid; pp. 613-16.
28. Ibid; pp. 617-622.
29. Ibid; pp. 642-49.
30. Ibid; pp. 712-19.
31. Ibid; pp. 746-47.
32. Ibid; pp. 719-21.
33. Ibid; pp. 593-608.
34. Ibid; pp. 723- 34.

Chapter 14.

1. William Still, *The Underground Railroad,* pp. 748- 55.
2. Ibid; p.749.
3. Ibid; pp. 39-40.
4. W.E.B Dubois, *John Brown* (New York; International Publishers, 1909) p.155.

5. Ibid; p. 156.
6. Ibid.
7. Norwood, Alberta S., Negro Welfare Work in Philadelphia, etc., p. 38. *Public Ledger, 14* December 1902, General Mulholland's Recollections of a Momentous period.
8. Ibid; Douglass, Frederick, John Brown, An Address, 23.
9. Ibid; pp. 38-9. Information from Miss Frances Ellen Still
10. Ibid; p. 39. Douglass, Frederick, An Address, 26; Villard, Oswald Garrison, 412, 413;Wilson, H. P. *John Brown,* 328; Leech, Samuel V., *The Raid of John Brown,23;* Sanborn, F.B; *John Brown,* 539
11. Ibid; Wilson, H.P., *John Brown,* 349-350; Sanborn, F.B., *John Brown,* 539; Warren, R.P., *John Brown,* 329; Douglass, Frederick, *Life and Times of Frederick Douglass, 390.*
12. Ibid; p. 40. Villard, Oswald Garrison , *John Brown,* 78.
13. Ibid; Douglass, Frederick, *John Brown.* An Address, 26; Villard, Oswald Garrison, *John Brown,* 412, 413; Sanborn F. B. *Life and letters of John Brown,* 538, 539; Douglass, Frederick, *Life and Times of Frederick Douglass, 390.*
14. Ibid; Alberta S. Norwood, Negro Welfare Work in Philadelphia, etc., pp. 40-41; Villard, Oswald Garrison, John Brown, 408.
15. Ibid; p.41; 472-73.
16. Ibid; 473.
17 Ibid. 474.
18 Ibid; Douglass, Frederick, John Brown, An Address, 14.
19. Ibid; 567; Villard, Oswald Garrison, *John Brown,* 529-30.
20.. Ibid; pp. 41-2. Villard, Oswald, Garrison, *John Brown,* 533-34; Still, William, Underground Railroad. xxii.
21. Ibid; p. 42; Still, William, Underground Railroad, xxii.
22. Ibid; pp 42-3, Underground Railroad, xxiii, xxiv.
23. Ibid; *Philadelphia Ledger,* xxiv.
24. Ibid; 14 December 1902, General Mulholland's Recollection of a Tumultuous Period.
25. Ibid; p.44. Annie Brown, North Elba, New York, 20 December 1859, to William Still, Philadelphia. Lock of John Brown's hair included in the letter.
26. Ibid; Letter in the William Still Collection of letters.

Chapter 15.

1. Carroll Quigley, *The Evolution of Civilizations: An Introduction to Historical Analysis* (Indianapolis, Indiana: Liberty Fund) 1979. p.134.
2. Luke 10: 1-20 *Holy Bible* King James Version.
3. Alberta S. Norwood, Negro Welfare Work in Philadelphia, etc., p.43 Still, William, The *Underground Railroad,* xxiv.
4. William Still, Philadelphia, to Rev. Samuel J. May, Syracuse, New York. Garrison papers, Boston Public Library.
5. Ibid; 2 March 1860. Vol. 8, No.7.
6. Ibid; 7 March 1850. Vol. 8. No. 9.
7. Ibid; 8 March 1860. Vol. 8. No. 10.
8. Ibid; 10 March 1860. Vol. 8 No. 12.
9. Ibid; 16, 17 March 1860. Vo.30. p. 30, 32.
10. Alberta S. Norwood, Negro Welfare Work in Philadelphia, etc. p.52. Still, William A Brief Narrative of the Struggle for the Rights of the Colored People of Philadelphia in the City Railroad Cars, and a Defense of William Still, Philadelphia. In the Pamphlets-Printed Matter section of the Norwood Thesis. Last seen in the possession of Mr. Ellwood Heacock, a former Secretary of the Pennsylvania Antislavery Society, Philadelphia. From the Collection of William Still.
11. Ibid; pp.52-55. Philadelphia, 30 August 1859. Still, William, "A Brief Narrative, etc; 314. *North American and United States Gazette,* 31 August 1859.
12 Ibid; p.55. Still, William, "A brief Narrative, etc;" 4.
13 Ibid; pp.55-56. *North American and United States Gazette,* 14 September 1859.
14 Ibid; pp.56-57. Still, William, *The Underground Rail Road* LIII.
15 Ibid; p.57. Ibid; LIV. Information from Miss Frances E. Still.
16. Ibid; Still, William, *The Underground Railroad;* A Brief Narrative, *etc; 5, 6.*
17. Ibid; p.46. Philadelphia *Public Ledger,* 14 December ,"General Mulholland's Recollection of a Tumultuous Period."

18. Ibid; Appendix 6, pp. 129-131.G. E. Stephens, 54th Massachusetts Infantry, Morris Island, South Carolina, 19 September 1863, to William Still, Philadelphia.
19. Ibid; pp.47-48. Still, William, The *Underground Railroad*, XXIX, XXX.
20. Ibid; p.48. Appendix 7, p. 132. George E. Baker, National Freedman's Society, Washington, D.C., 18 November 1862, to William Still, Philadelphia.
21. Ibid; pp.48-49. Still, William, The *Underground Railroad*, LXIX.
22. Ibid; p. 49.Appendix 8, p.133. Adjutant General's Office, Wash. D.C. to William Still, Esq. Care of Hon. William D. Kelley, House of representatives, Washington, D. C., By Order of the secretary of War, James W. Hardie. Still, William, The *UndergroundRail Road,*L.
23. Ibid; pp. 49-50. Still, William, The *Underground Rail Road,* L.
24. Ibid; pp. 57-58. Still, William, "A Brief Narrative, etc; 7, 8 9. Still, William, The *Underground Railroad*, LI, LIII; Philadelphia *Press*, 15 December 1863.
25. Ibid; Still, William, "A Brief narrative, etc; 9.
26. Ibid; pp.58-59. Still, William, The *Underground Railroad*, LIII; Still, William, "A Brief Narrative etc; 9, 10.

27 *Atlantic Monthly*, Vol. 17, February 1866. Rossetti, W. M., "English Opinion on the American War."

28. Ibid; pp.59-60; Ibid; 149.
29. Ibid; p.60. , Manuscript History, Book III, 310; Still, William, "A Brief Narrative, etc; 14, 15, 16.
30. Ibid; pp.60-61. Philadelphia *Press*, 8 December 1864; Still, William, "A Brief Narrative, etc; 10, 11.
31. Ibid; p. 61. Ibid; 2.

Chapter 16.

1. Alberta S. Norwood, Negro Welfare Work in Philadelphia, etc., p. 61; Still, William, A Brief narrative, etc., Still, William, A Brief Narrative, etc; 12.
2. Ibid; pp.61-62; ibid, 14, 15.

3. Ibid; p.62; ibid; 20.
4. Ibid; pp.62-63; Ibid; 21.
5. Ibid; p. 63; ibid; 23.
6. Ibid; Manuscript History, Book 3, 320.
7. Ibid; pp. 63-64;, 9 February 1867.
8. Ibid; *Press*, 1 April 1867.
9. Ibid; pp. 64-5; Manuscript History, Book 3, 321.
10 Ibid; p. 65; 323.
11 Ibid; pp. 65-6, Manuscript History, Book 3, 324.
12 Ibid; p. 66; Constitution of Pennsylvania, Article 10. Section 1.
13 Ibid; pp. 66-7. Still, William, The Underground Railroad, LVII; Financial Records of the Statistical Society. In possession of Miss Frances E. Still.
14 Ibid; p. 67. Appendix 4. pp. 124-25.
15 Ibid; Still, William, The Underground Railroad, LVIII.
16 Ibid; pp. 67-8. Appendix 9C, p. 136; 9D; p. 137; 9E, p. 138.
17 Ibid; p. 68. Still, William, The Underground Railroad, LVIII.
18 Ibid; LIX.
19 Ibid; LIX; First Annual Report of the Home for Aged and Infirm Colored Persons, 1.
20 Ibid; 14.
21 Ibid; pp. 68-9. Still, William, The Underground Railroad, LIX; Recollections of Miss Frances E. Still, Appendix 10. P. 139.
22 Ibid; p. 69; Appendix 11.pp. 140.
23 Ibid; p. 69. The Constitution, By-Laws, and the Rules of the Home for Aged and Infirm Colored Persons; Seventh Annual Report, 17, Newspaper clippings, etc., 7.
24 Ibid; 6.
25 Ibid; Appendix 12, p. 141. Mercantile Library Company of Philadelphia, 10 May 1872, to William Still, Philadelphia, p.141.
26 Ibid; p. 69-70. Still, William, The Underground Railroad, LX.
27 Ibid; p. 70.
28 Ibid; Recollections of Rev. Henry L. Phillips.
29 Ibid; Still, William, The Underground Railroad, LX. Appendix 13, p. 142

30 Ibid; Original records from which *The Underground Railroad* was written.
31 Ibid; pp. 70-1. Ledger in possession of Miss Frances E. Still.
32 Ibid; p. 71. Still, William, The Underground Railroad, XXX.
33 Ibid; Appendix 14. Pp. 143-44.
34 Ibid; pp. 71-2. Still, William, The Underground Railroad, XXXI.
35 Ibid; p. 72. Appendix 15; 15B. Letter to William Still from W.P. Garrison, 28 September 1871, from the office of *The Nation.* Enclosed was a receipt for Still's subscription.
36 Ibid; p. 72. *American Literature.* Part II, 1920, 326;*The Cambridge History of.*

Chapter 17.

1. James Still, *Early recollections and Life,* etc. pp.70-71.
2. Ibid; pp.72-5.
3. Ibid; pp.76-83.
4. Ibid; pp.83-4.
5. Ibid; pp.85-9.
6. Ibid; pp.94-5.
7. Ibid; pp.105-09.
8. Ibid; pp.149-151.
9. Ibid; pp. 153-56.
10. Kenneth R. Johnson, *A slave Family's Struggle for Freedom.* http://www.Rootsweb.com/~alcober/aa.struggle.htm.
11. Samuel J. May, Syracuse, 20 February 1861 to Peter Still, Burlington, New Jersey. Peter Still Papers.
12. James Still, Early Recollections and Life, etc pp.153-55.
13. Ibid; p. 156.

Chapter 18.

1. Tour Guide African American Sites, Burlington, New Jersey. http://www.burico.lib.nj/county/culturalheritage/african american/. P.1
2. Ibid.

3. Henry Charlton Beck, *Forgotten Towns of New Jersey (*New Brunswick, New Jersey: Rutgers University Press) 1983. pp. 138-163.
4. James Still, *Early Recollections and Life*, p. 157.
5. bid; p. 158.
6. Burlington County Courthouse, Burlington, County, New Jersey. Wills, Marriages, Deaths, Land Records, etc.
7. James Still, Early Recollections and Life, p. 159.
8. William Still, Anti-Slavery Office, Philadelphia, 10 ? 1852, to Peter Still, Burlington, New Jersey.
9. James Still, Early Recollections and Life, pp. 159-60.
10. Catalogue of the Harvard Medical School, Vol. 2. Alumnae Roll, 1788-1905. See also, Harrington, Francis Thomas, M.D., (Class of 1888)--Vol. 3, Entry No. 2002,- J.T. Still, M.D..; 1871, Medford, New Jersey.
11. Cushing Academy Alumnae Records, (May have been destroyed in a fire at the school in the 1890's) Ashburnham, Massachusetts. Student, Emmaretta Still, Medford, New Jersey.
12. New Jersey State Department of Vital Statistics, Trenton, New jersey, 02625.
13. James Still, Early Recollections and Life, pp. 161-64.
14. Ibid; p. 165.
15. Ibid; p. 180-81.
16. Ibid; 182-84.
17. Ibid; 193.
18. Ibid; pp. 201-03.
19. Ibid; pp. 207-08.
20. Alberta S. Norwood, Negro Welfare Work in Philadelphia, etc., p. 78; Still, William, Underground Railroad, XXXV.
21. William Still, The Underground Railroad, (Philadelphia: Porter & Coates,) 1872. Preface.

Chapter 19

1. Alberta S. Norwood, Negro Welfare Work in Philadelphia, etc., p. 78; Still, William, The Underground Rail Road, XXXV; ibid. pp. 78-9, Appendix 16A; John Hunn, Beaufort, South

Carolina, 19 October 1871, to William Still, Philadelphia; 16B; ibid; 21 November 1871.

2. William Still, The Underground Rail Road (Philadelphia: Porter & Coates), 1872. Title page.
3. Ibid; Appendix 1B; Dedication.
4. Ibid; Appendix 1C; Frontispiece. Signed photograph of William Still.
5. Ibid; Appendix 1D; Preface, pp. 1-6.
6. Ibid; Appendix 1E. List of Illustrations. pp. 7-8.
7. Ibid; 1F; pp.613-780.
8. Ibid; Contents. pp. 9-10.
9. Ibid; pp. 23-38; Seth Concklin.
10. Ibid; pp. 39-44; Underground Railroad letters. pp. 39-44.
11. Ibid; p. 39: Thomas Garrett, (U.G.R.R. Depot), Wilmington, 23 March 1856 to William Still.
12. Ibid; pp. 30-40; Miss Grace Anna Lewsi (U.G.R.R. Depot), Kimberton, 28 October 1855 to William Still.
13. Ibid; p. 748-49.
14. Ibid; p. 689.
15. Ibid: William Still, Philadelphia, 24 November 1855 to E.F. Pennypacker, Phoenixville, Pennsylvania. Friends Historical Society, Swarthmore, Pennsylvania.
16. Ibid; 2 November 1857.
17. Ibid; Ibid; 6 November 1858.
18. Ibid; 20 November 1858.
19. Ibid. p. 40: E.L. Stevens, Esq., Wash., D.C., 11 July 1858 to William Still.
20. Ibid; pp. 40-1; S.H. Gay, Esq., New York, 17 August 1855 to William Still.
21. Ibid; p. 41; John H. Hill, Hamilton, Ontario, 15 September 1856 to William still.
22. Ibid; p. 41; J. Bigelow, Esq., Wash. D.C., 22 June 1854 to William still.
23. Ibid; Ham & Eggs, a slave, (U.G.R.R. Agn't,) Petersburg, Virginia, 17 October 1860 to William Still.
24. Ibid; (U. G.R.R.) Professor C.D. Cleveland, Agn't.) p. 42; St. Catharines C. W. July 1855 to William Still.

25. Ibid; p. 43. Joseph C. Bustill, Harrisburg (U.G.R.R., Depot). 24 March 1856 to William Still.
26. Ibid; p. 43; Letter from a slave in Richmond, 18 October 1860 to William Still.
27. Ibid; p. 44; John Thompson, A fugitive to his mother, 6 Jeny, to William Still.
28. Ibid; pp. 44-45; "Wm. Penn" (of the bar), Wash., D.C., 9 December to William still.
29. Ibid; p. 81-6; Henry Box Brown.
30. Ibid; pp. 723-34. Prof. C.D. Cleveland.
31. Ibid; pp. 51-4. Death of Romulus Hall.
32. Ibid; pp. 368-77. William and Ellen Craft.
33. Ibid; pp. 86-97. Jane Johnson.
34. Ibid; pp. 296-99. Harriet Tubman.
35. J.M. McKim, New York City to William Still, Antislavery Office at Philadelphia, 10 November 1871. Bruce Catty Papers, New York Public Library.
36. Alberta S. Norwood, Negro Work in Philadelphia, etc., p. 69; Still, William, The Underground Railroad, XXVI.
37. Ibid; Information given by Miss Frances E. Still, the younger sister of Dr. Caroline Still Wiley Anderson.

Chapter 20.

1. Still, William, Journal of Fugitive Slaves who Passed Through station 2 of The Underground Railroad (1852-1857), The Pennsylvania Society for Promoting The Abolition of Slavery, etc., Minutes (1775-1787).
2. William Lloyd Garrison, Roxbury, Massachusetts, 7 April 1872 to William Still, Philadelphia. Peter Still Papers, Rutgers.
3. William Still, *The Underground Rail Road,* Contents; P.64.
4. Ibid; p. 68.
5. Ibid; p. 97
6. Ibid; p. 154.
7. Ibid; p. 240
8. Ibid; p. 250.
9. William Still, Preface, The *Underground Rail Road* (Philadelphia: Peoples' Publishing Co., 1878. 2nd ed., xviii.

10. Ibid; (Medford, New Jersey: Plexus) 2005. 5th. Ed., also, Preface to the 2nd Edition, xvii.
11. Ibid; William Still, *Still's Underground Railroad Records,* Philadelphia: by William Still,) 1883. 3rd. ed., Biographical Sketch of William Still, by William P. Boyd.
12. Ibid; Preface. *The Underground Rail Road,* (Medford, New Jersey; Plexus), 2005; 3rd. ed.
13. Alberta S. Norwood, p.67. Still, William, *Underground Rail Road.* LVIII.
14. Ibid; pp.67-68. Ibid; Appendix 9C; 9D; and, 9E.
15. Ibid; p.68. ibid ; LVIII.
16. Ibid; LIX.
17. Ibid; LIX. First Annual Report of the Home for Aged and Infirm Colored Persons, I.
18. Ibid: 14.
19. Ibid: pp. 68-9; William Still The Underground Railroad, LIX; Recollections of Miss Frances E. Still. Appendix 10.
20. Ibid; p. 69. Appendix 11.
21. Ibid; Constitution, "By-Laws, and Rules of the Home for Aged and Infirm Colored Persons, Seventh Annual Report. 17, Newspaper clippings the Seventh Report at the Old Folks Home opposite 17; Ninth Annual Report, 7.
22. Ibid; p. 69; Seventh Annual Report of the Home for Aged and Infirm Colored persons, 6.
23. Ibid; Appendix 12.
24. Ibid pp.69-70. Still, William, Underground Railroad, LIX .
25. Ibid; LX.
26. Ibid; Recollections Rev. Henry L. Phillips.
27. Ibid; Still, William, Underground Railroad, LX.
28. Ibid; pp. 70-71. Original record from which The Underground Railroad was written.
29. Ibid; p. 71. Ledger in possession of Miss Frances Ellen Still.
30. Ibid; Still, William, The Underground Railroad, XXX.
31. Ibid; Appendix 14.
32. Ibid; pp. 71-2. Still, William, The Underground Railroad, XXXI.

33. Ibid; p. 72. Ibid; XXXI. Appendix 15A; 15B; Letter from the office of *The Nation.*
34. Ibid; *American Literature, The Cambridge History of,* Part 2, 1920, 326.
35. Ibid; pp. 72-4. Still, William, The Underground Railroad, LIX.
36. Ibid; P. 74. Ibid; LIX.
37. Ibid; Recollections of Miss Frances E. Still.
38. Ibid: pp. 74-5. Ledger in possession of Miss Frances E. Still.
39. Ibid; p. 75. Recollections of Miss Frances E. Still.

Chapter 21.

1. John Hope Franklin, *Reconstruction : After the Civil War* (Chicago: University of Chicago Press), 1994. 2nd. Ed. P. 1-4; p. 36. Ibid; p.4.
2. Alberta S. Norwood, Negro Welfare Work in Philadelphia, etc., p. 80; 17A; 17B.
3. Ibid; p.89- 81. Copies of letters sent out by William still; Letters from various agents throughout the country. Now in possession of Miss Frances E. Still.
4. Ibid; p. 81. Also Appendix 18A; 18B.
5. Ibid; Letters from the collection of William Still.
6. Ibid; p. 82. Appendix 19.
7. Ibid; p. 82. Still, William, The Underground Railroad., 785.
8. Ibid; Executive Committee- the Pennsylvania Abolition Society, Minutes Book, 4, 85.
9. Ibid; Appendix 20.
10. Ibid; Appendix 21A; 21B.
11. Ibid; p. 85. The *Philadelphia Press,* 18 February 1874.
12. Ibid; Still, William, The Underground Railroad, LXI. Pictures in possession of Miss Frances E. Still; Recollections of Rev. Henry L. Phillips, and many other persons; The Philadelphia *Press* , 1 April 1867.
13. Ibid; pp. 85-6. Still, William, The Underground Railroad, LXI.
14. Ibid; p. 86. Still, William, An Address on Voting and Laboring- Delivered by William Still at Concert Hall, Philadelphia, 1874..

In possession of Miss Frances E. Still; Also in the Moorland-Spingarn Collection, Washington, D.C.

15. Ibid; p. 86-7. Still, William, An Address on Voting and laboring, I.
16. Ibid; p. 87. The *Philadelphia Press*, 11 March 1874, The *North American and United States Gazette*, 11 March 1874.
17. Ibid; pp. 87-8. Still, William, An Address on Voting and Laboring, 5.
18. Ibid; p. 88. 7.
19. Ibid; p. 89. 16.
20. Ibid; pp. 89-90. Appendix 23A; 23B; 23C; 23D; 23E; 23F; 23G.
21. Ibid; p. 90. Still, William, An Address on Voting and laboring.
22. Ibid; Recollections of Rev. Henry L. Phillips.
23. Ibid; *National cyclopedia of American Biography,* Vol. 6, 195.
24. Ibid; 195.
25. Ibid; p.91. Recollections of rev. Henry L. Phillips.
26. Ibid; N*ational Cyclopedia* Vol. 6; *Public Ledger*, 5 April 1881.
27. Ibid; Recollections of Rev. Henry L. Phillips.
28. Ibid; *National Cyclopedia,* Vol. 6, 195, 196.

Chapter 22.

1. William Still, *The Underground Rail Road,* pp. 611-12.
2. Irv. Brendlinger, *"Anthony Benezet: The True Champion of the Slave"http://www.Wesley.nnu.ed/wesleyan_*Theology/theo jan/31-35/32-1-7.html
3. Thomas Clarkson, "Against Slavery and the Slave trade" http://www.spartacus. Schoolnet.co.uk/Reclarkson.html
4. William Wilberforce, http://bbc.co.uk/historic figures/wilber force William
5. Thomas Fowell Buxton, "Evangelical from Great Britain. Dictionary of African Christian Biography. http://www.spartacus,schoolnet.co.uk/ Refowell.html
6. William Still, *The Underground Rail Road,* p. 593
7. Ibid; pp. 593-95.
8. Ibid; pp. 595-97.

9. Ibid; pp. 597-98.
10. Ibid; pp. 601-02.
11. "The Black Abolitionist Papers, Vol. I: The British Isles, 1830-1865, Edited by C. Peter Ripley. 24. Pages. The University of North Carolina Press. 85 "Speech by Martin R. Delany," delivered at City Hall, Glasgow, Scotland, 23 October 1860.
12. William Still, *The Underground Rail Road*, pp. 603-08.
13. The Concise Columbia Encyclopedia, 2nd. Ed., (New York: Columbia University press) 1889, p. 296.
14. David P. Currie, *The Constitution and the Congress*, 1829-1861, p. 170.
15. Alberta S. Norwood, Negro Welfare Work in Philadelphia, etc; pp. 75-6. Still, William, The Underground Railroad, LX; Recollections of Miss Frances Ellen Still.
16. Ibid; p. 76. Still, William, The Underground Railroad. LXI.
17. William Lloyd Garrison, 5 March 1875, Roxbury, Massachusetts, to William Still, Philadelphia.
18. "Friends and Fellow Laborers", 14 April 1875, The Friends Historical Library of Swarthmore, Pennsylvania. The Mott MSS, undated.
19. John Hope Franklin, Reconstruction After the Civil War, (Chicago: University of Chicago press, 1994), 1st. Ed. Citations taken from the 1991 ed.
20. Ibid;
21. Ibid; p. 211.

Chapter 23

1. The Concise Columbia Encyclopedia, 2nd. Ed. P. 169.
2. Norwood, Alberta S., Negro Welfare Work in Philadelphia, etc., p.99. Minutes Book 41, 95
3. Ibid; pp. 99-100. Minutes Book 4, p. 85.
4. Ibid; Book 3, 327.
5. Ibid; p. 100, 330.
6. Ibid; pp. 100-01. Manuscript History, Book 3, 340.
7. Ibid; p. 101. Appendix 25.
8. Ibid; p. pp.101-02. Manuscript History, Book 3, 340.
9. Ibid; pp. 72-4. Still, William, Underground Railroad, LIX.

10. Ibid; p.74. LIX.
11. Ibid; Recollections of Miss Frances E. Still.
12. Ibid; pp. 74-5. In possession of Miss Frances E. Still.
13. Ibid; pp. 91-2. Still, William, An Address on Voting and Laboring, 4.
14. Ibid; p. 92. Case in possession of Miss Frances E. Still.
15. Ibid; Still, William, Underground Railroad, LXIII. Recollections of Miss Frances E. Still.
16. Ibid; Recollections of Miss Frances E. Still.
17. Ibid.
18. Russell B. Nye, *William Lloyd Garrison and The Humanitarian Reformers*, (Boston: Little brown & Company, 1995), p. 105.
19. Ibid; p. 106.
20. Theodore D. Weld, *American Slavery As It Is: A Testimony of a Thousand Witnesses,* (The American Antislavery Office, Nassau Street, 1839.)
21. Russell B. Nye, *William Lloyd Garrison and the Humanitarian Reformers* , p. 111.
22. Ibid; pp. 62-3.
23. Ibid; pp. 41-2.
24. Ibid' p. 43.
25. Ibid; pp. 106-07.
26. Ibid; pp. 123-27.
27. Ibid; p. 129.
28. Ibid; pp. 130-31.
29. James McKim, Syracuse, May 1843 to Samuel J, May, 19:17. The Samuel J. May Papers in the William Lloyd Garrison papers, Boston Public Library.
30. A Declaration of Sentiments. The Women's Rights Convention held at Seneca Falls, New York, 19 July 1848.
31. Samuel J. May. The Rights and Conditions of Women, Sermon delivered at Syracuse, New York, November 1845. 3rd. ed. In a series of tracts printed by J.E. Masters. No. 20; Malcolm Block, Boston, Massachusetts. Boston Public Library.
32. Wendell Phillips, Esq., Women's Tracts No. 2. Speech given at the Convention held at Worcester, Massachusetts, 15, 16 October 1851.

33. Ibid; letter from Abby Kelley Foster.
34. Ibid; Letter from Harriet Martineau, 16 October 1851.
35. Ibid; Harriott Kezia Hunt, M.D., (Difficulties for Women to get a Proper Medical Education in Boston,) 15 October 1851.
36. Convention on Women's Rights, held at Syracuse, New York; Letter from Angelina Grimke Weld, 1852. Women's Rights Tract No. 8.
37. Convention on Women's' Rights, held at Worcester, Massachusetts, 1850. Syracuse, New York, September 1852. Women's' Rights tract No. 10.
38. Ibid.

Chapter 24.

1. William Still, *The Underground Rail Road* (Medford, New Jersey; Plexus Publishing Company, 2005), Still, William, Preface to the 1878 edition, Philadelphia, xvii.
2. Ibid; xviii.
3. John Hope Franklin, *Reconstruction: After The Civil War* (Chicago: University of Chicago Press, 1961), p. 38. Hereafter *Reconstruction.*
4. Wendell Phillips, To The Freedmen! Boston, Massachusetts, 16 July 1865. William Lloyd Garrison Papers, Boston Public Library.
5. John Hope Franklin, *Reconstruction,* p. 38.
6. Caroline Still (Anderson), (1864-1868). Necropsy for the year 1919-1920. Archives of Oberlin College, Oberlin, Ohio. (1848-1919).
7. Frances Ellen Still, (1874-1876), sister of Caroline Still (Anderson). Archives, Oberlin College, Oberlin, Ohio. (1857-1944).
8. Facts on the History of Oberlin College, Oberlin, Ohio- http://en.wikipedia.org/wiki/Oberlin_college.
9. Lincoln University, Langston Hughes memorial Library. Archives, William Wilberforce Still, and Robert George Still.
10. Ibid.
11. Oberlin College, Oberlin, Ohio. http://en.wikipedia.org/wiki/Oberlin _college.

12. Caroline Virginia Still Anderson. Material taken from the Alumnae Folder, Archives and Special Collection on Women in Medicine. Women's' Medical College of Pennsylvania, Philadelphia, Pennsylvania.
13. Sterling M. Lloyd, Assoc. Dean for Administration and Planning., (May 2006), A Short History of Howard University College of medicine.
14. http://www.med.howard.edu/nuHoward University/history.html.
15. Rachel L. Bodley, Dean, Twenty-Eighth Annual Announcement of the Women's Medical College of Pennsylvania, Philadelphia. Session of 1877-1878. (Philadelphia; Grant, Faires & Rodgers, 1877.)
16. History of the Women's medical College, Philadelphia, Pennsylvania 1850-1950. Reviewed by Mary Louise Marshall. http://www.pubmedcentral_nih.gov,pagerender.fegi?artid==195126&pageindex=1. Book reviews and Journal Notes; Alsop P. Guielma Fell, *History of the Women's Medical College of Pennsylvania,* Philadelphia 1850-1950 (Philadelphia: J.B. Lippincott, 1950).
17. Ibid; Emily Barringer Dunning, *Bowery to Bellevue: The Story of New York's First Woman Ambulance Surgeon* New York: W.W. Norton & Co., Inc. 1950).
18. Arnold J. Toynbee, *A Study of History:* Abridgement of Vols. I-VI, by D.C. Somervall (New York: Oxford University Press, 1960). Pp. 402-03.
19. William Still, *The Underground Rail Road* . p. 697.
20. Drexel University College of medicine, The medical College of Pennsylvania, p.11. http://www.drexelmed.edu/Alumni/colleges/ medical college of Pennsylvania/tabid/1086/D...4/30/08.
21. Drexel University College of medicine. http://en.wikipedia.org/wiki/Drexel_University_college_of_medicine.
22. Female Medical College & Homeopathic Medical College of Pennsylvania. Presented by Sylvain Cazalet. http://homeoint.org/cazelet/histopennsyfem.html. pp. 1-7. Homeopathic medical College of Pennsylvania.

23. Ibid; pp. 7-11.
24. Ibid; pp. 11-13.
25. Ibid; pp. 13-21.
26. Caroline Still Wiley (Anderson). The Archives on the Special Collection on Women in Medicine. The Women's Medical College of Pennsylvania, Philadelphia, Pennsylvania.

Chapter 25.

1. American Renaissance News: Race and the American Identity. http://www.com/mthews/archives?July30/2000/02/race_and_am_phP
2. Negro Women Internes. New England Hospital Collection, Folder 26. May-GoddardAmes Collecton. History of Women in Medicine- Box1-2. Schlesinger Library on the History of Women, Radcliffe Institute for Advanced Study, Harvard University, Cambridge, MA; Sophia Smith Collection on the History of Women, (New England Hospital Collection). Box7, Folder 26. Smith College, Northampton, MA.
3. New England Hospital Report for the Year Ending 30 September 1879. Box 2. Sophia Smith Collection.
4. Ibid; Negro Women Internes, 1846-1911. Folder 26, Box 7.
5. FOCUS, 29 October 2004. School History Book Forum Recognize Achievement of African Americans at HMS. http:// focus/hms.harvard. edu/2004/Oct_29_2004_/school_history.html. pp. 1-2; A Broad Foundation.http://www.countway.harvard.edu/chm/rarebooks/exhibits/broad_foundation.7/21/08. P.8.
6. Alumni Roll, 1872. Entry no. 2002. James Thomas Still, M.D. , 1871; Catalogue of the Harvard Medical School, Vol.2, 1855-1871. The Harvard Medical School's Countway Library of Medicine, Boston, MA.
7. Francis Harrington, M.D., A History, Narrative, and Documentary-1792-1905, (N.Y.1905). Countway Library of medicine.
8. Harry K. Beecher, M.D., and Marc Altschuler, M.D., Medicine At Harvard (Hanover, NH: University of New England press, 1977). P. 991.

9. Ibid; pp.991-992.
10. Ibid; 1044.
11. Ibid.
12. Henry Charlton Beck, The Roads of Home: Lanes and Legends of New Jersey."Forgotten Towns of New Jersey." (New Brunswick, NewJersey : Rutgers, 1983). p.138.
13. James Still, Early Recollections and Life. pp. 117-120.
14. African American History Timeline: 1800-1900/ The Blackpast remembered and R... http:/www.blackpast.org/?=timelines-african-american-history-timeline-1800-1900. pp. 13-15.
15. William Still 1821-1902. Capabilities of Colored Men. Appendix D. National Conference of Colored men, the proceedings of "Opportunities and capabilities of Educated Negroes," read at Fisk University, Nashville, TN, 6,7,8,9, May, 1879. P.56. Dictionary of the Arthur Spingarn catalogue of the Collection of Negro Authors, Vol.2, L-Z.; also (Boston: G.K. Hall &Co.,).
16. Ibid p.57.
17. Ibid. pp.57-58.

Chapter 26.

1. William Still, Opportunities and Capabilities of Educated Negroes. Appendix D. pp. 56-65., Conference of Colored men, Nashville. Proceedings of the National Conference of Colored men in the The United States, held in the Capitol at Nashville, Tennessee, May 6,7,8,9, 1879. (Washington, D.C.: Rufus H. Darby, 1879). 107pp. Catalogue of the Arthur B. Spingarn, Collection of Negro Authors. Howard University, Washington, D.C.
2. Ibid.
3. Ibid.
4. Ibid.
5. Ibid.
6. Ibid. pp. 58-9.
7. Ibid; pp. 59-60.
8. Ibid; p. 60.
9. Ibid; pp.60-62.
10. Ibid; pp.62-64.

11. Ibid; pp.64-65.

Chapter 27.

1. James Still, *Early Recollections and Life of Dr. James Still* 1812-1882 (Medford, New Jersey: Medford Historical Society, 1971) Facsimile ed.pp.3-9. Original edition self published (Philadelphia: J.B. Lippincott, 1877).
2. Ibid; pp.250-264.
3. Ibid; p.265.
4. J.T. Still, *Boston Evening Transcript.* Monday 24 June 1895. Obit.
5. Annual Report of the School Committee, Boston. 1875 (Boston: Rockwell & Churchill Printers), 1875.
6. Ibid.
7. Ibid.1876.
8. Ibid; 1877.
9. Ibid; 1878. Document No. 25.
10. Ibid.
11. *Boston Evening Transcript,* 24 June 1895. Boston Street addresses of Dr. James Still.
12. Commonwealth of Massachusetts Archives and Division of Vital Records. B-1021 Birth Record of Henrietta Eliza Still, 10 March 1876. Parents: James T. Still, Boston, father; Elizabeth Still,Philadelphia, mother.
13. Probate Court of Massachusetts, in and for the County of Suffolk, Boston, MA. Vol.729- P. 482. Minor children of Elizabeth and James T. Still, M.D living in Boston, MA on April 1897.
14. William Still, *The Underground Rail Road* (Philadelphia: Porter& Coates, 1872) 1. 1st. ed., Preface, pp. 1-6.
15. William Still, *The Underground Rail Road.*(Medford, N.J.: Plexus Publishing Company 2005) 3rd. ed. Preface. pp. xvii-xxiii.
16. Ibid.
17. Alberta S. Norwood, Negro Welfare Work in Philadelphia. p. 93. Anderson, Matthew,*Presbyterianism: its Relation to the Negro.* 6.

18. Ibid; 16.
19. Ibid; pp.93-94; Anderson, Matthew, Presbyterianism, 17.
20. Ibid; pp.94; 24.
21. Ibid; pp.94-95; Anderson, Matthew, Presbyterianism, 242.
22. Ibid; p. 95. 245.
23. Ibid; p.96. Memorial service to John McGill- late Treasurer of the Berean Building and Loan Association, 28, 29.
24. Ibid; p. 96. Information from Miss Frances Ellen Still and Mr. Basil Wood, Secretary.
25. Professor Joe Lockhard, "William Still and Philadelphia's African American Underground Railroad," presented at Temple University's English Department, 23 February 2005.P.16; Lurey Khan *One Day Levin...He Be Free*, (New York: E.P. Dutton, 1972).
26. Norwood, Negro Welfare Work in Philadelphia. pp. 96-97. Recollections of Rev. Phillips.
27. Ibid.

Chapter 28.

1. Arnold Toynbee, *A Study of History* (New York: Oxford University Press:1946). P. 402.
2. Ibid; pp.402-403.
3. Church and Community: The Berean Enterprise. http://www.history. Pecusa.org/exhibits/berean/index.html. p.1.
4. Minutes of the Forty-Fourth Annual Report of the Woman's Medical College of Pennsylvania. p.11- 12.
5. Aetna: African American History Calender:1998: Caroline V. Still Anderson. http://www. Aetna. com 6. African Americans-Caroline Still Wiley Anderson. http://www.africanamericans.com/caroline still, html.
7. Ibid; p.2.
8. Church and Community: The Berean Enterprise. Index 2, html. P.1.
9. Ibid; index 3. Html. P.1.
10. Ibid; p.2.
11. Caroline Virginia Still, (1848-1919). Necrology. Archives and Special Collections, Oberlin College, Oberlin, Ohio

12. Darlene Clark Hine, *Co-laborers in the Work of the Lord: Nineteenth Century Black Women Physicians.* Send Us a Lady Physician Women Doctors in America, 1835-1920. Ed. Ruth J. Abram (New York: WW Norton, 1985). P.111; Matthew Anderson, Presbyterianism: Its Relation to The Negro (Philadelphia: John Magill, White, and Co., 1899).
13. Helen Anderson (Still) Waller Papers, The Samuel Paley Endowment Fund. Rare Books and Manuscripts, Collections department. Temple University, Feb.1985, No. 1. Cases 1-2 Still Family, william Still.
14. Ibid; Dr.James Still.
15. Ibid: Case3. Anderson-Still Family. Caroline Still.
16. Lincoln University-Archives. William and Daniel Anderson., Lincoln University, West Chester, Pennsylvania.
17. Ibid; Case 4. Anderson-Still Family.
18. Ibid.; Case 1-2. Still Family, William Still.
19. Recollections of Lurey Khan.
20. James Still, *Early Recollections and Life of Dr. James Still,* (Medford, New Jersey: Medford Historical Society, 1971) Facsimile edition. "The Doctor of the Pines", p.vii; Henry Charlton Beck, *Forgotten Towns of Southern New Jersey,* (New Brunswick, N.J.: Rutgers) 1985. pp 138-163.
21. Catalogue of the Children of Levin and Charity Still, Peter Still Papers. Rutgers, New Brunswick.
22. Ibid; James and Henrietta Still.
23. Recollections of Lurey Khan.
24. Ibid.
25. Ibid.
26. Ibid.
27. Frank W.H. Convery, Feature Articles on the life of James Still, part 2. Mt. Holly, New Jersey Herald, (Thursday 11 January 1862).
28. Margery Cridland, Historical Sketch, in *Early Recollections and Life of James Still* (Medford, New Jersey: Medford Historical Society,1971).pp. v-viii.
29. Ibid; Henry Charlton Beck, *Forgotten Towns of Southern New Jersey. p.v2.*

30. Ibid; E.M. Woodward,*Woodward and Hagerman's History of Burlington and Mercer Counties, p. viii.* Photo of James Still's office. In the Mt.Holly, N.J Library.
31. Ibid; Stephen O'Keefe, feature article in the Camden-Courier Post (May 20 1971).p. viii.
32. Ibid; Lester King, M.D., "For the Social Historian the Book Presents Vividly , the Picture of Poverty in Rural New Jersey. JAMA April 1972.p. viii.

Chapter 29.

1. James T. Still, M.D. "Uncle Sam's Reverie!" or "What Shall be Done With the Pickininnies?" A Humorous Lecture. Under a different cover, the same text appears as: "Don't Tell White Folks," or "Light Out of Darkness." (West cedar St., Boston, Mass., 1889).
2. Ibid; dedication.
3. Ibid; Preface.
4. Ibid; p. 8.
5. Ibid; p. 10.
6. Ibid; pp. 11-12.
7. Ibid; pp. 12-14.
8. Ibid; pp. 14-16.
9. Ibid; pp. 18-20.
10. Ibid; p. 21.
11. Ibid; p. 29.
12. Ibid; pp. 30-31.
13. J.T. Still, M.D., Opinion in *The Afro-American press And Its Editors* (Springfield, Mass: Willey & Co., Publishers, 1891).
14. Ibid; p. 454.
15. *Boston Evening Transcript,* Obituary of J.T. Still, M.D., 24 June 1895.
16. Cedar Grove Cemetery , 920 Adams Street, Dorchester, Mass. Oak Hill section, Range H., Grave No. 12.
17. Suffolk County probate Court of Massachusetts, Boston, Mass., petition for the Guardianship of Mrs. Elizabeth Still, for Wendell Phillips and Mary Elizabeth Still. Vol. 729, p. 482, 29 April 1897.

18. Ibid; Administration of the estate of Dr. J.T. Still, by his wife, Elizabeth486. 11 March 1897.
19. Ibid; Petition No. 10430 entered by Mrs. Elizabeth Still.
20. Ibid; Notice of the Administration of the estate of Dr. J.T. Still, Vol. 727, 7 March 1897. Address of Mrs. Elizabeth still given as 15 Mount Vernon street, Boston, mass.

Chapter 30.

1. http://en.wikipedia.org/wiki/Fourteenth_Amendment_to_the_United_Stat. http://en./wikisource.org/wiki/Civil_Rights_Act_of_1866
2. Specie payment (American finance)—Britannica Online Encyclopedia.http://www.britannica.Com/eb/topic_5586471/specie-payment.
3. Ian Haney Lopez, *White By Law: The Legal Construction of Race,* 10th Anniversary updated edition (New York: New York University press,2006).p.28; Charles Gordon, and Stanley Mailman, Immigration Law and Procedures SS 92.03 [1],[b] (rev.ed.1992).
4. Ibid; p.29. Dred Scott v Sanford, 60 U.S. (19 How.) 393 (1857). For an insightful role of the development of American citizenship, see James Kettner, The Development of American citizenship, 1680-1870,at 300-333 (1978); see also Kenneth L. Karst, Belonging to America: Equal Citizenship and the Constitution 43 61 (1989).
5. Ibid; Civil Rights Act of 1866, ch.31, 14 Stat. 27.
6. Ibid; U.S. Const. amend.XIV.
7. Ibid; 169 U.S. 649 (1898).
8. Ibid; 112 U.S. 94 (1884).
9. William Still, *Underground Rail Road Records* (Philadelphia: 1883) with A Biographical Sketch of William Still: His Life Work to This Time by James P. Boyd.
10. Wayne E. Homan, P1.The Underground Railroad. Historical Society of Berk's County- The Underground Railroad http://www.berkshistory.org/articles/underground.html.
11. Ibid; Siebert, Wilbur H. *Mysteries of Ohio's Underground Railroad,* Columbus, Ohio: Long's College Bookstore Co.,

1951; *The Underground Railroad Railroad: From Slavery To Freedom* (New York: MacMillan Co., 1898); *The Underground Railroad in Massachusetts,*Proceedings of the American Antiquarian Society, Vo. 45 (April 17, 1935); *Vermont's Anti-Slavery and Underground Railroad Record.* Simmons, William J. *Men of Mark: Eminent progressive and Rising* ,Cleveland :M. Rewell & Co., 1887; Smedley, Robert C. *History of the Underground Railroad in Chester and the neighboring Counties of Pennsylvania,* Lancaster, PA: Office of the Journal, 1883.

12. Larry Gara , *The Liberty Line The Legend of the Underground Railroad* (Lexington, Kentucky: University of Kentucky Press, 1961). P.177; Wilber H. Siebert, *"The Underground Railroad in Michigan", Detroit Historical Monthly 1:10 (March 1923).* An article on Underground Railroad routes.
13. Frederick Douglass to Wilbur H. Siebert, 27 March 1893 *"The Underground Railroad in Mass. & N.Y."* MSS 116, Box 96. Siebert Manuscript Collection, Scrapbook of the Siebert Papers in the Archives- Library Division, Ohio Historical Society, Columbus, Ohio.
14. Ibid; William Still to Wilbur H. Siebert, 18 November 1893. "The Underground Railroad in Pennsylvania, Vol. 3." MSS 116, Box 118. The Ohio Historical Society
15. Wilbur H. Siebert, *The Underground Railroad: From Slavery to Freedom* (New York: Macmillan, 1998) reprint of orig. 1898 text by Siebert. (New Pratt Free Library, Baltimore, Maryland. http://www.exfl.net//sec/afam/undergrail.html.
16. Wayne E. Homan *The Underground Railroad in Berk's County.* P.1-2. The Historical Society of Berk's County.
17. Ibid; p.2. Smedley, Robert C., *History of the Underground Railroad in Chester and the Neighboring Counties of Pennsylvania.* Lancaster, PA; Office of the Journal, 1883.
18. Larry Gara, *The Liberty Line: The Legend of the Underground Railroad* (Lexington, KY: University of Kentucky Press). pp. 85-86; p.174.

19 William Still, Philadelphia, to S.L. Cratty, 27 March 1885 A request for Still's autograph for him" to be enrolled with the

letters of some of the noblest and bravest abolitionists." in The John Edward Bruce Papers. Schomberg Center for Research in Black Culture, Lenox Avenue, New York City.

20. Ibid; Dear Friends and Fellow Laborers on the Fiftieth Anniversary of the American Anti-Slavery Society," 14 April 1875. Signed Lucretia Mott, et al Friends Historical Library, Swarthmore College, Swarthmore, Pennsylvania.
21. Grace Anna Lewis, Media, Pennsylvania, 7 January 1898, to William Still, Pennsylvania. Pennsylvania Historical Society, Philadelphia.
22. William Still, Philadelphia to John Edward Bruce, 1 August 1893. Request for a copy of Frances [Ellen Watkins} Harper's *Iola Leroy, or Shadows Uplifted.* Phila., Garriques Brothers, 1892. Bruce-Cratty Papers. Schomberg Center for Research in Black Culture, Lenox Avenue, New York City

Afterword.

The Passing of William Still and the Underground Railroad.

1. *Appleton's Annual Cyclopedia* 1902-1903, pp. 490-98; William Still. Cragman, W.J., *The Colored American*, 1902.
2. B.W. Austin, Dallas, Texas, to William Still, Philadelphia, 19 December 1888. Garrison Papers, Boston Public Library.
3. William Still to B.W. Austin, Dallas, Texas, ? December 1888; Ibid.
4. Alberta S. Norwood, Negro Welfare Work in Philadelphia, etc., p. 102; Manuscript History, Book 3, 344.
5. Ibid; Letters to William Still, Appendix 26A, B, C, D, E, F. pp. 176-180.
6. Ibid; Appendix 27, pp. 182-3. Booker T. Washington, Tuskegee Normal School for Training Colored Teachers, to William Still, Philadelphia, 30 December 1888.
7. Ibid; Appendix 28A, B, C., pp. 184-86. Letters to William Still.
8. Ibid; 29, p. 187. C.J. Gibbons to William Still 18 March 1889.
9. Minutes of the Pennsylvania Anti-Slavery Society 1847-1916. The Pennsylvania Historical Society.

10. Alberta S. Norwood Negro Welfare Work in Philadelphia, etc., p. 102; Appendix 31, pp. 188-89. Still et al to William McKinley, president of the United States, 29 June 1889.
11. Ibid; pp. 102-03.
12. Ibid: 103.
13. Recollection of Lurey Khan to the gravesite of William, Letitia, and Frances E. Still, at the Eden cemetery in June 2006.
14. *Who Was Who in America, 1897-1902.*
15. *Journal of Pennsylvania History.* The Pennsylvania Historical Society, Philadelphia, Pennsylvania. John Coleman, editor. "William Still and the Underground Railroad", Gara, Larry, Vol. xviii, No. 1. (Jan. 1961) Easton, Pennsylvania.
16. *Dictionary of American Negro Biography*, Villard, Harold G., "William Still 1821-1902. Part 2:22-3; 1935-1936.
17. The Medford Historical Society, Church Road, Medford, New Jersey. Information re the addition of the office of James Still in the State of New Jersey and the National Register of Historical Sites.

BIBLIOGRAPHY.

Alsop, Guilema Fell, M.D. *History of the Women's Medical College of Pennsylvania,* 1850-1950. Philadelphia: Lippincott, 1950.

American National Biography. "William Still." VXX: 775-76. Drexel University College of Medicine. The medical College of Pennsylvania: Philadelphia.

Anderson, Matthew. *Presbyterianism: Its Relation to the Negro.* Philadelphia: John Magill White and Company.

Annual Reports of the New England Hospital for Women and Children, 1862-1967. Sophia Smith Collection. Smith College, Northampton, MA.

Annual Reports of the Massachusetts General Hospital, 1875-1901. Countway Library of Medicine, Harvard Medical School, Boston, MA.

AnnuaL Reports of the School Committee of the City of Boston. Boston: Rockwell & Churchill, 1875-1878.

Apolonia, Thornton. Boston Public Schools. *Past and Present with Some Reflections on Their Characteristics.* Boston: Wright & Potter, 1923.

Bacon, Benjamin. *"Statistics of the Colored People of Philadelphia."* Published per the Order of the Board of Education of the Pennsylvania Abolition Society , 1859. Historical Society of Pennsylvania, Philadelphia.

Beck, Henry Charleton. *The Roads of Home: Lanes and Legends of New Jersey.* New Brunswick, NJ: Rutgers University Press, 1983.

Beecher, Harry K M.D., and Altschuler, Marc, M.D. *Medicine at Harvard.* Hanover, NH: The University Press of New England, 1977.

Beltz, Herman, ed. *The Webster-Hayne Debate on The nature of The Union Selected Documents.* Indianapolis: Liberty Fund, Inc., 2000.

Bentley, Judith, *"Dear Friend," Thomas Garrett and William Still" Collaborators on the Underground Railroad,* New York: Dutton, 1997.

Bibliography of the Negro in Africa and America. "William Still and the Underground Railroad." 1st. ed. New York: Farrar, Strauss, and Giroux, 1928. Reprint. Tuskegee, Alabama: Tuskegee Institute, 1970.

Blackwell, Elizabeth. *Pioneer Work in the Opening of the Medical Profession to Women.* New York: Dutton, 1895

Bodley, Rachel., A.M., M.D. The College Story." Valedictorian Address to the 29th Graduating Class of The Woman's medical College of Pennsylvania. Philadelphia: Grant, Faires, T. Rodgers, 1881

Bordewich, Fergus M. *The Underground Railroad and the War for the Soul of America.* New York: Harper Collins, 2005.

Boston School Committee 1875-1878. James T. Still M.D. In the Annual Report 1875, 1876, 1877. Boston: Rockwell & Churchill, 1875-1877.

Bowditch, N.I. *A History of the Massachusetts General Hospital* [to Aug. 1851]. 2nd. ed. With a continuation to 1872. Boston: Trustees of the Bowditch Fund, 1872.

Bowditch, Vincent Y. Editor. *Life and Correspondence of Henry Ingersoll Bowditch.* 2 Vols. Boston, 1902.1:101

Brown, Henry Box. *Narrative of the Life of Henry Box Brown.* New York: Oxford University Press, 2002.

Convery, Frank, W.H. "The Life and times of James Still." *Mt. Holly Herald* (January-February 1962).

Cook, Samuel DuBois. Understanding Negro History. "On Turner, Beard, and Slavery," Staugh to Lynde, pp.106-07. *Journal of Negro History,* XL, xiii No. 4. (October 1963), 235- 240. Ibid;Introduction to Frederick Jackson Turner, United States, 1830- 1845: *The Nation and Its Sections,* [New York, 1935], p. vii

---------. Understanding Negro History, "A Paradox,"36-39. *Journal of Negro History,* XLV, No.4 (October 1960). 219-240.P.39. Ibid; 35-6. Walter Rauschenbush, "The Christianizing of the Social Order". (New York, 1912), 418.Cook, Samuel Dubois. "A Tragic Conception of Negro History." The paradox. *J. of Negro History* XIV, no. 4 (Oct. 1950), 219-240.

---------. *Understanding Negro History.* A Tragic Conception of Negro History. The Current Situation, Progress, and tradition." Edited with commentary by Dwight D. Hoover. Chicago: Quadrangle Books, 1968.

Cowen, David L. *Medicine and Health in New Jersey: A History.* Princeton, New Jersey: Van Nostrand, 1964. (Distributed. By Rutgers University Press, New Brunswick, N.J.

Cromwell, Otelia. *Lucretia Mott.* Cambridge, MA: Harvard University Press, 1958.

Current, Richard N. *Reconstruction.* Eyewitness Acounts of American History Series- Experts on the Civil War Era. Englewood Cliffs, NJ: Prentice Hall, 1965.

Currie, David. *The Constitution in Congress* Descent Into the Maelstrom *1829-1861.* Chicago: University of Chicago Press, 2005.

Dictionary of American Biography. Edited by Dumas Malone. Vol. IX. Still, William, (7 Oct.1821-14 July 1902.) Published under the Auspices of the American Council of Learned Societies. NY: Charles Scribner's Sons, 1935-1936

Directory of Afro-American resources. State of New Jersey University Library at Rutgers, New Brunswick, N. J.

Douglass, Frederick. Letters to William H. Siebert, New York, 27 March 1893. In the Siebert Collection, Vol. 13, Mss 116, Box 96. The Ohio Historical Society, Columbus, Ohio.

Dumont, Dwight L. *A Bibliography of Antislavery in America.* Ann Arbor: University of Michigan, Press,1961.

Fehrenbacher, Don E. *The Slave-holding Republic. An Account of the United States Government's Relations to Slavery.* New York: Oxford University Press, 2000.

Ghosts of By-Gone Glories Haunt Quiet Lanes and Memories of Bastow's Old-Timers. First published in *The Newark Star Ledger,* June 22, 1947 Reprinted with permission, Transcribed by Ben Ruset.Ghost Towns, written by Henry Charlton Beck; An Introduction to the New Jersey Pine Barrens, by Ben Ruset. Flexner, Abraham. *Medical Education in the U.S. and Canada.* Carnegie Foundation for the Advancement of teaching. Bulletin 4. Carnegie Foundation, 1910.

Franklin, Benjamin. *Address to the Public, 1789.* Pennsylvania AbolitionSocietyPapers,HistoricalSocietyofPennsylvania, Philadelphia.

Franklin, Benjamin. *"The Abolition of Slavery."* An Address to the public from the Pennsylvania Society for Promoting the Abolition of Slavery, and the Relief of Free Negroes Unlawfully Held in Bondage. Read by Charles F. Jenkins, President, for Franklin, the President of the Society ,in 1787.

Franklin, John Hope. *Reconstruction: After the Civil War.* Chicago: University of Chicago Press,1961.

Gara, Larry. "William Still and The Underground Railroad." *Pennsylvania History,* Coleman, John V., editor. Vol. xxviii, No. 1. (Jan. 1961). Easton, Pennsylvania. In the *Journal of the Pennsylvania Historical Society,* Easton, PA.

--------."William Still Reformer—The Underground Railroad." *The Dictionary of Negro Biography.* New York: Norton, 1981.

---------.*The Liberty Line: The Legend of The Underground Railroad,* 1st. ed. Lexington, Kentucky: University of Kentucky Press, 1961. Repr. By publisher, (1967, 1969).

Garrison, William Lloyd Papers. Letters to William Still. Vol. 36. 13 May 1870; Vol. 37, 1 June 1871.

---------. Letter to William Still, Philadelphia 7 April 1875. Peter Still Papers, Rutgers. Also in *The Negro in New Jersey 1754-1964.* Rutgers University Library- Afro-American Resources . New Brunswick, N.J.

Gleen, Robert W. *Black Rhetoric: A Guide to African American Communications.* Metuchan, NJ: Scratecrow Press, 1976.

Hampton Institute, Collis P. Huntington Library, Hampton, VA.

Harrington, Thomas Francis, M.D. *Harvard Medical School: A History narrative, and Documentary, 1792-1905.* New York: 1905. Countway Library of Medicine, Harvard Medical School, Boston, MA.

Hendrick, George Willene, ed. With Intro. *Fleeing For freedom:* Stories of the Underground Railroad as told by Levi Coffin and William Still.Chicago : Ivan R. Dee, 2004.

Higginson, Thomas Wentworth. *Army Life in a Black Regiment,* with an Introduction by Howard Mumford Jones. Ann Arbor, MI Michigan State University Press, 1960.

Hine, Darlene Clark. *Co-Laborers in the Work of the Lord.* Nineteenth Century Black Women Physicians. South Carolina State Press: date?.

Historical Society of Pennsylvania Manuscripts, #646. William Wells Brown (1816-1884). Letters. Philadelphia, PA.

------------ Society of Pennsylvania Manuscripts. *"Social, Cultural and Statistical Association of the Colored People of Pennsylvania,"* in Afro-American resources. Philadelphia, PA.

Howard University, Washington, D.C. Library of the Moorland-Foundation. *Dictionary of the Catalogue of the Jesse E. Moorland Collection of Negro Life and History.* Boston: G.K. Hall,1970. 9v.

Hunt, Harriott K. M.D. Letter. "Taxation Without Representation." Read before the Convention held at Worcester, Massachusetts, 16 October 1851. Boston Public Library.

Hunt, Harriott K., M.D. *"Glimpses and Glances: or Fifty Years Social Including Twenty Years Professional Life."* Boston: J.P. Jewett, 1856.

Jacobi, Mary Putnam. *"Women in Medicine."* Ed. Annie Nathan Myers, *Women's Work in America,* New York: Holt, 1891.

Johnston, Rev. N.R. Beginnings of Geneva College. Milestones, Vol. 10, No. 2-Spring, 1985 Boston Public Library.

Kennett, Frances. *Folk Medicine- Fact and Fiction. Age old Cures. Alternative medicine.* "Natural Remedies." NY: Crescent Books, 1962.

King, Lester, M.D. "For the Social Historian [Dr. James Still's Book] *Presents vividly the Picture of Rural Poverty in New Jersey"* JAMA (April 1872). Countway Library of Medicine, Harvard Medical School, Boston, Ma.

Lamb, Daniel Smith. *Howard University Medical Department: An Historical, Biographical, and Statistical Souvenir.* Moorland-Spingarn Collection on Negro History. Howard University, Washington, D.C.

Library of Congress. General Reference and Bibliographic Division. Washington, D.C.

Logan, Rayford W. *Howard University. The First Hundred years, 1867-1967.* New York: New York University press, 1969

---------. and Winston, Michael R., Editors. *Dictionary of American Negro Biography.* "William Still and the Underground Railroad." Norton, 1982.

Loguen, Jermaine W. *The Rev. J.W. Loguen, As a Slave, and As a Freeman.* Syracuse: J.G.K. Truair & Co., 1859.

Lloyd, Sterling M. Associate. Dean for Administration and Planning., (May 2006). A Short History of Howard University College of Medicine.

Mann, Peggy, and Siegel, Virginia. *The Man Who Bought Himself The Story of Peter Still.* NY: MacMillan, 1975.

Massachusetts Volunteer Militia. *Military Order of Loyal Legion, 1870-1900.* James Thomas Still, M.D.-1871-1874, Surgeon. Archives in the Massachusetts State House, Boston, Ma.

May, Samuel J. *Some Reminiscences of Our Antislavery Conflict. 1st ed.* Boston, Massachusetts, 1869. Reprinted, Miami, Florida: Mnemosyne, 1969. In the Fisk Library of Negro Collections, Nashville, Tn.

----------. "The Rights and Conditions of Women." Woman's Rights Tract No. 1. Syracuse, New York, 1845. Boston: J.E. Masters, No. 20. Malcolm Block, 1853. Boston Public Library.

McPherson, James M. Abraham Lincoln and the Second American Revolution. NY: Oxford University Press, 1991.

Merrill, Walter M. ed. *The letters of William Lloyd* Garrison, Vols. 1, 3, 4. Cambridge: Harvard University press, 1971.

Miller, Randall M., and Smith, John David. *Dictionary of Afro American Slavery.* "William Still and The Underground Railroad." 707-08. NY: Greenwood Press, 1988.

National Cyclopaedia of American Biography. Vol.2. New York, 1899.

Needles, Edward, An Historical Memoir of the Pennsylvania Society for Promoting the Abolition of Slavery, the Relief of Free negroes, Unlawfully Held in Bondage, and For Improving the Condition of the African Race." Philadelphia 1848. Historical Society of Pennsylvania, Philadelphia.

New England Hospital for Women and Children, Boston, MA. *Annual Report [September 1879-1880]; included are the 1862-1967; 1875-1879.*The Sophia Smith Collection. Smith College, Northampton, MA.

-----------. Annual Report for the Year Ending 30 September 1879. West Newton: Boy's Home Press, 1879.

-----------*Fiftieth Anniversary of Boston:* George H. Ellis, 1913. May-Goddard-Ames

---------*History and Description of Boston: W. L. Orland, 1876. May-Goddard-Ames Collection. Radcliffe College, Cambridge, MA.*

-----------.Records 1859-1960s. 7 Boxes. Countway Library of Medicine. Harvard Medical School, Boston, MA.

-----------Records 1862-1908, 135 Vols. Countway Library of Medicine. Harvard Medical School, Boston, MA.

New Jersey Library Association. *New Jersey and the Negro, A Bibliography, 1715-1966.* Trenton,NJ.

New York Public Library. Schomburg Collection of Negro Literature and History-Dictionary Catalogue. Boston:

G.K. Hall, 1862. 9v. in the Guide to Reference Books, 9th ed. American Library Association, Chicago, 1876.

Norwood, Alberta S. "Negro Welfare Work in Philadelphia Especially as Illustrated by the career of William Still 1775-1930." MA Thesis. University of Pennsylvania, Philadelphia, 1931. On microfilm in the Van Pelt Library.

Nye, Russell. *William Lloyd Garrison and the Humanitarian Reforms.* Boston: Little Brown, 1955.

O'Keefe, Stephen. "Doctor of The Pines Philosophy Could Heal Today's Ills." *Camden-Courier Post*, Camden: New NJ. (20 May 1971).

Packard, Francis R., M.D. Editor, *Annals of Medical History.* Vol. 1. New York" Hafner, 1963.

Penn, Garland, I.Editor. *Afro-American Press and Its Editors.* Springfield, Massachusetts: Willey & Co., 1891. "Opinion of James Still, M.D." In Gleen, Robert W. *A Guide to African American Communications.* Metuchen, NJ: Skatecrow Press, 1876.

Pennsylvania Society for Promoting the Abolition of Slavery, etc., Papers 1748-1916. Circa 12,000 items Correspondence, legal documents, minutes, ledgers books, and lists of members of the Society. Also Mss, letters, and microfilm Accounts of the Vigilance Committee of Philadelphia, and the Journal written by William Still, an agent in the Historical Society of Pennsylvania, in Philadelphia, founded in 1824. Found in the Directory of Afro-American Resources. Rutgers University Library, New Brunswick, NJ.

Pennsylvania Abolition Society Manuscript Collection. V1. 1748-1749; Vol. 2. 1789-1790; Vol. 1791-1793. Historical Society of Pennsylvania, Philadelphia.

----------Minutes of the Pennsylvania Society for Promoting the Abolition of Slavery, 1827-1847. Historical Society of Pennsylvania, Philadelphia.

----------Manuscript History. Books 1, 2, 3. Historical Society of Pennsylvania.

----------Minutes of the Executive Committee, 1847-1916. Historical Society of Pennsylvania.

---------*Journal of the Convention, 1837.* Historical Society of Pennsylvania.
---------William Still Papers and Letters—1852-1902. Reel 32. Historical Society of Pennsylvania.
---------Minutes of the Executive Committee. Book 4, 1856-1870. Historical Society of Pennsylvania.
----------Minutes 1860-1867. Manuscripts and By-Laws, 1775-1787. Historical Society of Pennsylvania.
----------Items pertaining to the History and Activities of Abolition Societies, and the Influence.Exerted by Quakers and Other Abolitionists. Historical Society of Pennsylvania, Philadelphia. Also found in the Directory of Afro-American Resources, Rutgers University Library, New Brunswick, NJ.
---------Manumission Certificates 1765-1865. Manumission Books 1780-1851.
---------Indenture Books 1758-1835.
---------Minutes of the American Convention 1794-1809.
---------Census Books on the Negro Population of Philadelphia ca. 1840-1847.
---------Education and Employment Statistics. 1849-1856.
---------Minutes of the Executive Committee of the Pennsylvania Abolition Society. Book 4. 1856-1870.
---------Material on the Philadelphia Supervisory Committee for recruiting Colored Regiments; and 17 Vols. on the Education of Negroes among which are extensive records of the Clarkson School 1819- 1861.
---------Petition for the Colored People of Philadelphia to Ride in the Cars. Signed Document, 1866.
--------Social, Cultural, and Statistical Association of the Colored people of Pennsylvania. Manuscript of the Constitution, By-Laws, Roll, and Minutes 1860-1867.
--------Society for the Relief of Free Negroes Unlawfully Held in Bondage. Articles and Minutes 1775-1787.
--------William Still's *Journal of Fugitive Slaves Who Passed Through Station No. 2 of The Underground Railroad 1852-1857.*
--------Sojourner Truth, Letter (as dictated to her grandson, William) to William Still. 1876.

--------Vigilance Committee of Philadelphia. Minute Book and Record of Cases kept by Jacob C. White, Jr. 1839- 1844.

---------Letter signed by the editor of the *Commonwealth,* by Moncure O. Conway.

Phillips, Wendell, Esq., Speech. Woman's Rights Tracts. No.2 Boston Public Library.

---------. "To The Freedman!" On Learning to Read and Write. 16 July 1865. William Lloyd Garrison Papers. Boston Public Library, Boston, MA.

Pickard, Kate E.R. *The Kidnapped and the Ransomed.* The Story of Peter Still. 1st ed. Syracuse: Hamilton, 1856. Also listed as NY: E.O. Jenkins, 1856. Reprinted 1970. Jewish Publication Society of America.

Pope, Emily F., M.D. Call, Emma, M.D., and Pope, Augusta. *The Practice of Medicine by Women in the United States.* Boston: Wright & Potter, 1881.Presented before the American Social Science Association at Saratoga, New York. Radcliffe College, Cambridge, MA.

Proceedings of the 9th Convention for Promoting the Abolition of Slavery, and For Improving the Condition of the African Race. Assembled at Philadelphia. 10-15 October 1818 (Phila. 1818).

--------Proceedings of a Convention of Delegates from the Abolition Societies, 1798. In "Documents: The Appeal of the American Convention of Abolition Societies." The *Journal of Negro History, April 1921* (V1), 213.

Proceedings of the Antislavery Convention of American Women. Held in Philadelphia, 15,16,17,18 May 1838. (Phila.1838), passim. 18 May 1838. Plus 183,9, 23 May 1839.

Proceedings of the Ninth Convention for Promoting the Abolition of Slavery, and for Improving the Condition of the African Race 10-15 Oct.1818 (Phila).

Proceedings of a Convention of Delegates from the Abolition Societies, 1798.In"Documents: The Appeal of the American Convention of Abolition Societies." The *Journal of Negro History, April 1921* (V1), 213.

Quarles, Benjamin, *Black Abolitionists,* New York: Oxford University Press,1969.Repr. (paperback) New York: Da Capo, 1969.

Renehan, Edward, J., Jr. *"The Secret Six." The true Tale of the Men who Conspired with John Brown.* New York: Crown, 1995.

Quigley, Carroll.*The Evolution of Civilizations: An Introduction to Historical Analysis* (Indianapolis, Indiana: Liberty Fund) 1979.

Quinquennial Catalogue of Harvard University, 1636-1930. Harvard University Library, Cambridge, Massachusetts.

Rosetti, W.M. "English Opinion on the American War." *Atlantic Monthly* Vol. 17 (February 1866).

Schomburg Collection.*Negro Literature and History. Dictionary Catalogue,* Boston:G.K. Hall, 19629v.supplement, 1st ed. Boston, 1967-1972. 2 v., 4v. New York Public Library.

Sears, Lorenzo.*Wendell Phillips,Orator and Agitator,* New York: Benjamin Blom, 1909.Reissued 1967.

Sewell, Richard H. *A House Divided: Sectionalism and the Civil War. 1848-1865.* Baltimore, Johns Hopkins University Press, 1988.

Shadd, Mary Ann Papers. Moorland-Spingarn Research Center, Howard University, Washington, D.C.

Siebert,Wilbur."The Underground Railroad in Massachusetts." *New England Quarterly, 9.*(September 1936.)

---------."The Underground Railroad in Pennsylvania." *Siebert Scrapbook.* Vol.3. (Nov. 1893). Ohio Historical Society, Columbus, OH.

--------. *The Underground Railroad: From Slavery to Freedom* (New York:Macmillan, 1998). reprint of orig. 1898 text by Siebert. (New York).African American Geneology-African American department, Enoch Pratt Free Library, Baltimore, Maryland.

"Underground Railroad in Massachusetts. *American Antiquarian Society. XLV* (April 1935): 25-100. Harvard University Library, Cambridge, Massachusetts.

"Underground Railroad in Michigan." *Detroit Historical Monthly.* Vol. 1 (March 1923): 10, Michigan Historical Society,

Detroit."Underground Railroad in Pennsylvania." In the Scrapbook of WH Siebert, Vol3. Wilbur H. Siebert papers in the Ohio Historical Society, Columbus, Ohio.

Smedley, Robert C. *History of the Underground Railroad in Chester and the Neighboring Counties of Pennsylvania.* Lancaster. Journal, 1883.

Smith, Gene, *American Legacy-Pathfinders.* "The Greatest Station Master." Vol. 2. No. 3. Fall 1996.

Smith, Joseph Hutchinson. "Some Aspects of the Underground Railroad in the Counties of Southeastern Pennsylvania." *Bulletin of the Historical Society of Montgomery County of Pennsylvania.* Vol. 3 (Oct. 1941), 7.

Smith, Stephen, M.D. "A Woman Student in a [Man's] Medical College." In Memory of Elizabeth Blackwell and her sister, Dr. Emily Blackwell [a grad]. Of the Cleveland Medical School]. N.Y. Academy of Medicine, 1911. "In Her Own Words."Radcliffe College.Cambridge, MA.

Spiro, Howard M., M.D. "Myths and Mirths-Women in Medicine." "In Her Own Words." *New England Journal of Medicine* 292 (Feb. 1975): 354-356. History of Women in Medicine.May-Goddard-Ames Collection Radcliffe Institute. Cambridge, MA.

Stanton,Elizabeth Cady. Letter. "Declaration of Sentiments." Woman's Rights Tracts. No. 10. Woman's Rights Convention, Worcester, Massachusetts. 20 October 1850. Boston Public Library.

---------Speech. Woman's Rights Convention, Syracuse, New York, September 1852. In Seneca Falls, New York, September 1852. Boston Public Library.

---------,Anthony, Susan B., Gage, Matilda Jocelyn.*History of Women's Suffrage,* (4 Vols.) 1881-1902. Rochester, N.Y.: Susan B. Anthony in Box 1, Box 2. Ames Collection. Radcliffe Institute. Cambridge, MA.

Sterling,Dorothy. *We Are Your Sisters,* New York:Feminist Press, *1984.*

---------.*Ahead of Her Time* .Abby Kelly and the Politics of Antislavery. NY: Norton, 1991.

Still James, *Early Recollections and Life of Dr. James Still 1812-1885.* 1st edition, self published ,Philadelphia: Lippincott, 1877. Reprinted, Medford, NJ. Medford Historical Society.1971.

Still, James Thomas MD (Harv) 1871 *The Afro-American Press and its Editors.* Ed. I Garland Penn. "Opinions of Negroes on the Subject of Black Journalists." Springfield, MA: Wiley & Co., 1891.

-------. "Uncle Sam's Reverie! Or What Shall Be Done With the Pickininnies?" also entitled, "A Humorous Lecture.Don't Tell White Folks. Pamphlets by J. T. Still, M.D, Boston, Massachusetts 1889.

Still, William. "Voting and laboring.' Delivered at Concert Hall, Philadelphia, 10 March 1874. Moorland-Spingarn Research Center, Howard University, Washington, D.C.

-------. "Opportunities and Capabilities of Educated Negroes." Read at the National Conference of Colored Men. In the Proceedings of, held at Fisk University, Nashville, TN, 6-9 May 1879. *Dictionary Catalogue of the Arthur B. Spingarn Collection of Negro Authors.* Howard University, Washington, D.C.: Rufus H. Darby, 1879. [Moorland-Spingarn Research Center, Vol. 2, L- Z. Boston: G.K. Hall& Co.].

------- "A Brief Narrative of the Struggle for the Rights of the Colored People of Philadelphia in the City Railway Cars, and a Defense of William Still." Philadelphia, 9 February 1867. In possession of Frances E. Still, 1930.

--------.*Accounts of the Philadelphia Vigilance Committee of the Pennsylvania Abolition Society,854-1857.* Historical Society of Pennsylvania, Philadelphia.

--------.Papers. Leon Gardner Collection in the Philadelphia Abolition Society. Historical Society of Pennsylvania, Philadelphia." Delivered at Concert Hall. 10 March 1874. Philadelphia: J.P. Rogers, 1874. Spingarn Research Center. Howard University, Washington, D.C. in the Historical Society of Pennsylvania, Philadelphia.

--------. *Journal of the Philadelphia Vigilance Committee.* Station 2 of the Underground Railroad. Reel 32. Historical Society of Pennsylvania, Philadelphia. *The Underground Rail Road.* 1st ed. Philadelphia: Porter & Coates, 1872.

--------.*The Underground Rail Road. 2nd ed.* Reprinted by the author, Philadelphia: People's Publishing Company, 1878.

--------. *Still's Underground Rail Road Records,* 3rd ed.Philadelphia" self published by the author, 1886.

-------*Underground Rail Road,* 4th ed. Reprinted Medford, New Jersey: Plexus Publishing, 2005.

Toynbee, Arnold J. *A Study of History: Abridgement of Vols. 1-10.* By D. C. Somervell. New York: Oxford University Press, 1957.

Villard, Harold G. "William Still and the Underground Railroad." Dictionary of American Biography. [18: 23.] 1936. Part 2:22-3, [1935-36.]

Weld, Angelina Grimke Letter. Woman's Rights Tracts No. 8. Convention held at Syracuse, New York, September 1852. Boston Public Library.

Weld, Theodore D. *Slavery As It Is: Testimony of a Thousand Witnesses.* New York: American Antislavery Office, Spring& Nassau Streets, 1839.Repr. Arno Press, 1968.

Woodward & Hagerman. *History of Burlington and Mercer Counties.* Burlington Bounty, NJ. In the Mount Holly Library.

Women's Rights tracts. No. 2. Convention held at Worcester, MA, 15, 16 October 1851.

-----------------------------No. 8 Convention held at Syracuse, NY, September 1852.

---------------------------No 10. Held at Seneca Falls, NY, October 1850. Women's Rights Tracts. 22 October 1855.

Selected Reading.

African American Autobiography. A Collection of Critical Essays. Ed. By Andrews, William L.,New Century Views. Richard Broadhead, Maynard Mack. Series editors. Englewood Cliffs,NJ : Prentice Hall, 1993.

Akhil Reed, Amar. *America's Constitution. A Biography.* New York: Random House, 2006.

Andrews, William L., ed. *African American Biography : A Collection of Critical Essays.* Englewood Cliffs, NY: New Century Views, 1993.

Anthony, Katherine Susan. *Susan B. Anthony. Her Personal History and her Era.* NY: Doubleday, 1954. Schlesinger Library, Radcliffe Institute. Cambridge, MA.

Aptheker Bettina. *Woman's Legacy: essays on race, Class, and Sex in American History.* Chapter- "Quest for Dignity: Black Women in the professions, 1885-1900. Amherst: University of MA Press, 1859.

Armstrong, Karen. *The Battle for God.* NY: Knopf, 2000.

Aptheker, Herbert, compiler. *A Documentary History of the Negro People in the United States:* From the Reconstruction Era to 1910. (NY, 1951). Vol. 2. 625- 26.

Barrett, David V., *Secret Societies: From the Ancient and Arcane to the Modern and Clandestine.* "The Ku Klux Klan."182-185. NY : Sterling, 1997. Prev. Publ. by Blandford, London.

Bettman, Otto L., Ph.D. *A Pictorial History of medicine.* 3rd ed. Springfield, IL: Charles C. Thomas, 1962.in the May-Goddard-Ames Collection in the Schlesinger Library, Radcliffe Institute. Cambridge, MA.

Birney, James Gillespie. 1831-1857.(2 Vols. NY, 1938).

Blackwell, Elizabeth, M.D. *Pioneer Work in Opening the medical Profession to Women.* London: Longman's Green, 1895

Blanchard, Paula. Margaret Fuller: From Transcendentalism to Revolution.Reading, Massachusetts: Addison-Wesley Publishing Company, 1987.

Blight, David W. *Black Memory and Progress of the Race. The Civil War and American Memory.* Cambridge, MA :Harvard University Press, 2001.

Brieger, Gert H. *Medicine in America in the Nineteenth Century.* Baltimore :Johns Hopkins Press, 1872.

Bluestein, Burton. *The Culture of professionalism. The Middle Class and the Development of Higher Education in America.* NY : Norton, 1976.

Cowen, Tom, M.D., and Maquire, Jack. *Timelines of African American History, 500 Years of Black Achievement.* "Contemporary Events." [1821}, 52. Still, William- Writer and Lifetime Civil Rights Activist. Published an account of The Underground Railroad. NY : Roundtree Press/ Perigree Books, 1994.

David, Donald. *The Divided Union,* Boston: Little Brown, 1961.

Douglass, Frederick. John Brown. *An Address on the 14th Anniversary of Storer College,* Harpers Ferry, West VA. Dover, NH: 1881. Douglass, Frederick. *Life and Times of Frederick Douglass.* Revised. Edition, Boston: 1892.

Drachman, Virginia G. *Hospital With A Heart.* NY: Cornell University Press, 1984.

Dumond, Dwight L. Editor. *Letters of Theodore Dwight Weld, Angelina Grimke Weld, and Sarah Grimke.* 1822-1844. (2 Vols. NY 1934.)

Finkleman, Paul. *His Soul Goes Marching On Responses to John Brown and the Harpers Ferry Raid,* Charlottesville, Virginia: University of Virginia Press, 1995.

Flemming, George D. *Shamong, Images of America* Charleston, Sc; Arcadia Publishing, 2009.

Flexnor, Eleanor. *Century of Struggle: The Woman's Rights Movement in the United States.* NY: Atheneum, 1972.

Frederickson, George M. *Racism: A Short History.* Princeton, NJ: Princeton,

Garrison, Frances J., and Garrison, Wendell P. *William Lloyd Garrison,* 1805- 1879: The Story of His Life Told By His Children. (4 Vols.) NY: 1885-1889. ? Publisher.

Giddings, Paula. *When and Where I Enter. The Impact o f Black Women on Race and Sex in America* NY: Bantam Books, 1985. Orig. published. By William Morrow & Co., 1985

Hallowell, Anna Davis. *James and Lucretia Mott. Cambridge, MA:* Harvard University Press, 1884.

Harlan, Loius R. *The Negro in American History.* University of Cincinnati Publication No. 6. American Historical Association. 400 A Street, S.E. Washington D.C., 200

Johnson, Oliver. *William Lloyd Garrison and His Times.* Boston: Houghton Mifflin, 1885.

Leech, Rev. Samuel Vanderlip, D.D. *The Raid of John Brown at Harpers Ferry as I Saw It.* 1909.

McPherson, James. *Abraham Lincoln and the Second American Revolution,* Oxford:Oxford University press, 1991.

Morrison, Michael A. *Slavery and the American West: The Eclipse of Manifest destiny and the Coming of the Civil War.* Chapel Hill: University of North Carolina Press, 1999.

Reynolds, David S. *John Brown Abolitionist,* NY: Knopf, 2005.

Robertson, James I., Jr. *Civil war! America Becomes One nation.* NY: Knopf, 1992.

Truax, Rhoada. *The Doctors Jacobi.* Boston: Little Brown, 1952. "In Her Own Words." .May-Goddard-Ames Collection. Schlesinger Library. Radcliffe Coll;ege,Cambridge, MA.

Wilson, Dorothy, Clark. *Lone Woman. The Story of Elizabeth Blackwell, the First Woman Doctor.* Boston: Little Brown, 1970.

Women in Medicine. May-Goddard-Ames Collection. Schlesinger Library. Radcliffe College. Cambridge, MA.

Woodson, Carter G. *The Negro in Our History.* Washington, 1924. *Editor, Negro Orators*

Wollstonecraft, Mary. *Vindication of the Rights of Women. Published in England in 1792.*

Zakrzewska, Marie Elizabeth. *A Memoir.* Boston: New England Hospital for Women and Children, 1903.

Appendix.

Appendix 1. Catalogue of the Children of Levin and Charity Still. Peter Still Papers, Rutgers, New Brunswick, NJ.

Appendix 2. Letter from William Still to James O.Cousins 1852. Peter Still Peter Still Papers, Rutgers, New Brunswick, NJ.

Appendix 3. Preface to William Still. *The Underground Rail Road.* Philadelphia: Porter & Coates, 1872.

Appendix. 4. Preface.William Still.*The Underground Rail Road.* Philadelphia: The People's Publishing Company,1878.

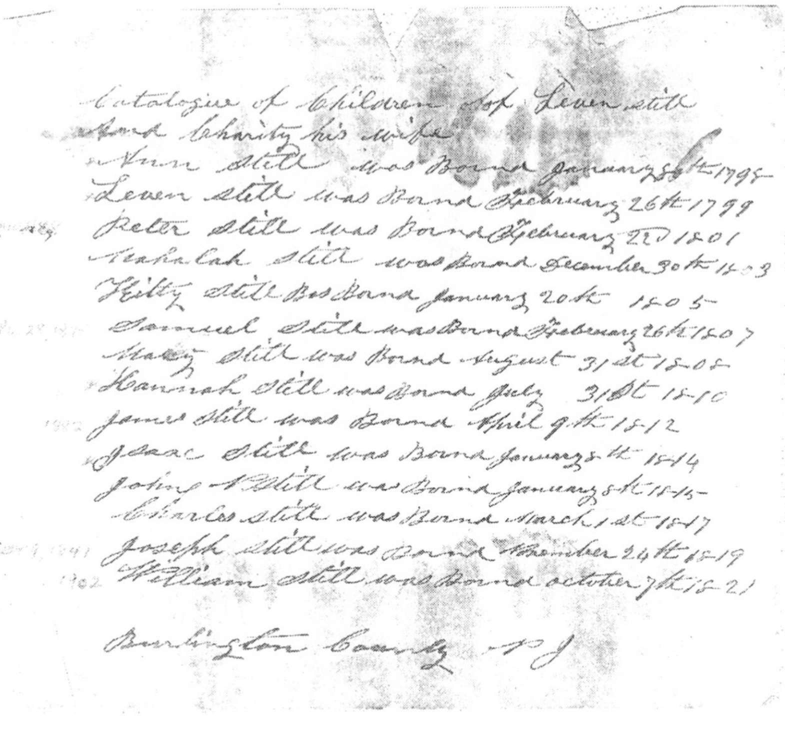
Catalogue of Children of Leven still
And Charity his wife
Ann Still was Born January 5th 1798
Leven still was Born February 26th 1799
Peter Still was Born February 22d 1801
Mahalah Still was Born December 30th 1803
Kitty Still Was Born January 20th 1805
Samuel Still was Born February 26th 1807
Mary Still was Born August 31st 1808
Hannah Still was Born July 31st 1810
James Still was Born April 9th 1812
Isaac Still was Born January 5th 1814
John N Still was Born January 5th 1815
Charles Still was Born March 1st 1817
Joseph Still was Born November 24th 1819
William Still was Born October 7th 1821

Burlington County NJ

Philadelphia August 7th 1850

Last Friday afternoon, Peter Freedman
was brought to this office by a man
whom I was partialy acquainted with,
object of Peter was to see if he could
gain some instruction how he might
find his parents & relatives, whome
he had been sold away from for
43 Years. The remarks made by the
Stranger much surprised me and I
soon began to make inquiries
as to his parents and their names,
He immediately gave the names
of his father, Mother, and the brother
who was also sold with him at
the same time. By this time I
perceived that a wonderful development was about to be made.
My feelings became ~~and~~ unuttera-
able, although I endeavored to suppress
them with much effort, but the
fact that this Peter was one of
my long absent brothers stared me
too full in the face to gainsay
or dispute the evidence for one
moment. Thus a Brother whom

whom I had never before seen
was introduced to me in this most
wonderful manner. It would
afford me much pleasure to
make further statement concerning
this matter but for want of time
I must forbare at present
Suffice it to say that Peter
found his Mother, 5 brothers &
3 Sisters situated comfortably in life

From Peter's Youngest Brother, Wm Still

No 31 North fifth St.

Philadelphia
Pa

PREFACE.

Whereas, The position of William Still in the vigilance committee connected with the "Underground Rail Road," as its corresponding secretary, and chairman of its active sub-committee, gave him peculiar facilities for collecting interesting facts pertaining to this branch of the anti-slavery service; therefore

Resolved, That the Pennsylvania Anti-Slavery Society request him to compile and publish his personal reminiscences and experiences relating to the "Underground Rail Road."

In compliance with this Resolution, unanimously passed at the closing meeting of the Pennsylvania Anti-Slavery Society held last May in Philadelphia, the writer, in the following pages, willingly and he hopes satisfactorily discharges his duty.

In these Records will be found interesting narratives of the escapes of many men, women and children, from the prison-house of bondage; from cities and plantations; from rice swamps and cotton fields; from kitchens and mechanic shops; from Border States and Gulf States; from cruel masters and mild masters;—some guided by the north star alone, penniless, braving the perils of land and sea, eluding the keen scent of the blood-hound as well as the more dangerous pursuit of the savage slave-hunter; some from secluded dens and caves of the earth, where for months and years they had been hidden away waiting for the chance to escape; from mountains and swamps, where indescribable suffering from hunger and other privations had patiently been endured. Occasionally fugitives came in boxes and chests, and not infrequently some were secreted in steamers and vessels, and in some instances journeyed hundreds of miles in skiffs. Men disguised in female attire and women dressed in the garb of men have under very trying circumstances triumphed in thus making their way to freedom. And here and there when all other modes of escape seemed cut off, some, whose fair complexions have rendered them indistinguishable from their Anglo-Saxon brethren, feeling that they could endure the yoke no longer, with assumed airs of importance, such as they had been accustomed to see their masters show when traveling, have taken the usual modes of conveyance and have even braved the most scrutinizing inspection of slave-holders, slave-catchers and car conductors, who were ever on the alert to catch those who were considered base and white enough to practice such deception. Passes have been written and used by fugitives, with their masters' and mistresses' names boldly attached thereto, and have answered admirably as a protection, when passing through ignorant country districts of slave regions, where but few, either white or colored, knew how to read or write correctly.

Not a few, upon arriving, of course, hardly had rags enough on them to cover their nakedness, even in the coldest weather.

It scarcely needs be stated that, as a general rule, the passengers of the U. G. R. R. were physically and intellectually above the average order of slaves.

They were determined to have liberty even at the cost of life.

The slave auction block indirectly proved to be in some respects a very active agent in promoting travel on the U. G. R. R., just as Jeff. Davis was an agent in helping to bring about the downfall of Slavery. The horrors of the block, as looked upon through the light of the daily heart-breaking separations it was causing to the oppressed, no pen could describe or mind imagine; hence it will be seen that many of the passengers, whose narratives will be found in this work, ascribed their first undying resolution to strike for freedom to the auction block or to the fear of soon having to take their chances thereon. But other agencies were at work in the South, which in various ways aided directly or tacitly the U. G. R. R. cause.

To refer in detail to any considerable number of these agents would be impossible, if necessary. Some there were who nobly periled their all for the freedom of the oppressed, whose sufferings and deeds of bravery must have a fitting place in this volume.

Where in history, modern or ancient, could be found a more Christlike exhibition of love and humanity, of whole-souled devotion to freedom, than was proven in the character of the hero, Seth Concklin, who lost his life while endeavoring to rescue from Alabama slavery the wife and children of Peter Still?

So also do the heroic and faithful services of Samuel D. Burris demand special reference and commemoration, for his connection with the U. G. R. R. cost him not only imprisonment and the most barbarous treatment, but likewise the loss of his freedom. He was sold on the auction block.

Here too come the overwhelming claims of S. A. Smith, who at the sad cost to himself of many of the best years of his life in the Richmond penitentiary, boxed up Henry Box Brown and others in Richmond, and committed them to Adams' Express office, to be carried in this most extraordinary manner to freedom.

We must not omit from these records the boldness and the hazard of the unparalleled undertakings of Captains Drayton, Lee, Baylis, &c.

While the Vigilance Committee of Philadelphia was in no wise responsible for the suffering incurred by many of those who helped the slave, yet in order to show how men were moved to lend an ear to those hungering and thirsting for freedom, and to what extent the relentless spirit of Slavery would go in wreaking vengeance upon them—out of the many who were called upon to suffer thus, the individual cases here brought forward must suffice. Without introducing a few of such incidents the records would necessarily be incomplete.

Those who come after us seeking for information in regard to the existence, atrocity, struggles and destruction of Slavery, will have no trouble in finding this hydra-headed monster ruling and tyrannizing over Church and State, North and South, white and black, without let or hindrance, for at least several generations. Nor will posterity have any difficulty in finding the deeds of the brave and invincible opposers of Slavery, who in the language of Wm. Lloyd Garrison, declared without concealment and without compromise: "I am in earnest, I will not equivocate—I will not excuse—I will not retreat a single inch—and I will be heard."

While this resolute spirit actuated the hearts of all true abolitionists, it was a peculiar satisfaction and gratification to them to know that the slaves themselves were struggling and hungering for deliverance. Hence such evidence from this quarter never failed to meet with hearty sympathy and aid. But here the enemy was never willingly allowed to investigate.

The slave and his particular friends could only meet in private to transact the business of the Underground Rail Road ground. All others were outsiders. The right hand was not to know what the left hand was doing.

Stockholders did not expect any dividends, nor did they require special reports to be published. Indeed prudence often dictated that even the recipients of our favor should not know the names of their helpers, and *vice versa* they did not desire to know theirs.

The risk of aiding fugitives was never lost sight of, and the safety of all concerned called for still tongues. Hence sad and thrilling stories were listened to, and made deep impressions; but as a universal rule, friend and fugitive parted with only very vivid recollection of the secret interview and with mutual sympathy; for a length of time no narratives were written. The writer, in common with others, took no notes. But after the restoration of Peter Still, his own brother (the kidnapped and the ransomed), after forty years' cruel separation from his mother, the wonderful discovery and joyful reunion, the idea forced itself upon his mind that all over this wide and extended country thousands of mothers and children, separated by Slavery, were in a similar way living without the slightest knowledge of each other's whereabouts, praying and weeping without ceasing, as did this mother and son. Under these reflections it seemed reasonable to hope that by carefully gathering the narratives of Underground Rail Road passengers, in some way or other some of the bleeding and severed hearts might be united and comforted; and by the use that might be made privately, if not publicly, of just such facts as would naturally be embraced in their brief narratives, re-unions might take place. For years it was the writer's privilege to see many travelers, to receive from their own lips the most interesting and in many cases exceedingly thrilling accounts of their struggles for liberty, and to learn who had held them in bondage, how they had been treated, what prompted them to escape, and whom that were near and dear to them they had left in chains. Their hopes, fears and sufferings were thus recorded in a book. It scarcely need be added with no expectation, however, that the day was so near when these things could be published.

It is now a source of great satisfaction to feel that not

only these numerous narratives may be published, but that in connection therewith, for the completeness of the work, many interesting private letters from fugitives in Canada, slaves in the South, Underground Rail Road conductors and stockholders, and last and least, from slaveholders, in the bargain—all having a direct bearing on the mysterious road.

In the use of these various documents, the writer begs to assure his readers that the most scrupulous care has been taken to furnish artless stories, simple facts,—to resort to no coloring to make the book seem romantic, as he is fully persuaded that any exaggerations or additions of his own could not possibly equal in surpassing interest, the original and natural tales given under circumstances, when life and death seemed about equally balanced in the scale, and fugitives in transit were making their way from Slavery to Freedom, with the horrors of the Fugitive Slave-law staring them in the face.

Thousands were either directly or indirectly interested in this enterprise, and in all probability two generations will pass away before many who are now living witnesses to the truth of these records will cease to bring vividly to mind the hour and circumstance when for the first time they were led to resort to this road to escape the "barbarism" of Slavery.

Far be it from the writer to assume, however, that these Records cover the entire Underground Rail Road operations. Many local branches existed in different parts of the country, which neither time nor limit would allow mention of in this connection. Good men labored and suffered, who deserve to be held in the highest admiration by the friends of Freedom, whose names may be looked for in vain in these pages; for which reason some may be inclined to complain. With respect to these points it may here be remarked that in gathering narratives from unwritten sources—from memory simply—no amount of pains or labor could possibly succeed in making a trustworthy history. The writer has deemed it best, therefore, to confine himself to facts coming within his personal knowledge, and to the records of his own preserving, which, by the way, are quite too voluminous to be all used in this work. Frequent abridgements and omissions must be made.

The writer is fully conscious of his literary imperfections. The time allotted him from other pressing duties is, moreover, exceedingly limited. Nevertheless he feels that he owes it to the cause of Freedom, and to the Fugitives and their posterity in particular, to bring the doings of the U. G. R. R. before the public in the most truthful manner; not for the purpose of amusing the reader, but to show what efforts were made and what success was gained for Freedom under difficulties. That some professing a love of liberty at this late date will be disposed to criticise some of the methods resorted to in aiding in the escape of fugitives as herein recounted, may be expected. While the writer holds the labors of Abolitionists generally in very grateful appreciation, he hopes not to be regarded as making any invidious discriminations in favor of the individual friends of the slave, whose names may be brought out prominently in this work, as it is not with the Anti-Slavery question proper that he is dealing, but simply the Underground Rail Road. In order, therefore, fittingly to bring the movements of this enterprise to light, the writer could not justly confine himself to the Acting Committee, but felt constrained to bring in others—Friends—who never forsook the fugitive, who visited him in prison, clothed him when naked, fed him when hungry, wept with him when he wept, and cheered him with their warmest sympathies and friendship. In addition to the names of the Acting Committee, he has felt constrained to beg the portraits of the following stockholders and advisers of the Road, whose names will be found on the next page, and in thus presenting a brief sketch of their labors, he feels that the true friends of the slave in recognizing them in this connection with many of the once Fugitives (now citizens), will regard it as a tribute to the Anti-Slavery cause rather than the individuals themselves.

WILLIAM STILL.

PHILADELPHIA, *January*, 1872.

PREFACE TO THE 1878 EDITION

Like millions of my race, my mother and father were born slaves, but were not contented to live and die so. My father purchased himself in early manhood by hard toil. Mother saw no way for herself and children to escape the horrors of bondage but by flight. Bravely, with her four little ones, with firm faith in God and an ardent desire to be free, she forsook the prison-house, and succeeded, through the aid of my father, to reach a free State. Here life had to be begun anew. The old familiar slave names had to be changed, and others, for prudential reasons, had to be found. This was not hard work. However, hardly months had passed ere the keen scent of the slave-hunters had trailed them to where they had fancied themselves secure. In those days all power was in the hands of the oppressor, and the capture of a slave mother and her children was attended with no great difficulty other than the crushing of freedom in the breast of the victims. Without judge or jury, all were hurried back to wear the yoke again. But back this mother was never resolved to stay. She only wanted another opportunity to again strike for freedom. In a few months after being carried back, with only two of her little ones, she took her heart in her hand and her babes in her arms, and this trial was a success. Freedom was gained, although not without the sad loss of her two older children, whom she had to leave behind. Mother and father were again reunited in freedom, while two of their little boys were in slavery. What to do for them other than weep and pray, were questions unanswerable. For over forty years the mother's heart never knew what it was to free from anxiety about her lost boys. But no tidings came in answer to her many prayers, until one of them, to the great astonishment of his relatives, turned up in Philadelphia, nearly fifty years of age, seeking his long-lost parents. Being directed to the Anti-Slavery Office for instructions as to the best plan to adopt to find out the whereabouts of his parents, fortunately he fell into the hands of his own brother, the writer, whom he had never heard of before, much less seen or known. And here began revelations connected with this marvellous coincidence, which influenced me, for years previous to Emancipation, to preserve the matter found in the pages of this humble volume.

And in looking back now over these strange and eventful Providences, in the light of the wonderful changes wrought by Emancipation, I am more and more constrained to believe that the reasons, which years ago led me to aid the bondman and preserve the records of his sufferings, are to-day quite as potent in convincing me that the necessity of the times requires this testimony.

And since the first advent of my book, wherever reviewed or read by leading friends of freedom, the press, or the race more deeply represented by it, the expressions of approval and encouragement have been hearty and unanimous, and the thousands of volumes which have been sold by me, on the subscription plan, with hardly any facilities for the work, makes it obvious that it would, in the hands of a competent publisher, have a wide circulation.

And here I may frankly state, that but for the hope I have always cherished that this work would encourage the race in efforts for self-elevation, its publication never would have been undertaken by me.

I believe no more strongly at this moment than I have believed ever since the Proclamation of Emancipatión was made by Abraham Lincoln, that as a class, in this country, no small exertion will have to be put forth before the blessings of freedom and knowledge can be fairly enjoyed by this people; and until colored men manage by dint of hard acquisition to enter the ranks of skilled industry, very little substantial respect will be shown them, even with the ballot-box and musket in their hands.

Well-conducted shops and stores; lands acquired and good farms managed in a manner to compete with any other; valuable books produced and published on interesting and important subjects—these are some of the fruits which the race are expected to exhibit from their newly gained priveleges.

If it is asked "how?" I answer, "through extraordinary determination and endeavor," such as are demonstrated in hundreds of cases in the pages of this book, in the struggles of men and women to obtain their freedom, education and property.

These facts must never be lost sight of.

The race must not forget the rock from whence they were hewn, nor the pit from whence they were digged.

Like other races, this newly emancipated people will need all the knowledge of their past condition which they can get.

The bondage and deliverance of the children of Israel will never be allowed to sink into oblivion while the world stands.

Those scenes of suffering and martyrdom millions of Christians were called upon to pass through in the days of the Inquisition are still subjects of study, and have unabated interest for all enlightened minds.

The same is true of the history of this country. The struggles of the pioneer fathers are preserved, produced and re-produced, and cherished with undying interest by all Americans, and the day will not arrive while the Republic exists, when these histories will not be found in every library.

While the grand little army of abolitionists was waging its untiring warfare for freedom, prior to the rebellion, no agency encouraged them like the heroism of fugitives. The pulse of the four million slaves and their desire for freedom, were better felt through "The Underground Railroad," than through any other channel.

Frederick Douglass, Henry Bibb, Wm. Wells Brown, Rev. J. W. Logan, and others, gave unmistakable evidence that the race had no more eloquent advocates than its own self-emancipated champions.

Every step they took to rid themselves of their fetters, or to gain education, or in pleading the cause of their fellow-bondmen in the lecture-room, or with their pens, met with applause on every hand, and the very argument needed was thus furnished in large measure. In those dark days previous to emancipation, such testimony was indispensable.

The free colored men were as imperatively required now to furnish the same manly testimony in support of the ability of the race to surmount the remaining obstacles growing out of oppression, ignorance, and poverty.

In the political struggles, the hopes of the race have been sadly disappointed. From this direction no great advantage is likely to arise very soon.

Only as desert can be proved by the acquisition of knowledge and the exhibition of high moral character, in examples of economy and a disposition to encourage industrial enterprises, conducted by men of their own ranks, will it be possible to make political progress in the face of the present public sentiment.

Here, therefore, in my judgment is the best possible reason for vigorously pushing the circulation of this humble volume—that is may testify for thousands and tens of thousands, as no other work can do.

WILLIAM STILL, AUTHOR.
PHILADELPHIA, PA.

SEPTEMBER, 1878.

John Henry Hill

Maria Weems Escaping In Male Attire

Hon. Abram Galloway
(Secreted in a vessel londed with turpentine)

Samuel D. Burris

William Craft

Ellen Craft

Jane Johnson

Passmore Williamson

John Hunn

Samuel Rhoads

William Whipper

Grace Anna Lewis

Mrs. Frances E.W. Harper

John Needles

Abegail Goodwin

Thomas Garrett

Daniel Gibbons

Lucretia Mott

J. Miller McKim

Rev. William H. Furness

William Lloyd Garrison

Lewis Tappan

Elijah F. Pennypacker

William Wright

Dr. Bartholomew Fussell

Robert Purvis

N.W. Depee

Jacob C. White

Charles Wise

Edwin H. Coates

Desperate Conflict In A Barn

Rescue Of Jane Johnson And Her Children

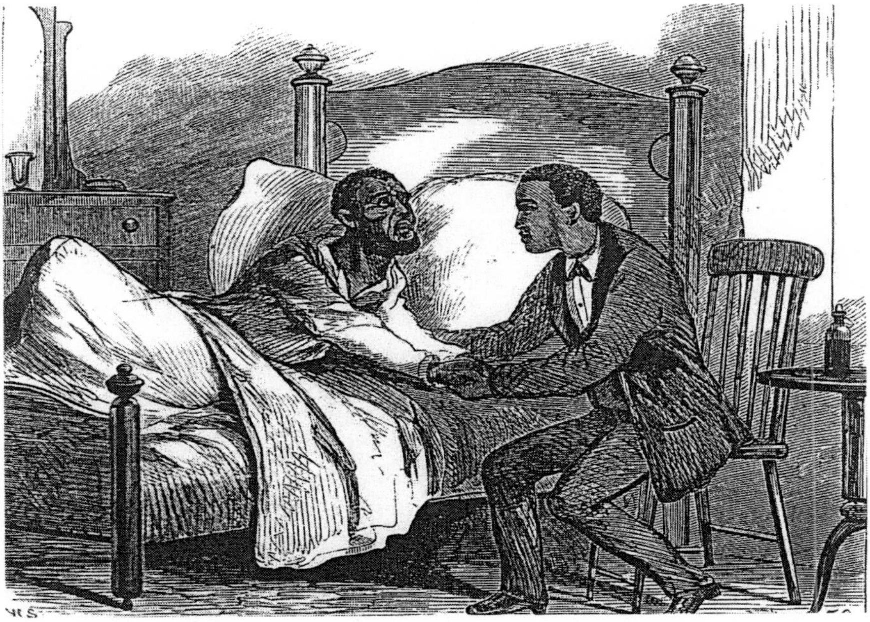

Death Of Romulus Hall

Resurrection Of Henry Box Brownb

A Bold Stroke For Freedom

Twenty-Eight Fugitives Escaping From The Eastern Shore Of Maryland

The Christiana Tragedy

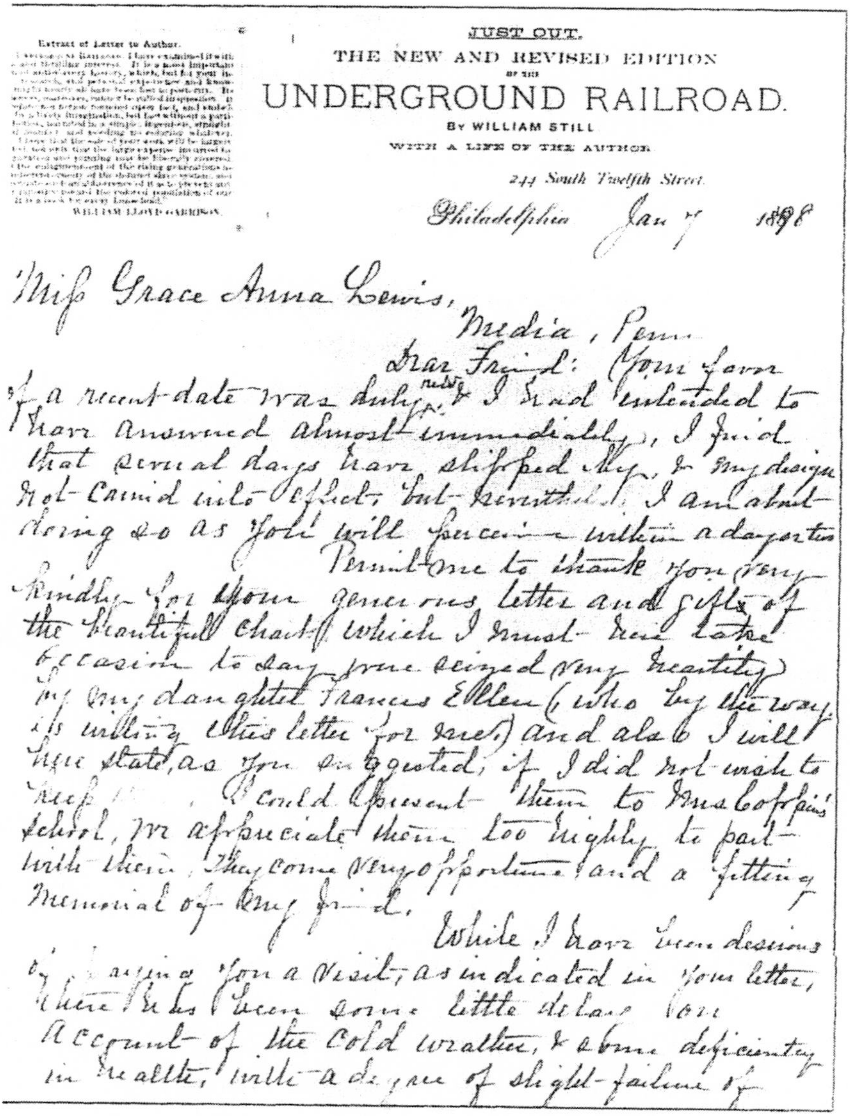
Extract of Letter to Author.

WILLIAM LLOYD GARRISON.

JUST OUT.

THE NEW AND REVISED EDITION OF THE

UNDERGROUND RAILROAD.

BY WILLIAM STILL

WITH A LIFE OF THE AUTHOR

244 South Twelfth Street.

Philadelphia Jan 7 1898

Miss Grace Anna Lewis,

Media, Penn

Dear Friend: Your favor of a recent date was duly rec'd & I had intended to have answered almost immediately, I find that several days have slipped by, & my design not carried into effect, but nevertheless I am about doing so as you will perceive within a day or two.

Permit me to thank you very kindly for your generous letter and gifts of the beautiful charts which I must now take occasion to say were received very heartily by my daughter Frances Ellen (who by the way is writing this letter for me,) and also I will here state, as you suggested, if I did not wish to keep [illegible], I could present them to Mrs Coffin's school, we appreciate them too highly to part with them. They come very opportune and a fitting memorial of my friend.

While I have been desirous of paying you a visit, as indicated in your letter, there has been some little delay on account of the cold weather, & some deficiency in health, with a degree of slight failure of

William Still's letter to Grace Anna Lewis

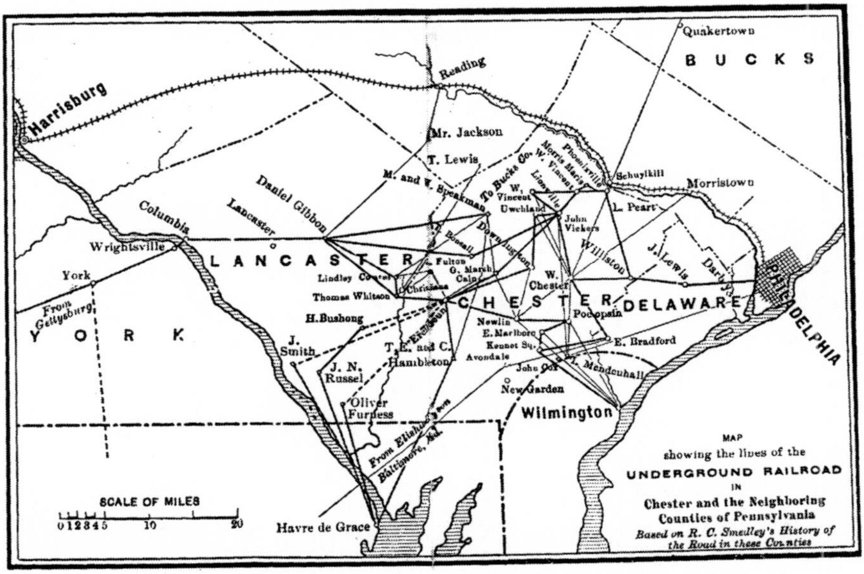

Map of Underground Railroad routes in Pennsylvania and Delaware, from William Sietbert book.

The photos and engravings are taken from William Still's 1872 edition of *The Underground* Rail Road. Photos in the public domain.

Engravings: Desperate Conflict in a Barn, Death of Romulus Hall, Rescue of Jane Johnson and Her Children, Commercial Value of Ten Negro Slaves as itemized in this invoice dated 1835.

Photographs: James McKim, William and Ellen Craft, Jane Johnson and Passmore Williamson, William Lloyd Garrison, Samuel Burris, Frances Ellen Watkins Harper, James McKim, Lucretia Mott. William and Ellen Craft.

Map. Underground Railroad Map of Chester and Neighboring Counties of Pennsylvania.